The Lost Gospel of Judas Iscariot

Also by Bart D. Ehrman

Peter, Paul, and Mary Magdalene:
The Followers of Jesus in History and Legend

Misquoting Jesus: The Story Behind Who Changed the Bible and Why

The Text of the New Testament: Its Transmission,
Corruption, and Restoration, Fourth Edition
(with Bruce M. Metzger)

Truth and Fiction in The Da Vinci Code

The New Testament: A Historical Introduction
to the Early Christian Writings,
Third Edition

A Brief Introduction to the New Testament

The Apostolic Fathers: Volumes I and II

Lost Christianities: The Battles for Scripture
and the Faiths We Never Knew

Lost Scriptures: Books that Did Not Make It
into the New Testament

Christianity in Late Antiquity, 330–450 CE:
A Reader
(with Andrew Jacobs)

The New Testament and other Early Christian Writings:
A Reader, Second Edition

Jesus: Apocalyptic Prophet of the New Millennium

After the New Testament: A Reader in Early Christianity

The Orthodox Corruption of Scripture: The Effect of
Early Christological Controversies on the Text of the New Testament

Didymus the Blind and the Text of the Gospels

The Lost Gospel of
Judas Iscariot

⌘

A New Look at Betrayer and Betrayed

Bart D. Ehrman

OXFORD
UNIVERSITY PRESS

OXFORD
UNIVERSITY PRESS

Oxford University Press, Inc., publishes works that
further Oxford University's objective of excellence
in research, scholarship, and education.

Oxford   New York
Auckland   Cape Town   Dar es Salaam   Hong Kong   Karachi
Kuala Lumpur   Madrid   Melbourne   Mexico City   Nairobi
New Delhi   Shanghai   Taipei   Toronto

With offices in
Argentina   Austria   Brazil   Chile   Czech Republic   France   Greece
Guatemala   Hungary   Italy   Japan   Poland   Portugal   Singapore
South Korea   Switzerland   Thailand   Turkey   Ukraine   Vietnam

Published by Oxford University Press, Inc.
198 Madison Avenue, New York, NY 10016

Oxford is a registered trademark of Oxford University Press.

ISBN-10: 0-19-531460-3
ISBN-13: 978-0-19-531460-1

All photos by Kenneth Garrett / National Geographic Image Collection.

Printed in the United States of America

Contents

To Dale Martin,
friend and scholar extraordinaire,
who has always pushed me
to look at things differently

Preface

M ost of the Gospels from early Christianity have been irretrievably lost. Occasionally one turns up, found by trained archaeologists looking for them or, more commonly, by local peasants inadvertently coming upon a treasure that is, quite literally, beyond their dreams. It is rare—a once-in-a-lifetime experience at best—for a scholar to have the opportunity to be involved with the first evaluation, authentication, and publication of a newly discovered Gospel. As it turns out, I was lucky.

A series of unexpected phone calls, some of them from the National Geographic Society, alerted me to the discovery of a long-lost Gospel, the Gospel of Judas Iscariot. Scholars had known of the one-time existence of this Gospel from the writings of the early church fathers. But these ancient reports were bizarre and hard to believe. Could there be a Gospel of Jesus written from the perspective of his mortal enemy and betrayer, Judas Iscariot? And could such a Gospel actually paint Judas in a favorable light, claiming that, contrary to all tradition, he was in fact Jesus' closest disciple and confidant? National Geographic wanted me to help authenticate the Gospel and establish its historical significance. I jumped at the chance, and here I can tell the story.

This is a Gospel that seemingly has appeared out of nowhere, discovered in a tomb in Egypt some thirty years ago, and now available for the first time for readers intrigued with the history of early Christianity and the many forms of Christian belief and practice of the early centuries. It is in fact a Gnostic Gospel. And it is one of the most intriguing ever discovered. It is not a Gospel written by Judas or by anyone who actually knew him. It is not as ancient as Matthew, Mark, Luke, or John. But it is one of our earliest surviving non-canonical Gospels. And the tale it has to tell is remarkable.

In recounting the story I have incurred some debts that I would like to acknowledge. My thanks go to National Geographic, especially Terry Garcia,
Senior Vice President of Missions, for bringing me on board for the project,
and Betty Hudson, Senior Vice President of Communications, for all her support. Robert Miller, my friend and editor at Oxford University Press, gener-
ously agreed to publish my account and read my manuscript with a keen editorial
eye. Especially to be thanked are my friends in the field, scholars who have
read the following pages, saved me from egregious mistakes, and tried to save
me from many more: Dale Martin, of New Testament fame and fortune, from
Yale University, to whom I have dedicated this book; Andrew Jacobs, the bright-
est star on the horizon of Late Antique Christianity, at the University of California, Riverside; Zlatko Plese, my brilliant colleague at the University of North
Carolina at Chapel Hill, and Coptologist nonpareil; Herb Krosney, the investigative reporter who more than anyone else is responsible for making the
discovery of this Gospel known to the world; an anonymous but unusually
keen and insightful reader obtained by Oxford University Press, whose comments have made me think and think; and my wife, Sarah Beckwith, a medi-
evalist in the Department of English at Duke, whose perceptiveness and intellect
are uncanny.

Translations of the Gospel of Judas are by Rodolphe Kasser, Marvin Meyer,
and Gregor Wurst, in collaboration with François Gaudard, in *The Gospel of
Judas* (Washington, D.C.: National Geographic, 2006); translations of the New
Testament and other early Christian writings are my own, unless otherwise
indicated.

The Lost Gospel of Judas Iscariot

⌘

CHAPTER ONE

My Introduction
to the Gospel of Judas

I first saw the Gospel of Judas on Sunday, December 5, 2004, in a restoration studio just outside of Geneva, Switzerland. I was exhausted but exhilarated. The day before, I had given two lectures on the history of early Christianity for the Program in the Humanities at my home institution, the University of North Carolina at Chapel Hill. I then drove straight to the Raleigh-Durham airport for an overnight flight to Geneva. From there it was a quick taxi ride to the hotel. The schedule was tight: I didn't have time to unpack before meeting my contacts.

We met in the lobby of the hotel, and I was ushered into the backseat of a van along with six others. We were driven off to our rendezvous point, in Nyon, Switzerland, on Lake Geneva. It was a cold and dreary day, and tired as I was, I knew this trip was something special.

I was one of a small team of scholars assembled by the National Geographic Society to help them verify the antiquity and authenticity of a newly discovered Gospel. There was an air of secrecy about the meeting. Each of us had been required to sign a nondisclosure agreement. We were not to discuss with anyone—most especially the press—what we were about to see and hear. National Geographic was considering whether to make a large financial investment in the authentication, publication, and promotion of this Gospel, and they didn't want anyone leaking the news of just what it was.

It was allegedly an ancient manuscript containing an account of Jesus' ministry from the perspective of his betrayer, Judas Iscariot. No one thought the Gospel was actually by Judas himself. Judas was an illiterate peasant, like Jesus' other disciples. But there was the possibility that it was one of our oldest surviving Gospels: not as old as Matthew, Mark, Luke, and John, but possibly from the second Christian century. That century had seen a proliferation of

Gospels forged in the names of Jesus' disciples—Gospels written in the names of Thomas, Philip, and Mary, for example. This Gospel would be different, however. All the other surviving Gospels told the story from the perspective of Jesus' friends. This one allegedly was by his enemy. But according to the hints and rumors circulating in the early church, this lost Gospel named after Jesus' betrayer portrayed Judas Iscariot not as the rotten apple in the apostolic barrel but as the one disciple who understood Jesus' teaching and did his will. Was this the Gospel that had now been discovered? Did we now have that "other side" of the story available to us in an ancient manuscript?

It took me a while to piece together who was with me on this little expedition. In addition to Terry Garcia, executive vice president for missions at National Geographic, there was Herb Krosney, the investigative reporter who had first brought news of the potential story to the attention of National Geographic; John Heubusch, head of the investment programs for Gateway Computers and its Waitt Family Foundation, which was considering whether to make a sizeable contribution to the project; and the other two experts who had been flown in to provide National Geographic with the information it needed to decide if this was an authentically ancient manuscript or instead a modern (or medieval) forgery.

The three of us had very different areas of expertise. There was A. J. Timothy Jull, director of the National Science Foundation's Accelerator Mass Spectrometer Facility in Tucson, Arizona, a scientist who specialized in the carbon-14 dating of ancient manuscripts. Earlier in his career Jull had helped establish scientific datings for the Dead Sea Scrolls. There was Stephen Emmel, an American-born scholar who held a prestigious chair at the University of Münster in Germany in the field of Coptology—the study of the ancient Egyptian language Coptic, the language in which the document was allegedly written. And there was me, a scholar of the New Testament and early Christianity, with a particular interest in the "lost Gospels," that is, the Gospels of the early centuries that did not make it into the canon of Christian Scripture.

Our charge was to verify that the initial reports about the manuscript could be trusted, that this was indeed an ancient Coptic text that told part of the Gospel story from the perspective of Jesus' betrayer, Judas Iscariot.

The manuscript was being kept in the studio of one of Europe's leading experts in manuscript restoration and preservation, Florence Darbre, who was connected with the renowned Martin Bodmer Foundation in Switzerland. I must admit that when we arrived, I was a bit taken aback. Given the importance of Darbre's work, I was expecting a more lavish setting. Darbre's studio was in the most inauspicious spot one could imagine, on the second floor of a slightly dilapidated building above a pizza shop in a small, unimpressive Swiss town far removed from the cultural center of Geneva. But outward appearances can be deceptive. For within this studio was one of the world's treasures from antiquity, which Darbre had spent three years meticulously piecing together. This was a Gospel text that had appeared on the antiquities market some twenty-five years earlier but was virtually unknown to the world of scholarship, let alone to the public at large.

We filed out of the van, into the building, up the stairs, and into a large room with a large picture window overlooking an empty field and the industrial building next to it. Joining us there, along with Darbre, were Frieda Tchacos Nussberger, the antiquities dealer of Greek origin who owned the manuscript, and her legal counsel, the Swiss lawyer Mario Roberty, internationally known for his work with European clients interested in fine art and antiquities.

There was excitement in the air as the meeting began. After the introductions, Roberty made some preliminary remarks on the manuscript we were about to see. It had been acquired in 2001 by an organization that Roberty himself had founded some seven years earlier, called the Maecenas Foundation, which was dedicated to the restoration of ancient artifacts and to returning them to their nations of origin. The manuscript had originally been discovered in the late 1970s. Its early history was shrouded in mystery, but its whereabouts from 1983 to the present could be documented with relative certainty. The manuscript consisted of sixty-two pages of text, written on papyrus (the ancient equivalent of paper); it was a small anthology, containing several different texts from Christian antiquity. Two of these texts were already known to scholars from earlier manuscript discoveries in Egypt: a book called the Letter of Peter to Philip and another called the First Apocalypse of James, both of them apocryphal writings. The third was of immediate and enduring interest. It was an ancient Gospel. Like the other texts, this was a Coptic translation of a much earlier document. The manuscript itself, Roberty indicated, was from the fourth century, but the foundation had reason to believe that it was a copy of a document originally written in Greek as early as the mid-second century. It was in fact probably the Gospel referred to around 180 CE by the church father and heresy hunter Irenaeus, who mentioned a Gospel in use among a group of Christian "heretics" known to history as the Gnostics. Irenaeus called it the Gospel of Judas.

Roberty was sophisticated and urbane, and he spoke with authority in impeccable English. He was very interested in getting the experts' opinions on the document, although he and his colleagues had no doubt at all about its authenticity. For the past three years it had been meticulously studied and translated by one of the world's very senior Coptic scholars, Rodolphe Kasser, professor emeritus at the University of Geneva. Kasser was an authority of international status, and his word was gold. National Geographic wanted to know if we would agree with his assessment of the document and his evaluation of its significance.

Next to speak was Frieda Tchacos Nussberger, the antiquities dealer, in her late fifties. She had acquired the manuscript some years earlier; we did not know how. She gave us her greetings but kept her comments brief. She obviously was trying to interest National Geographic in contributing to its restoration and publication.

This was not just an antiquarian interest for her; she had large sums of money invested in the manuscript and was looking for a financial backer.

Then it was restoration expert Florence Darbre's turn. She spoke of the manuscript with special affection and let us know what a miserable state it had been in when it was first brought to her attention three years earlier. The manuscript had not been conserved and protected after it had been discovered and removed from (smuggled out of?) Egypt. By the time it came into her hands it had been manhandled; its fragile pages had broken and been senselessly reshuffled. It was literally falling apart. Her first step had been to place all the surviving pieces—full pages and small fragments—under protective glass, and then to begin the arduous process of arranging the pages in their original sequence and fitting the hundreds of small fragments together, much like reassembling an enormous jigsaw puzzle without knowing what the final picture might look like. In this work she had been assisted at every step by Rodolphe Kasser, who was able not only to help reassemble the manuscript but also to read and translate it.

While Darbre was still speaking we could hear the door open in the (closed) pizza parlor below us. Coming slowly up the steps was Kasser himself, who had made the trip from his home town of Yverdon-les-Bains in order to meet with us and discuss for the first time this text, into which he had poured three years of his life. In my twenty-five years as a scholar, I had never met Kasser, even though we have comparable fields of academic interest. He was principally involved with Coptology—the study of the Coptic language and the ancient texts written in it—and I was an expert in early Greek-speaking Christianity and the manuscripts (including those of the New Testament) that it had produced. I knew, of course, of Kasser's work, as he was one of the premier scholars in his field. And I knew that he must, by now, be an old man. What I did not know was that he was suffering from an advanced stage of Parkinson's disease. He moved slowly and his hand continuously twitched while Frieda Nussberger made the introductions. Nussberger clearly had a special affection for this eminent scholar, who had worked so long to restore and translate the precious manuscript she owned.

The only person that Kasser already knew there from the National Geographic team was Stephen Emmel, the American Coptologist brought along to verify Kasser's judgment that this was an ancient manuscript written in ancient Coptic. Though two decades his junior, Emmel was respected by the grand old master in the field. And as irony would have it, Emmel had actually laid eyes on this manuscript once before, over twenty years earlier in a hotel room in Geneva, under darker and less controlled conditions, as a previous owner was trying to arrange its sale to a group of Americans for a whopping $3 million. Emmel suspected that the manuscript he had seen then, as a young graduate student at Yale, was the same he was about to see now, as a seasoned scholar in the field. But he couldn't know until they brought it out for us to examine—

and through all these opening speeches and introductions he was getting noticeably edgy, wanting to see what we had come to see.

I too was eager—not because I had seen the document before, but because I knew full well its historical significance if it turned out to be what it purported to be. This would be a major find from early Christianity, easily the greatest of my lifetime.

After Kasser had been introduced, Emmel asked that we at last be allowed to see the manuscript. Frieda nodded to Darbre, who went into the next room, which contained her safe. She returned with several Plexiglas sheets that were protecting the ancient papyrus on which the text was written. And there it was, before our eyes.

I'm not a Coptologist. Coptic is one of those languages that I taught myself in my spare time over the years, mainly because I wanted to be able to read ancient Coptic translations of the New Testament and some of the Gnostic Gospels discovered in the twentieth century. I can hack my way through a Coptic text with a dictionary and enough time. But I do know something about ancient manuscripts, as I've worked at some length on Greek texts of the New Testament since my graduate days at Princeton Theological Seminary in the early 1980s. I know an ancient manuscript when I see one. What was placed before our eyes was an ancient manuscript. Was there any chance this could be a modern forgery? Almost none at all. This was the real thing.

As excited as I was, Emmel was nearly beside himself. This was the same manuscript he had seen twenty years earlier—he was sure of it. At the time he hadn't realized exactly what it was, as he had been given only a few minutes to look it over and had not been allowed to study or translate it. In those few minutes he had seen that it contained at least three texts, and he had been able to identify two of them as copies of documents known from earlier discoveries. The third was some kind of discussion between Jesus and his disciple Judas. At the time, back in 1983, Emmel had assumed that this disciple was Judas Thomas (sometimes known as Doubting Thomas). He hadn't suspected that it was none other than Judas Iscariot. And why *would* he suspect it? We have numerous Gospels that narrate Jesus' interactions with Judas Thomas—in fact, we have a very famous Gospel of Thomas. But there was no surviving extracanonical Gospel dealing primarily with Judas Iscariot. Until now.

As Emmel perused the manuscript lying before us on the table, someone asked him if this really was about Jesus and Judas Iscariot. Emmel turned to Kasser, who bent over the page, searching for the right words, and then pointed at them. There, right on the page in front of our eyes, were the Coptic words for Judas Iscariot. This was the lost Gospel of Judas.

A National Geographic film crew had been filming everything that had happened—our arrival, the opening speeches, the presentation of the manuscript pages, our initial examination of them. We, of course, wanted to see more pages and to have a chance to look over what was there at greater length and greater leisure. We were there not for our own scholarly interests, however, but to provide National Geographic with the information that it needed in order to decide whether it would be worth their while investing in a project on this text. And so they wanted some interviews on tape. They first posed some questions to Emmel, pressing him on the one point of their particular interest: could this be a modern forgery? If they had asked a hundred experts, they would have received the same answer, every time: absolutely no way. But they persisted: suppose someone *wanted* to forge a document like this? How many people in the world would be able to do it—that is, to compose a Gospel in Coptic to make it look like an ancient translation of a Greek original and then fabricate the document on ancient papyrus, passing it off as the real thing? Emmel first blurted out a number, but then paused and said, "No, in fact, I think there are four people in the world who could do it. And two of them are in this room."

My view was that no one could do it. There are modern forgeries, but they are nothing like this. This was an ancient papyrus manuscript written clearly in an ancient hand, similar in many ways to those of fourth- and fifth-century Greek manuscripts that I knew from my study of the texts of the New Testament.

The National Geographic team then wanted to film a discussion between Kasser and me, where I could probe a bit into the contents and meaning of this Gospel that he had been studying for so long, which no other living scholar had yet been able to examine, let alone read and translate. Despite my jet-lagged state, I was full of questions. What exactly did the Gospel say? Did it contain a secret revelation of Jesus, as do other Gnostic texts? Did it contain previously unknown conversations between Jesus and Judas Iscariot? Did it have an account of Jesus' betrayal, told from Judas's perspective? Was it probably the account mentioned by Irenaeus in the second century? How did it begin? How did it end? What was it about?

The questions came quickly to my mind, but I had to ask them patiently. Kasser's principal language is French, and he speaks English a bit reluctantly. And so we went slowly, in English, with the cameras rolling. Frieda Nussberger, the protective owner of the manuscript, was off in the other room with several others while Kasser and I talked. But when she realized what I was asking him, and that he was starting to divulge the secrets found within the manuscript—its actual contents—she hurried into the room, placed her hand on Kasser's shoulder, and gently told him that that was enough for now. She didn't want the world to know what was in the manuscript until she had been able to reach a financial agreement with National Geographic. If everyone knew what the text said, there would be far less urgency to acquire the rights to it.

Next in line for interview was Timothy Jull, who was to provide scientific evidence of the authenticity of the manuscript through carbon-14 dating. This would be hard evidence that the manuscript was what everyone had claimed it was, an ancient document. And his examination could be even more precise than that: from his laboratory in Arizona he could provide a date for the manuscript's writing material—the papyrus—to within about sixty years of its manufacture. The way carbon-14 dating works is this. Every living being, plant and animal, is made up of organic compounds that absorb the radioactive isotope carbon-14 from the atmosphere. When a living thing dies, the carbon-14 it contains begins to decay, and does so at a constant rate, so that after 5,700 years, half of what was originally present in the organism has dissipated. This is the half-life of carbon-14. If you don't know the age of the specimen, you can see how much carbon-14 is left in it; this will tell you how long it has been dead. In the case of ancient manuscripts, many of them—including this Gospel we were examining, and most other ancient Christian texts—were written on papyrus, a writing material that was manufactured out of the papyrus reeds that grew in Egypt beside the Nile. A carbon-14 dating can indicate with scientific precision when the papyrus was first cut, in preparation for using it to create the writing material. This would provide independent verification for the rough date estimated by Coptologists such as Kasser and Emmel on the basis of the style of writing found in the text.

For a carbon-14 analysis to be done, however, a small portion of the manuscript has to be processed. This requires cutting a tiny piece—about half a centimeter (approximately ¼ inch) square—and taking it back to the lab for analysis. The analysis destroys the piece. And so Jull, with the assistance of Florence Darbre and Rodolphe Kasser, had to choose some tiny bits to cut away from the surviving pages of the manuscript, bits that would then be lost forever. It was not an easy choice, and they certainly did not want to take any pieces that had any writing on them! They eventually chose five samples from different parts of the manuscript and its cover, to make sure that the entire manuscript was produced at the same time and that none of it was a more recent forgery.

After they had cut their fragments and carefully stored them for transport back to Arizona, we broke for lunch—pizza, of course—and continued talking about what we had seen. Emmel pleaded to be shown more of the manuscript, and so Darbre retrieved a number of Plexiglas-covered sheets for him to peruse. I sat across the table from him and looked to see what I could find. Every now and then Emmel would make an exclamation and show me something significant. A couple of things I could see on my own, especially the altogether important conclusion of the document we had been asked to verify. There it was, clear as day, understandable even for someone with limited experience reading Coptic manuscripts. The last line of the last page read: "And he received some money and turned him over to them." And then came the words *peuaggelion Nioudas*—"the Gospel of Judas." Here it was, sitting in front of me, above a pizza parlor in a small Swiss town near Lake Geneva: a text discussed and condemned by early church fathers, which had disappeared for centuries, only to be recovered by unknown circumstances and unknown figures in modern times, a lost Gospel that now had been found.

The people at National Geographic had what they needed for the day. We headed out to the van and drove back to the hotel. I was thrilled but bone-tired. Much of the afternoon remains a blur to me as we continued conversations and speculations. We had seen the physical manuscript—but what did the Gospel actually say? We had only a few hints from Kasser, a few tidbits picked out by Emmel in his perusal of some pages, and a few surmises. That evening we all went out to dinner in Geneva and over drinks made a friendly wager—experts, film crew, and everyone else—on the carbon-14 dating: how early could this thing be? Some proposed early fifth century; I guessed middle of the fourth. Some—notably Herb Krosney, the independent researcher who first uncovered the existence of the document and alerted National Geographic to its historical importance—were even more sanguine, thinking possibly early fourth century.

We were all wrong, but Krosney came the closest. Months later we learned that the carbon-14 dating put the manuscript much earlier, within sixty years, one direction or another, of 280 CE—late third century. If the mean dating is correct—if this document really was written around 280 CE—it would be our earliest datable Gnostic Gospel (assuming that it was in fact Gnostic), one of the earliest datable documents from early Christianity. The date of the production of the manuscript, of course, does not tell us when the Gospel itself was first composed (just as the Bible sitting beside me on my desk was manufactured in 1989, but the Gospels it contained were composed nineteen hundred years earlier). There still was the question of whether this was the actual Gospel of Judas known about from Irenaeus, and if so, what it contained that made it so threatening to church fathers that they condemned its use.

Emmel, Jull, and Terry Garcia left Geneva the next morning, but I stayed an extra day. National Geographic wanted to film an interview with me concerning the historical significance of the manuscript, assuming that it was what it was purported to be, the recovered Gospel of Judas. Wanting a historical site for the interview, the crew had learned of the ruins of a Roman theater not far from Geneva, in the town of Avenches, in Roman times called Aventicum. There the camera crew set up for the interview, with the partially restored ruins in the background. It was bitterly cold; between shoots we would head into the café across the street for coffee and warmth. Roberty was there—he wanted to hear what I would say about the precious document. And Herb Krosney had scripted a number of questions. The goal, of course, was to show why a find like this might matter—to National Geographic or to anyone else.

Once we got started, the questions came rapid-fire. What do we know about Judas? Was he actually one of the twelve disciples? Why was he called Iscariot? Do we have solid evidence that he betrayed Jesus? What exactly is it that he betrayed to the authorities: simply Jesus' whereabouts, or something else in

---

Facing page   The Codex containing the Gospel of Judas. This is the disheveled state of the manuscript before restoration; the bottom part of the page is the conclusion of the "Letter from Peter to Philip."

addition? Why would he betray his own teacher? What is said about Judas outside the New Testament? Why did later Christians use the story of Judas to cast aspersions on the Jewish people, so that in the Middle Ages Judas became the prototypical "Jew"—a greedy, thieving, demon-driven Christ-killer? Could a new discovery of a Gospel of Judas alter that portrayal? What do we know about a Gospel allegedly by Judas? What did Irenaeus say about it? Why did Irenaeus find it so dangerous? Is it possible that this newly discovered Gospel could be the one that Irenaeus condemned? Would its discovery be of interest only to scholars, or to a broader audience? If to a broader audience, why? Presumably Judas himself did not write the book, so why should we care what later authors imagined he would have said? And so on.

Many of my answers to these questions will be found in the pages that follow—as will be a fuller account of how the Gospel was first discovered and how it wound its way through the hands of various antiquities dealers, some of them unscrupulous (or at least incompetent), until it was purchased by Frieda Tchacos Nussberger and given over to the Maecenas Foundation, headed by Mario Roberty. The answers were a bit slow in coming. It took many months before everything fell into place—before I could read an English translation of the book and examine at leisure the Coptic text on which it was based, and months more before I could learn the story of the discovery and handling of the manuscript over the past years, based on the book eventually produced by Herb Krosney, who played the literary sleuth to piece all the details together.

But already during my interview on that cold day in Avenches, I could say a few things about Judas—whom, of course, I already had studied as a historical figure—and of the potential significance of a Gospel written in his name. It was clear to me that this newly discovered Gospel of Judas could be one of two things. Its importance and the breadth of its appeal would depend entirely on which of these two things it was.

On one hand, it could be a typical Gnostic Gospel that described a Gnostic view of the world, revealing the secrets of how this miserable world of pain and suffering came into existence as a cosmic disaster, and how those of us in the know (the term *Gnostic* comes from the Greek word for "knowledge") can escape the material trappings of this world to return to our heavenly home. We have a number of Gospels like this, many of them discovered in the twentieth century. If that is the kind of Gospel this one was, then its discovery would be important—but principally for scholars of early Christianity.

It was possible, however, that the Gospel was something else. Conceivably—I couldn't know at this point, not having been able yet to read it—it could be an account of the life of Jesus told from the perspective of Judas. If that's what it was, it would not merely be important. It would be huge. This would be the first Gospel ever discovered that told the story from the betrayer's perspective, from the point of view of one of Jesus' alleged enemies. What if in this account the betrayer of Jesus was portrayed as his closest friend and truest disciple? That would involve an alternative point of view from early Christianity, about which we find faint traces and rumors in our ancient sources, but for which we have no surviving evidence. If this Gospel contained that kind of perspective, it would be one of the truly significant discoveries of modern times, rivaling many of the documents discovered in 1945 near Nag Hammadi, Egypt.

What I had no way of knowing at the time of my interview was that my either/or hypothesis was wrong. For as it turns out, the Gospel is not one of these things. It is both. This is a Gospel that conveys a Gnostic message (which I will explain in later chapters) about the creation of the world, the coming of Christ, and the nature of salvation. But it is also a book that portrays the relationship of Jesus to his betrayer in ways completely contrary to the New Testament portrayals.

This alternative portrayal naturally leads the historian to ask yet again about the real, historical Judas Iscariot. Who was he? What was he like? What did he do? Why did he do it? And how can we know?

To begin answering these questions I need to establish some background information. And so, although the bulk of this book will be about the Gospel of Judas, discovered in the late 1970s and published now nearly thirty years later, we will need to start by learning about the portrayal of Judas in our other surviving sources—the Gospels of the New Testament and other ancient sources outside the Gospel. After I have set out that context, I will move to a full discussion of the Gospel of Judas—where and how it was discovered, how it moved around among antiquities dealers in Egypt, the United States, and Switzerland, how it came to be restored and translated, what it contains, and why its message should be so intriguing, both to scholars of early Christianity and to lay readers interested in knowing about the New Testament, the life of Jesus, and the history of Christianity after his death.

This will then lead me to undertake a historical exploration of what we can say about the historical Judas himself: who he was, what he did, and why he did it.

In many ways, Judas will remain an enigmatic figure for us. This new Gospel—as often happens—raises at least as many questions as it answers. But that is part of the excitement of historical research. Whenever we study the past, we find new avenues of exploration opened up to us. Ultimately we want to find answers, to be sure. The discovery of a new text, however, not only satisfies our longings to know more; it also fuels the fires of our curiosity. This is the kind of text the Gospel of Judas is. It is an old text with the power to generate new questions, questions about who Jesus really was, what he revealed, and what his mission involved; questions about Judas, what he did, and why he did it; and even questions about who we ourselves are, why we are here, and where we are going.

⌘

CHAPTER TWO

Judas in Our Earliest Gospels

F act may be stranger than fiction, but it is also harder to find. One of the
most interesting things about the people connected with the life of Jesus—
whether Judas Iscariot, Mary Magdalene, the disciple John, Pontius Pilate, or anyone else—is that numerous legends survive about them, but few certifiable facts.

Just take Mary Magdalene, for example.[1] People today typically think of
her as a reformed prostitute who was a particularly close disciple of Jesus—
closer than most of his male disciples. Those who (think they) know even more
about her recognize her as the one who anointed Jesus' head with costly perfume prior to his betrayal and arrest; some think of her as the woman who was
caught in an act of adultery and whom Jesus saved from being stoned to death
by saying, "Let the one without sin among you be the first to cast a stone at
her." Recently, because of the blockbuster success of Dan Brown's page-turning
thriller *The Da Vinci Code,* people have come to think of her not just as Jesus'
adoring disciple but as his adoring spouse, with whom he had sex and fathered
a child.

How much of this portrait of Mary is fact and how much fiction? In actual-
ity, it is all fiction, every bit of it. Or at least if it is fact, it is not fact that can be
found in our earliest sources—the Gospels of the New Testament that give us
the only testimonies from the first century about this woman. In all of the
Gospels of the New Testament, Mary Magdalene is mentioned only one time
during Jesus' entire public ministry prior to his crucifixion, and in that one
reference we are simply told that she was one of three women who accompanied Jesus and his disciples during his itinerant preaching ministry and who
gave them the funds they needed to survive (the other two were Joanna and
Susanna).[2] That's it! There are no references to her being a prostitute, having
anointed Jesus (that was a different, unnamed woman), or having been the

woman caught in adultery (that was yet a different unnamed woman)—let alone having been Jesus' wife and lover. Where, then, do people get their ideas about the Magdalene from? From legends told about her many decades or even centuries after her death. These are stories that are made up—sometimes (for example, in the case of her having Jesus' baby) made up in modern times by novelists or "independent researchers" who want to sell books.

What does this have to do with Judas Iscariot? In his case as well we have few historical facts but numerous later retellings of his story. Some of these retellings come from sources long after his day—for example, in medieval legends that arose centuries after his death. Some of them are from merely decades later, for example, in the Gospels of the New Testament. To be sure, in some instances the tales told about Judas can provide us with historical information about who he really was, what he did, and why he did it. But in many instances it is hard to separate the fact from the fiction—especially because our very earliest sources tell us so little when we want to know so much.

Judas in Our Earliest Source

It comes as a surprise to many people to learn that our earliest source for knowing about the life of Jesus is not one of the Gospels of the New Testament but the writings of the apostle Paul. Even though the Gospels are placed first in the New Testament, that does not mean they were the first to be written—the New Testament is arranged not according to when the books were written but according to genre, with the Gospels first, then the book of Acts, then the letters (of Paul and others), and then the book of Revelation. Although they are placed in the middle of the New Testament, Paul's letters were the first of the New Testament books to be written. In fact, they are the earliest Christian writings that we have, of any kind whatsoever. And so, in asking about figures in the life of Jesus, it is always helpful to look at our earliest author to see what he has to say about them. This is especially the case given what we will see later: the Gospels of the New Testament were written thirty-five to sixty-five years after the life of Jesus, and they don't always agree in everything they say about it. If we can find an earlier source, such as Paul, that provides independent information about Jesus' life (it is independent because the Gospel writers hadn't read Paul's writings, and he couldn't have read theirs, as they hadn't written yet), then we can know what Jesus said, did, and experienced with greater certainty.

The problem is that Paul rarely mentions any of the figures known from the Gospel accounts of Jesus' life—he never mentions Mary Magdalene, for example, or the disciple John, or Pontius Pilate. Or Judas Iscariot. Scholars debate why it is that Paul says so little about the characters known from Jesus' life—or indeed, even more striking, about Jesus' life itself. Some scholars think that Paul had other matters on his mind and so didn't bother to mention such things; others think that he assumed that his readers knew all about them; yet others think he doesn't mention incidents and characters from Jesus' earthly life because he simply didn't know about them. He was writing, after all, before the Gospels, and he was not one of Jesus' earthly followers—so maybe he didn't know the stories that were later to become part of the Christian Scriptures.[3] In any event, even though Paul is the earliest Christian source, he doesn't say much about the life of the one to whom he was devoted as his Lord.

He does say a few things, however, and hints at several others, and these statements and hints are eagerly pounced upon by scholars who want to know what actually happened during Jesus' life. Some scholars have thought that Paul does refer to Judas Iscariot in a veiled way in an off-the-cuff remark in one of his letters.[4] In his first letter to the Corinthians, Paul is upset for a number of reasons, mainly because the Corinthian Christians were misbehaving in lots of ways: he indicates that they formed cliques that contended with one another over which of their leaders was spiritually superior; their worship services had grown chaotic; there was rampant immorality, with some men visiting prostitutes and bragging about it in church (they were saved already, so why did it matter how they behaved?), and one fellow was living in sin with his stepmother. Paul writes 1 Corinthians to deal with these and other problems.

One of the problems was that the Corinthians' weekly communion meal, held in commemoration of Jesus' death, had gotten out of control. This was not like communion in modern Christian churches—whether Catholic, Orthodox, or Protestant—where worshipers eat a wafer or small piece of bread and take a small sip of wine or grape juice. It was more like a potluck supper where food and wine were shared in recollection of the Last Supper Jesus had with his disciples before his betrayal, arrest, and crucifixion. This meal was meant to commemorate what Jesus had done for the sake of others and to reflect the love he had shown to all. But at Corinth the meal had evolved into something else. Paul indicates that some members of the congregation were coming early and eating all the food and getting drunk on the wine, and others—those who had to work late—were finding nothing left to eat or drink. For Paul this was not good. He deals with the problem in his letter, upbraiding the Corinthian Christians for their disorderly conduct and reminding them what the meal was supposed to be all about. In that context, he reminds his readers how Jesus himself held his Last Supper—and it is here that Paul may, in the opinion of some readers, make a reference to Judas Iscariot. Paul begins his recollection with the following (this is how the passage is sometimes translated):

> For I received from the Lord that which I also handed over to you, that the Lord Jesus, on the night in which he was betrayed, took bread, and after giving thanks, broke it and said, "This is my body given for you." (1 Cor. 11:23–24)

The key phrase for us, of course, is the statement that this took place "on the night in which he was betrayed." Surely this is a reference to the betrayal of Jesus by Judas Iscariot, so even though the betrayer is not mentioned by name, it is clear that Paul knows all about the incident.

But in fact the matter is not so clear. The problem has to do with the Greek word that Paul uses when he says that Jesus was "betrayed" (Paul, and all the other authors of the New Testament, wrote in Greek). The word is common in the New Testament—Paul himself uses it over fifteen times in his letters, including one other time in the passage I just quoted. When Paul says that the information he is now relating is what he also "handed over" to the Corinthians, it is the same word he uses when he indicates that Jesus was "betrayed." The Greek word is *paradidomi*—and it literally means "to give or hand someone or something over to someone else."

Is Paul referring, then, to Judas Iscariot handing Jesus over to the ruling authorities for trial? Probably not, for in every other instance that Paul uses *paradidomi* with reference to Jesus, it refers to the act of God, who "handed Jesus over" to death for the sake of others. This can be seen, to choose just one passage, from Romans 8:32:

> What then shall we say to these things? If God is for us, who is against us? He who did not spare his own son, but handed him over [*paradidomi*] for all of us—how will he not give us all things with him?

Since Paul doesn't specify that he is talking about the betrayal of Jesus by Judas in 1 Corinthians 11:23–24, the translation I gave of the passage may be inaccurate. Probably it would be better to stick with how Paul uses the word in question elsewhere, and translate it as follows:

> For I received from the Lord that which I also handed over to you, that the Lord Jesus, on the night in which he was handed over [by God, to face death], took bread, and after giving thanks, broke it and said, "This is my body given for you." (1 Cor. 11:23–24)

If this translation is correct, then there is no reference in any of Paul's letters to Judas Iscariot or to his act of betrayal. In fact, there is one passage that might suggest that Paul did *not* know about Judas and his betrayal. Later in the same book, Paul is discussing the appearances of Jesus to various groups and individuals after his resurrection (1 Cor. 15:3–8), and here he states that "[Christ first] appeared to Cephas, and then to the Twelve." This clearly refers to Jesus' twelve disciples, but how could he have appeared to all of them if Judas was no longer among their number? Either Paul is using the term "the Twelve" as a shorthand reference to Jesus' closest disciples—so he doesn't really mean there were exactly twelve of them—or he doesn't know the tradition that one of the Twelve had betrayed his master and departed from the group.

In any event, what this means is that our earliest knowledge of Judas comes not from our earliest Christian author but from the Gospels of the New Testament, written thirty-five to sixty-five years after the events they narrate. This makes it difficult to know what Judas actually did in betraying Jesus, let alone why he did it. Our later sources, the Gospels, have varying accounts of the deed and its motivation. I won't worry about trying to establish the historical facts, however, until much later, in the final chapters of this book. For now we can turn to the accounts themselves to see how each of the Gospel authors portrays Judas and his nefarious deed. As we will see, each of them gives a different portrayal.

Judas in the Gospel of Mark

To make sense of how each of the Gospel writers portrays Judas, it is important to understand more broadly how they portray Jesus and his disciples. As it turns out, the distinctive emphases of each Gospel come to be reflected in what they have to say about Judas. That is to say, the traditions about Judas and what he did are molded in such a way as to reflect what the authors are trying to say about Jesus more broadly. The Gospel writers are not simply presenting us with historical facts. They are telling stories about Jesus, shaping the stories in such a way as to convey their own views about who he is and why he matters. The stories of the secondary figures in their accounts—the disciples in general, for example, and Judas Iscariot in particular—are told in light of these views.

This can be seen with particular clarity in the Gospel of Mark, our earliest surviving account of Jesus' life.[5] Mark has always been my favorite Gospel, in part because its view of Jesus is so understated and the literary artistry is so profound. Earlier scholars, such as the great Augustine, minimized the importance of Mark, thinking that it was simply a condensation of the Gospel of Matthew—a kind of *Reader's Digest* version of the more complete account. But since the nineteenth century, scholars have realized that this is not the case, that Mark was probably the first Gospel to be written, later to be expanded by Matthew and Luke.[6] Unfortunately, the early scholars who thought this made an unwarranted step and concluded that since Mark was the earliest, it was a bare-bones factual statement about what Jesus really said and did, which came to be expanded later. In their view, Mark was just concerned with the facts.

Since the early twentieth century, scholars have come to a different view, realizing that Mark is just as theologically interested in his view of Jesus as any of the other Gospel writers.[7] He is not simply stating historical facts but is telling a story. His understanding of Jesus has affected how he tells the story. Mark is fairly subtle in how he conveys his theological points about Jesus— and this is what makes reading and understanding Mark so challenging and so interesting. Beneath the surface of the narrative is a theological agenda, which affects everything he says about Jesus. In particular, this agenda affects how he portrays Jesus in relationship to others, especially to his disciples, including Judas Iscariot.

Mark's Portrayal of Jesus

When you read Mark's Gospel carefully, it is clear that he wants to portray Jesus as the messiah of the Jews, the Son of God, who was destined to die for the sins of others. What is striking is that almost no one in the entire narrative understands Jesus' identity, not even the disciples.

Who does know who Jesus is in this Gospel? Jesus himself obviously knows. When he gets baptized in the very opening of the account, a voice comes from heaven that declares, "You are my beloved Son, in whom I am well pleased" (1:11). This voice comes not to the crowds who are gathered but only to Jesus (it does not say "This is my Son," as it says, for example, in the Gospel of Matthew). In addition, since this is the voice of God declaring Jesus' identity, God obviously knows who Jesus is. Moreover, Mark knows, since he's writing the account. And you know because you're reading it. Who else knows? The demons know, because when he casts them out of a demoniac, they cry, "You are the son of God" (3:11). Jesus orders them to be silent and not to tell anyone. No one else seems to know.

The people from his hometown can't understand how he can say and do such wonderful things—isn't he just the local carpenter (6:1–6)? His mother, brothers, and sisters think he's gone out of his mind, and they try to remove him from public view (3:20–21). The leaders of his people think that he is inspired and empowered by the Devil (3:22). Even his own disciples don't understand who he is (6:52), as he repeatedly laments, for example, in 8:21: "Do you not yet understand?"

The misunderstanding of the disciples is one of the key themes of this Gospel. Halfway through the Gospel—after Jesus has been delivering amazing teachings and performing astounding miracles—it becomes clear that the disciples have some sense that Jesus is someone special, but their understanding of who he really is is completely wrong. This is shown in the famous episode of the confession of Peter. Jesus asks his disciples, "Who do people say that I am?" (8:27). They reply that some consider him to be John the Baptist raised from the dead, or Elijah of Old Testament fame come back to life, or one of the other prophets. Jesus then asks who *they* think he is, and Peter, representative of the group, replies with what you might think is the right answer: "You are the messiah" (8:29). Jesus responds by instructing them not to tell anyone (he constantly tries to keep his identity under wraps in this Gospel); he then indicates that he must journey to Jerusalem to be rejected by the Jewish leaders and crucified. Peter shows his complete misunderstanding of Jesus' identity by rebuking him for saying such a thing. Jesus in turn rebukes Peter and calls him "Satan," spurning him for thinking like a human, not like God (8:33).

What does all this mean? Peter and the others appear to know that Jesus is the messiah, but they don't know what kind of messiah he is. To make sense of this, we have to understand what first-century Jews thought about the messiah. Many Jews probably didn't think about the messiah at all, but those who did had a range of ways of thinking about him. Some thought he would be a great military leader who would overthrow the foreign oppressors and make Israel a great nation again, as it had been under the rule of King David in the past (this appears to be Peter's view). Others thought he would be a divine-like being who would come in judgment on the earth to overthrow the forces of evil and set up God's good Kingdom on earth. Yet others thought he would be a divinely inspired priest who would lead the Jewish people in following the laws of God. To our knowledge, however, no one thought that the messiah would be someone who would be crucified—crushed by God's enemies as a helpless criminal.[8]

For Mark, however, that is precisely who Jesus was. He was the messiah—but he was the messiah who would suffer. That view would have seemed to be nonsense to most Jews. The messiah was to be great and powerful, not weak and helpless. He was to rule God's enemies, not be squashed by them. Peter, representing the disciples, has a normal expectation of who the messiah would be. If Jesus is the messiah, then obviously he will not be rejected and crucified. But according to Mark, this was a serious misunderstanding. Jesus was to be a suffering messiah.

On two later occasions in Mark's Gospel Jesus indicates that he will go to Jerusalem to be killed (9:31; 10:33–34), and on both occasions the disciples again show that they don't understand: they think Jesus as messiah will rule, and that they will rule with him (9:32; 10:35). In the first instance, the disciples begin arguing among themselves which one of them is the greatest (if Jesus is the great and powerful messiah, which of them is next in line?); in the second, James and John want to know if they can sit at his right and left hands in his glorious coming Kingdom. Both times Jesus expresses some frustration with the disciples: they don't understand that being his followers means suffering, not glory. Those who are truly his disciples will "take up their cross" in order to follow him.

It is striking that the disciples never do get it in this Gospel. Despite their claims that they will stick with Jesus through thick and thin, when he is arrested they all flee. Peter, again representing them all, denies three times that he even knows Jesus. They are not there to stand up for him at his trial. They are not there to lend support when he gets crucified. They do not offer to give his body a decent burial. They do not visit the tomb afterward.

Instead, it is other people—not the disciples—who prove faithful at the time of crisis. Before his arrest, an unknown woman anoints his head in an extraordinary and generous gesture, which he takes as an anointing of his body for his imminent burial (14:3–9; the disciples, characteristically, voice their objections). It is Simon of Cyrene, an otherwise unknown person, who "takes up his cross" and carries it to the place of crucifixion (15:21). It is a group of women who watch him get crucified (15:40–41). It is the unnamed Roman centurion in charge of the crucifixion who sees him die and confesses that he is "the Son of God" (this centurion seems to be the only one in the entire text who really understands that it is in his death that Jesus is God's son). It is Joseph of Arimathea, another unknown figure, who provides him with a decent burial (15:43). And it is the women, Mary Magdalene and two others, who visit the tomb on the third day (16:1). Strikingly, they are told by a man at the empty tomb to go tell "the disciples and Peter" that Jesus has been raised from the dead, but they flee the tomb "and don't tell anyone anything, for they were afraid" (16:8).[9] The disciples never do figure it out.

Mark's Portrayal of Judas

How does all this relate to Judas Iscariot? Judas is not mentioned much in the Gospel of Mark. His name occurs only three times. But in some ways, his story is the story of the other disciples. He also is someone who doesn't "get it." Unlike the others, he does something about his misunderstanding. He is the one who turns Jesus over to the authorities. But in keeping with Mark's stark narrative—where he typically refers to incidents without explaining their deeper meaning—we are not told what motivated him to do so.

Judas is first mentioned early in Mark's narrative, when Jesus chooses his twelve disciples and calls them "apostles" (i.e., those sent on a mission) (3:13, 19). These were his twelve closest followers, whom he wanted to "be with him" and whom he authorized to go forth "to preach" and "to have authority over the demons." The final one chosen is "Judas Iscariot, who betrayed him" (or "who handed him over"). There is nothing in this first reference to suggest that Jesus put Judas in a different camp or that he recognized Judas would have a role different from the others.' Judas had the same calling, the same responsibilities, the same authority, the same mission as everyone else. And so, from here on out, one has to assume that for Mark, Judas was one of Jesus' closest, most devoted followers.

But if one of Mark's overarching points is that all the disciples misunderstood Jesus and failed to remain faithful to him in the end, then Judas too misunderstood and failed. In his case the failure is simply more obvious. Later in the Gospel we're told that Jesus knew that one of his chosen ones would betray him, predicting the betrayal in the scene at the Last Supper: "Woe to that one through whom the Son of Man is turned over. It would have been better for that one not to have been born" (14:20). Judas is not named here, but the reader knows exactly whom Jesus is referring to. In no small measure this is because Judas by this point has already agreed to do the evil deed.

Immediately before this account of the Last Supper comes the story I referred to earlier, when an unnamed woman anoints Jesus' head with costly perfume. Jesus takes this as a kindly act: she, at least, has understood that he must die, even if the disciples do not grasp this. The disciples themselves, in a characteristic act of miscomprehension, do not appreciate her act. "Some of those who were there" (I assume this is the disciples, though it doesn't actually say this) were outraged that the woman had wasted such expensive ointment, when it could have been sold for nearly a year's wages and given to the poor. Jesus, as is his wont, rebukes their failure to understand:

> Leave her alone; why do you trouble her? She has done a good deed for me. For you will always have the poor with you, and whenever you want you can do good for them; but you will not always have me. She has done what she could: she has anointed my body ahead of time for burial. Truly I tell you, wherever the gospel is preached throughout the world, what she has done will also be spoken of, in memory of her. (Mark 14:8–9)

And then comes the next fateful verse, the second of the entire Gospel in which Judas is explicitly named:

> And Judas Iscariot, one of the Twelve, went out to the chief priests in order that he might betray him to them. Those who learned of it rejoiced and promised to give him money. So he was looking for an opportunity to betray him.[10]

We are not told what it is, exactly, that Judas has agreed to betray. Somewhat earlier, immediately before the anointing, we learn that the chief priests and scribes—evidently because Jesus was winning popularity among the crowds in Jerusalem by his preaching—were seeking a way to "arrest him by stealth and to kill him." But they did not want to do it "during the [Passover] feast, lest that lead to a riot among the people" (14:1). It appears, then, that Judas is willing to give them information that they need to make the arrest without anyone noticing.[11]

What is more striking is that Mark gives us no explicit motive for Judas's decision. We are told that the Jewish leaders (the "chief priests") agree to give Judas money for the betrayal. But we are not told that money is why Judas went to them in the first place. As we will see, Matthew explicitly states that this was Judas's motive, and John implies it. But in Mark there is no motive at all, unless we can infer one from the context.

Up to this point the narrative is modeled to show that the disciples—all of them, Judas included—fail to understand who Jesus is, thinking that he must be a great and powerful figure, not one who is to be arrested, tried, and crucified like a common criminal. Then this unnamed woman anoints him with oil. Did they misunderstand this act as well?

In ancient Israel, the divinely appointed kings were anointed with oil during their inauguration ceremonies, as a sign of God's favor upon them. In fact, the kings were sometimes called "God's anointed one." In the Hebrew language, the word for "anointed one" is *mashiach,* from which we get our word *messiah.* In Greek, the language of the New Testament, the translation of *mashiach* is *christos,* whence we get our word *Christ.* For the disciples, if Jesus is the messiah (Christ), that must mean that he is God's future king. But instead of interpreting his anointing as a kingly act, Jesus indicates that he has been anointed for his "burial." That is, he takes this woman's kindly gesture as an indication that he is soon to die. After all the other instances in Mark where Jesus tries to explain to his disciples that he is the messiah who must suffer, they patently display their misunderstanding. Is it possible that this is what Mark means us to infer in this instance as well? In this case it is not Peter who shows he doesn't get it, as in Mark 8; and it is not James and John, as in Mark 10. It is Judas Iscariot.

Since Mark doesn't tell us what motivated Judas, it appears to have been this immediately preceding act. But what conclusions are we to draw? There are several options that we might consider, none of them completely satisfactory:

1. Is it that, for Mark, Judas believed that Jesus was to be the future king, and agreed to turn him over to the authorities because he was tired of waiting for Jesus' public declarations of his intentions and thought that he could force his hand by putting Jesus in a situation where he was more or less compelled to take action, call for the crowds to rally in his support, and assert himself as their leader? As attractive as this option is, it doesn't seem to gel with the rest of Mark's narrative. If that was his motivation (remember, I'm talking not about what the historical Judas did, but only about what Mark wanted us to understand that he did), why doesn't Judas in Mark stir the crowds at Jesus' trial to rise in opposition to the Roman authorities?

2. Or is it that Judas now, finally, of all the disciples, did come to understand what Jesus had been saying all along, that he was not to be the anointed king but the crucified messiah, and in order to assist him to that end, he did Jesus' will and handed him over to his death? This is an intriguing possibility, but it overlooks the fact that Jesus earlier declared that the one who "handed him over" would be condemned, not blessed, for his actions: "It would be better for that one not to have been born" (14:20).

3. Is it that Judas now came to understand Jesus' intention—of being tried and executed—and out of frustration decided to turn traitor to the cause? According to this interpretation, Mark's Judas thought that Jesus really should seek the throne of Israel, but once he realized that was not the plan, he became Jesus' mortal enemy and betrayer.

Unfortunately, we may never know what Mark wanted us to think about the betrayal, other than the fact that Jesus condemned the one who was to do it and that Judas made the necessary arrangements with the Jewish leadership in Jerusalem.

The final reference to Judas in Mark's Gospel comes in the betrayal scene itself. After the Last Supper, Jesus has gone out with his disciples (without Judas? Or did Judas sneak off by himself later?) to the Garden of Gethsemane to pray. Here again those closest to him prove faithless. He asks Peter, James, and John to stay alert and watch for him while he prays in private, but three times he comes back to find them asleep. The third time he tells them that "the hour has come. See, the Son of Man is betrayed into the hands of sinners. Arise, let us go. See, the one who betrays me is near" (14:41–42). And immediately Judas Iscariot arrives with an armed crowd from the chief priests, scribes, and elders. He had indicated how he would identify Jesus to them: with a kiss. He comes to Jesus, calls him "rabbi," and then kisses him. The crowd lays hands on Jesus and arrests him with only a brief skirmish before the disciples all flee. Judas tells them to take Jesus away "securely" (14:44)—but it is not clear what he means. Is he afraid Jesus might try to escape? Or does he want Jesus to be protected from the mob?

Scholars have long noticed the parallels that Mark appears to be drawing between Judas, the one who betrayed Jesus, and Peter, the one who denied him. Both failed their master. Peter in his bravado had sworn at the Last Supper that he would never desert Jesus. But then in Jesus' hour of need, he fell asleep instead of staying awake to watch for him—and not just once, but three times. When Jesus was arrested, he along with the other disciples fled the scene. And later, when charged with being one of Jesus' followers, again he proved faithless, denying that he knew him, again not once but three times.

Mark provides some hints that Peter will be restored to a right standing with Jesus. After he denies Jesus for the third time he remembers that Jesus had predicted it would happen, and he breaks down, weeping (14:72). Later, after the crucifixion, when the women go to the tomb to find it empty, they are instructed to go "tell the disciples and Peter" that Jesus had been raised and that he would meet them in Galilee (16:7). Why is Peter specifically mentioned along with the other disciples? No doubt because Jesus wanted him to know that he stood forgiven.

What about Judas? Mysteriously, but characteristically, Mark leaves it to his readers' imaginations what happened to him. He is never mentioned after betraying Jesus with a kiss. But one can scarcely hope for his repentance and return to Jesus' good graces, for Jesus has already indicated that it would have been better for him "not to have been born" (14:20). Peter then is restored, but Judas is evidently lost. And that's all Mark has to say about the matter.

Judas in the Gospel of Matthew

Whereas the Gospel of Mark was written about thirty-five or forty years after Jesus' death (possibly 65–70 CE), Matthew was composed about ten or fifteen years later (80–85 CE). For over a century scholars have argued that Matthew used Mark as one of its sources. One of the best ways to study Matthew is by seeing how his stories about Jesus are different from Mark's—seeing, that is, what Matthew has added to Mark, taken away from Mark, or altered in Mark. By noticing what Matthew has changed we get a clear idea concerning what he wants to emphasize in ways different from his earlier source.[12]

Matthew's Differences from Mark

For our purposes here, I don't need to give a full account of Matthew's alterations of Mark but can simply point out three kinds of changes that are particularly relevant for understanding the way Matthew chose to portray Judas Iscariot in his account.

1. For one thing, Matthew is a much longer Gospel than Mark, mainly because he has added large sections of Jesus' teaching, not found in the earlier Gospel. So, for example, only in Matthew do we get the famous Sermon on the Mount (Matt. 5–7). In this sermon, Jesus delivers some of his best-known teachings, not found in Mark, including the Beatitudes ("Blessed are the poor in spirit"), the Lord's prayer ("Our Father"), the Golden Rule ("Do to others as you would have them do to you"), and so on. In some of the most distinctive sayings of the sermon, Jesus instructs his followers to be concerned for the spiritual things in life, not for material things.

   > Do not lay up treasures for yourselves on earth, where moth and rust destroy and where thieves break in and steal; but lay up treasures for yourselves in heaven. . . . For where your treasure is, there your heart will be also. (6:19–21)

   > You cannot serve both God and riches. (6:24)

   > Do not be anxious about your life, what you eat or drink, nor about your body, what you wear . . . Look at the birds of heaven: they do not sow or reap or gather crops into the barn, but your Father feeds them. Are you not worth much more than they? (6:25–26)

2. Matthew is often thought of as the most "Jewish" of the Gospels of the New Testament, in that here Jesus places a greater emphasis on following the Jewish law than in Mark (or the others). Here alone does Jesus say:

   > Do not think that I came to destroy the law and the prophets. I did not come to destroy but to fulfill. Truly I say to you, until heaven and earth pass away, not an iota, not a stroke of a letter will pass away before it has all been fulfilled. Whoever therefore looses one of the least of these commandments and teaches others to do likewise will be called least in the Kingdom of Heaven; but whoever does them and teaches them will be called great in the Kingdom of Heaven. (5:17–19)

   In this Gospel there is a special emphasis that the things Jesus said, did, and experienced were all "fulfillments" of prophecies of the Jewish Scriptures—starting with his birth to a virgin mother (1:20–23; cited as a fulfillment of Isaiah 7:14) in Bethlehem (2:6; cited as a fulfillment of Micah 5:2), including his sojourn as an infant in Egypt (2:13–15; cited as a fulfillment of Hosea 11:1), and moving on through his public ministry (8:17, where his healing ministry is cited as a fulfillment of Isaiah 53:4) to his death. All of these references are found in Matthew but not in Mark, and all of them are said to have been a "fulfillment of the Scriptures."

3. At the same time, Matthew can be seen as the most "anti-Jewish" of the early Gospels, in that here it is the Jewish leaders in particular who are portrayed as Jesus' harshest enemies, whom he vigorously opposes on numerous occasions, lambasting their hypocrisy and constant inclinations to do evil and to lead the Jewish people astray (most stridently in Matthew 23). This opposition between Jesus and the Jewish leadership comes to a head in the accounts of Jesus' trial and crucifixion. Whereas in Mark, both the Roman governor Pontius Pilate and the Jewish leaders (chief priests and scribes, etc.) are responsible for handing Jesus over to death, in Matthew the focus is shifted. It is the Jewish leaders who are responsible, who rally the Jewish people to call out for Jesus' crucifixion, even though Pilate firmly declares him to be innocent and proclaims that he himself is "innocent of this man's blood." In response the Jewish crowd, stirred up by the Jewish leaders, makes that infamous cry that has led to such hateful acts of anti-Semitism over the ages, where they take responsibility for the death of Jesus and pass that responsibility on to their descendants: "His blood be upon us and our children" (27:25).

These changes in emphasis that we find in Matthew's Gospel are reflected in the ways that he tells the stories about Judas Iscariot. As with Mark, Judas is not a central player in most of the stories of the Gospel; here his name occurs only five times. As with Mark, prior to Jesus' betrayal and arrest, Judas is mentioned only once, as one of the twelve disciples whom Jesus called "to have authority over the unclean spirits so as to cast them out, and to heal every illness and every disease" (10:1, 4). Still, the stories about Judas that Matthew took over from Mark have been changed in slight but significant ways, and he has added a story of his own about what happened to Judas after the betrayal.

Judas's Motivation in Matthew

We saw that in the Gospel of Mark, there was no explicit indication of why Judas betrayed Jesus. That is not the case in Matthew. Here the matter is crystal clear: Judas did it for the cash.

As in Mark, Judas's decision to betray Jesus comes immediately after the unnamed woman anoints his head with expensive oil. In Matthew's account of the story, however, it is not simply "some people" who object to this lavish waste of fine ointment. It is "the disciples" who object (26:8). Matthew suggests further that this is what tipped Judas over to the other side. After the account we are now told that "then" Judas went to the high priests.

That is to say, Matthew has made a clearer connection between the two stories, both of them involving money spent on Jesus. The difference between the stories is that the unnamed woman spent what she had to honor Jesus, and

Judas earned what he could to betray him. In the verse that describes his meeting with the chief priests, Judas's motivation is stated:

> Then one of the Twelve who was called Judas Iscariot went to the chief priests and said, "What do you wish to give me, if I hand him over to you?" And they paid him thirty pieces of silver. And from then on he was seeking an opportunity to hand him over. (26:14–16)

This motivation of greed fits in with Matthew's broader agenda in telling the story of Jesus. In Matthew's earlier account of Jesus' teaching, not found in Mark, Jesus had stressed the importance of being more concerned with having treasure in heaven than on earth; he had taught them not to be concerned about the material things of this world; he had told them that it was impossible to serve both God and riches. He had also taught them that they should treat others as they wanted to be treated themselves. In Matthew's version of Jesus' arrest, not only does Judas betray his master, but in doing so he shows that he stands completely against everything that Jesus stood for. He was more interested in earthly treasure, in material things, in riches. And he certainly was not treating Jesus in the way he himself would have wanted to be treated. Matthew's Judas is the negative example of discipleship.

The Fulfillment of Scripture in Matthew

Sometimes Matthew explicitly states that what Jesus did or experienced was a fulfillment of the prophecies of Scripture. On eleven separate occasions Matthew indicates that an event occurred "in order to fulfill what was written in the prophet[s]." None of these passages can be found in Mark.

But there are yet other occasions where Matthew changes a story of Mark without calling attention to the fact that his altered account alludes to a passage of Scripture. This appears to be the case in the passage cited above from Matthew 26:15, where Judas is paid "thirty pieces of silver" in exchange for agreeing to betray Jesus. This is an allusion to the Jewish Scriptures and is part of Matthew's overall plan of showing that everything in Jesus' life was a fulfillment of prophecy.

The payment of thirty pieces of silver appears to be a reference to the Old Testament prophet Zechariah 11:12: "So they weighed out as my wages thirty shekels of silver." Evidence that Matthew has this very passage in mind comes later in his story, in the account that we will be considering next, where Judas repents of his deed and throws the thirty pieces of silver down in the Temple, but the chief priests refuse to take them back. Matthew indicates explicitly in that case that this is a fulfillment of the very next verse in Zechariah: "So I took the thirty shekels of silver and threw them into the treasury in the house of the Lord" (Zech. 11:13).[13]

Interpreters have wrangled over the years concerning what this reference to the prophecy of Zechariah actually signified for Matthew. The problem is that the passage in Zechariah is itself very confusing—hardly anyone can make heads or tails of it. In it we are told that a "shepherd" is appointed to watch over the houses of Israel, but because he is despised, he gives up the job and tells his employers to pay him if they see fit. They pay him thirty pieces of silver, and the Lord instructs him to throw this "lordly price at which I was valued by them" into the treasure of the house of the Lord.

Zechariah is probably being sarcastic when he calls the thirty pieces of silver a "lordly price." According to the Law of Moses, this was the price owed for a slave who was gored by a neighbor's ox (Ex. 21:32). Apart from that, it's hard to know what Zechariah meant by his little story. It appears that for Matthew, at least, this so-called shepherd was a bad person who was getting paid for doing a bad job, and that he then relinquished his payment. And that's what Judas did.

Judas's betrayal, in other words, functions on two levels for Matthew. On the human level, Judas simply wanted to see what he could make off the wicked deed. But on the divine level, in betraying Jesus Judas fulfilled what Scripture predicted would happen. This may have been implied in Mark as well, as readers familiar with Scripture may have thought that Jesus' betrayal by one of his most intimate disciples, who ate bread with him at the Last Supper, could be a fulfillment of what was stated in Psalms of the Jewish Bible: "Even my bosom friend in whom I trusted, who ate of my bread, has lifted the heels against me" (Psalm 41:9). And the fact that Judas betrayed Jesus with a kiss may have been seen as a reference to Proverbs 21:6: "Well meant are the wounds a friend inflicts, but profuse are the kisses of an enemy." Or perhaps the betrayal by a kiss was meant to refer to 2 Samuel 20:9–10, where one of the soldiers of King David, Joab, meets another of his own men, Amasa, who had been delinquent in carrying out David's orders. Joab is said to have grabbed Amasa by the beard with his right hand to kiss him, while with the left hand he drove a sword into his belly, eviscerating him.

Whether or not Mark understood Judas's act to be a fulfillment of Scripture, that is certainly what Matthew thought—and so he added the claim that Judas did it for thirty pieces of silver, the price of a gored slave.

The Death of Judas in Matthew

There are other small changes that Matthew makes in Mark's account of Judas, but there is one very major difference between the two stories. Unlike Mark, Matthew tells us what Judas did after the betrayal. When he saw "that [Jesus] was condemned," he repented of his deed and brought the thirty pieces of silver back to the chief priests, telling them, "I have sinned by betraying innocent blood" (27:3–4). When they refused to take the money, he threw it down in the Temple and "went out and hanged himself."

The story doesn't quite end there, however. The chief priests decide they can't return the money to the Temple treasury, since "it is blood money"—that is, since it has been connected with the execution of a convicted criminal. And so they use it to purchase "the potter's field" as a place to bury strangers. Because it was a field purchased with blood money, we're told that the place came to be "called the Field of Blood." Matthew indicates that all of this was to fulfill what was spoken by the prophet Jeremiah: "And they took the thirty pieces of silver, the price set of the one on whom the some of the children of Israel had set a price, and they gave these for the potters' field, just as the Lord commanded me" (Matt. 27:9–10).

Scholars have long puzzled over why Matthew indicates that this Scripture passage comes from Jeremiah when it appears to come from Zechariah.[14] It may be that, as in other instances in the New Testament, the author has blended quotations from two different sources and named only one of them.[15] In any event, there are interesting similarities between what Judas does and what the Old Testament prophet Jeremiah did in several passages (see Jer. 18, 19, and 32). In one, for example, Jeremiah is told to take a "potter's jug" to the "Potsherd Gate" going into Jerusalem, and to smash it, in order to show what God is going to do to his people in Jerusalem—destroy them—because they have forsaken him and "filled this place with the blood of the innocent." If Matthew is alluding to this passage in Jeremiah, his message is dire: he is predicting that Jerusalem will be destroyed in retribution for the killing of the innocent Jesus. This interpretation is not at all far-fetched: Matthew intimates a similar claim earlier in his book, for example in 22:7 and 41. For Matthew, living years after the Romans had sacked Jerusalem and destroyed its Temple, this was God's punishment of Jews for the rejection of the messiah. Small wonder later readers would charge Matthew with fueling the fires of anti-Semitism.

In any event, the overarching point that Matthew is trying to make in his story of Judas's death is that even he, Jesus' own betrayer, recognized the error of his ways and came to proclaim that Jesus in fact was innocent and not worthy of "condemnation." The phrase that Matthew uses when he indicates Judas's remorse at betraying "innocent blood" is the same phrase he uses later when Jesus is put on trial before Pilate. Pilate, as we have seen, points out that Jesus has done nothing to deserve death, but the "chief priests and elders" urge the people to call for his crucifixion (Matt. 27:22–23). To show his own view of the matter, Pilate calls for water and washes his hands before the crowd, declaring that he is "innocent of this man's blood."

Matthew's point could not be clearer. If the one who betrayed Jesus indicates that he is innocent, and if the Roman governor who condemned him to death declares him innocent, who is responsible for his death? It is those who forced the governor's hand—the crowds in Jerusalem, driven on by their leaders, the chief priests and elders.

Over the years scholars have disagreed on the genuineness of Judas's repentance. Was he really sorry for what he had done? If so, why didn't he try to secure Jesus' release by standing up for him at his trial? The question may be unanswerable, and it may never even have occurred to Matthew, for a good reason. Even though the Gospel writers often changed the stories that they narrated in order to emphasize the points they wanted to stress, there were limits to what they could say. In this particular case, Matthew may well have known (or at least have heard) that Judas died (or disappeared) after his act of betrayal. And so he told the story in a way that emphasized his overarching point: even the one who turned Jesus in recognized that his condemnation was not just.

In the next chapter we will see that we have other accounts of Judas's death that are strikingly different from this one in Matthew—notably in one of our other canonical sources, the book of Acts, written by the same author who composed the Gospel of Luke. In none of these other stories is Judas said to have hanged himself. The question of what actually happened to Judas is one that we will want to address later, after we have examined all of the early portrayals of his deed and its aftermath.

Judas in the Gospel of Luke

Like Matthew, the Gospel of Luke was written about ten or fifteen years after Mark, and its author also used Mark as one of his sources. Unlike Matthew, Luke wrote a sequel to his Gospel account of Jesus' life, in the book of Acts, a narrative of the early years of Christianity after the death and resurrection of Jesus up through the ministry of the apostle Paul. We will be exploring the book of Acts in the next chapter, since it too mentions the death of Judas but portrays it very differently from the Gospel of Matthew. There is no reference to Judas's death in Luke's Gospel, however, and it is the Gospel that we will focus on here in this chapter.

Luke's changes to Mark are quite different from those of Matthew, but once again they are reflected in the way Luke tells the story of Judas.[16] Judas is not a major player in most of the Gospel. His name occurs only four times in the narrative: when he is called to be one of the Twelve and then at the end, when he decides to betray Jesus and then does the deed.[17] In some respects Luke's account of these latter events is very similar to Mark's. But there are key differences as well, related to the overall changes Luke makes in his Markan source.

The Role of Satan in Luke

One change Luke makes in Mark's portrayal of Jesus occurs at the beginning of his narrative of Jesus' public ministry. As readers of the Gospels have long noticed, even though Mark states at the beginning of his Gospel that after his baptism Jesus was tempted by the Devil for forty days, Mark does not actually describe the famous three temptations in the wilderness, where Jesus is first tempted to turn the stones into bread to assuage his hunger, then to jump off the pinnacle of the Temple to be rescued by the miraculous intervention of God, and then to worship Satan in order to be given rule over all the kingdoms of earth. These three temptations are described in Matthew and Luke but not in Mark.[18]

One of the striking differences between Matthew's and Luke's accounts of the temptation is that the order of their second and third temptations is reversed: the order I summarized above is Matthew's. Luke puts the temptation in the Temple last. But more striking for our purposes here is what happens after Jesus had for the third time spurned the temptation and rebuffed Satan. Luke indicates that after the final temptation, "the Devil left him until an appropriate time" (Luke 4:13).

What a tantalizing statement. What would be the appropriate time for Satan to reappear on the scene? In fact, throughout Luke's account of Jesus' ministry the Devil is noticeably absent. To be sure, Jesus encounters demons on numerous occasions, but he always overcomes them and defeats them. Satan appears powerless during the ministry—and not only at the hands of Jesus but also at the hands of his disciples. After Jesus sends them out on their mission to preach the gospel, heal the sick, and cast out demons, they return with great stories of their success, whereupon Jesus informs them that he has observed "Satan falling from heaven" (10:18; see also 13:16). In other words, the power of the Spirit that allowed Jesus to overcome the Devil in his temptation was at work in his authorized representatives as well. During Jesus' entire ministry, Satan faces one defeat after the other.

And what has that to do with Judas Iscariot? We saw that in Mark there was no motivation stated for his decision to betray Jesus, although there were hints that it was somehow connected with the lavish waste of expensive ointment by the unnamed woman who anointed Jesus. In Matthew, on the other hand, the motivation was clearly stated: Judas wanted the money. Not so in Luke. On one hand, his decision to betray Jesus is not driven by the anointing, for Luke has shifted this story to a different part of the narrative. Here Jesus is not anointed just before his arrest and trial; instead the anointing—again by an unnamed woman—occurs relatively early in his ministry (7:36–50). And the account of the anointing is so different in most of its details from the story in Mark and Matthew that some have questioned whether in fact it is even the same story. In any event, none of the disciples, nor anyone else, is said to be upset about the lavish expense. Instead, Jesus' host, a Pharisee, is upset that he allows himself to be touched by a "sinful" woman. We're not told how she's sinful: the idea that she must have been a prostitute came only later. In the New Testament a "sinful" person was simply anyone who didn't follow the law of Moses scrupulously. She may have been inclined to eat nonkosher foods, for all we know. In any event, it is not this that sets Judas off to betray Jesus.

Nor is he driven by greed. As in Mark, after Jesus' public teaching in Jerusalem, Judas goes off to confer with the "chief priests" to discuss how he might betray him, and they agree to give him money. But Luke does not say that he did it for the cash. What, then, motivated him? For Luke, it was the Devil himself.

Then Satan entered into Judas called Iscariot, who was a member of the Twelve; he went out and consulted with the chief priests and soldiers how he might betray him. (Luke 22:3)

For Luke's Gospel, the betrayal and, ultimately, crucifixion of Jesus was a Satanic plot. Just as Satan had opposed him at the beginning of the Gospel, now he opposes him again at the end. During Jesus' public ministry Satan was at the mercy of Jesus' Spirit-driven power, but in the end Satan reasserts himself. The death of Jesus was a Satanic act to lash back at the Son of God. He used Judas as his henchman to do his dirty work. For Luke, however, it was not Satan and his allies who would have the last word. God would raise Jesus from the dead (at the end of the Gospel) and empower his followers to overcome Satan (at the beginning of Acts). As you would expect from a Christian author, Luke thinks that God ultimately triumphs over the senseless evil wreaked by his enemy, the Devil.

Jesus in Control in Luke

An even more striking change that Luke has made in his source has to do with the way Jesus is portrayed as going to and facing his death. Luke's source, the Gospel of Mark, is a powerful but lean narration of the events leading up to and including the crucifixion, a narration gripping in its sheer pathos. This is sometimes missed by readers who conflate the various Gospel accounts of the crucifixion, jumbling them all together so that the things that Jesus says and does in Mark are combined with what he says and does in all the other Gospels. The result of this conflation of accounts is that the distinctive emphasis of each Gospel is destroyed, while a brand-new account is created—not by one of the Gospel writers but by the reader of the Gospels, who makes Jesus say and do all of the things found in each of the accounts.

Mark's account, as with much of Mark's narrative otherwise, is stark and powerful. Jesus has been betrayed by one of his own followers and denied by another. All his companions have fled; none stands beside him in his hour of need. He is sent off to be crucified, and he is silent throughout the entire proceeding, almost as if in shock at what is happening. He is silent on the way to crucifixion, while being nailed to the cross, and while hanging on the cross. But others are not silent, for nearly everyone present verbally abuses and mocks him: the Jewish leaders, those passing by his cross, and even the two robbers being crucified with him. Here in Mark is a Jesus who has been betrayed, denied, condemned, rejected, mocked, and abandoned, even by God himself. At the very end Jesus cries out his only words of the entire proceeding, in his pathetic cry of dereliction, "*Eloi, eloi, lema sabbachthani*"—which translated (it is Aramaic) means "My God, my God, why have you forsaken me?" And then he dies.

We shouldn't think that this is not really how Mark wanted to portray Jesus because he is portrayed in other ways in other Gospels. Mark needs to be allowed to have his own say in how Jesus faced his death. It is not a pretty picture. Jesus dies in agony, wondering why all—including his God—have abandoned him.

Luke, however, provides a very different account, and the differences should not be passed over lightly. In Luke Jesus is not at all silent on his way to crucifixion. On the way to the site, he stops beside a group of women who are weeping, and he tells them, "Daughters of Jerusalem, do not weep for me but weep for yourselves and for your children" (23:27–31). Here Jesus is more concerned for their fate than for his own.

While being nailed to the cross Jesus is not silent in Luke. He instead prays for those who are doing this to him: "Father, forgive them, for they do not know what they are doing" (23:34). While on the cross, Jesus actually has an intelligent conversation with one of the others being crucified with him. One of the criminals mocks him: "Aren't you the Christ? Save yourself and us." But the other criminal rebukes him, since their condemnation is just, while Jesus "has done nothing wrong." He then asks, "Jesus, remember me when you come into your Kingdom." Jesus gives him the calm and reassuring words that he longs to hear: "Truly I tell you, today you will be with me in paradise" (23:43). Jesus in this account is calm and in control of the situation. He knows what is happening to him and why it is happening. And he knows what the outcome will be: he will wake up in paradise with this robber beside him.

Finally, most telling of all, rather than uttering his "cry of dereliction" ("Why have you forsaken me?"), in Luke Jesus instead breathes a final prayer: "Father, into your hands I commend my spirit" (23:46). The Jesus of Mark may have felt abandoned at the very end, even by God himself; but not the Jesus of Luke. Here Jesus feels the presence of God and the assurance that he is still with his Father, who will now receive his spirit. Here, in Luke, Jesus is fully in charge of his own death.

The same shift in emphasis can be seen in the earlier portrayal of Jesus immediately before his betrayal and arrest. It is striking that in Mark's Gospel, we are told that Jesus "was greatly distressed and disturbed" (Mark 14:33). Luke doesn't say that. In Mark Jesus tells his disciples that his "soul is terribly grieved, even unto death" (Mark 14:34). He says no such thing in Luke. In Mark Jesus goes off by himself and falls on his face to pray (14:35); in Luke he simply kneels down (Luke 22:41). In Mark Jesus asks God three times for the "cup" to pass from before him (i.e., that he not have to face his suffering); in Luke he asks only once, and prefaces his prayer by saying, "If you are willing." The net result of these changes is clear: here again Jesus is portrayed not as in deep anguish over his coming fate but as calm and in control of the situation.

This is the reason for another interesting change in Luke's story, this time in his account of the betrayal, which happens next. Many readers have not noticed the change because it is so slight. In Mark, of course, Judas betrays Jesus with a kiss—possibly in fulfillment of Proverbs 21:6. In Luke it is not at all clear that the kiss ever occurred. For here, unlike in Mark, Judas comes up to Jesus with the crowds "in order to kiss him," but Jesus evidently stops him: "Jesus said to him, 'Judas, are you betraying the Son of Man with a kiss?'" (22:48). A small skirmish immediately occurs, as mentioned in Mark. In both accounts one of the followers of Jesus pulls out a sword and strikes the slave of the high priest, cutting off his right ear. This earns Jesus' rebuke in both accounts, but in Luke Jesus does more than that: he reaches out to the slave and heals him on the spot.

Luke's Jesus is in complete control of the situation at his betrayal. He takes matters into his own hands, he appears to stop Judas from delivering the kiss, and he takes charge of the attempt to defend him with the sword. This is Luke's Jesus in a nutshell: calm and unflappable, facing the fate that lies ahead of him in full assurance of God's presence and care.

Conclusion: Judas in Our Earliest Gospels

What I have tried to show in these brief comments on the portrayals of Judas in our three earliest Gospels is that in every instance the literary and theological agenda of the author has affected the way he has retold the story of Judas and his betrayal. As I have suggested occasionally throughout the discussion, there are two kinds of conclusions that can be drawn from these observations, one literary and the other historical.

The literary conclusion is that as is the case with Jesus himself, so too with Judas. Every portrayal of him is different, and we do a disservice to the author of each account if we pretend that he is saying exactly what some other author is saying. If Matthew wants to say that greed is what drove Judas to do what he did, but Luke wants to insist that the Devil made him do it, it is not really fair to either author to argue that they mean the same thing. If that's what we think, we have, in effect, taken what Matthew says, combined it with what Luke says, and created then a mega-Gospel (for which we might as well throw in Mark and John as well, for good measure)—a Gospel found nowhere in the New Testament but simply in our own heads, as we write a Gospel of our own to substitute for the Gospels of the New Testament. In my view as a literary and historical scholar, that is not the best way to treat the early accounts of Jesus' (or Judas's) life.

The historical conclusion is that we have different accounts from different authors writing at different times to different audiences for different reasons. Given the differences of the accounts, we will eventually want to reexamine them to see if it is possible to draw some kind of historical conclusions about what *really* happened. In some cases, the differences between the accounts turn out to be irreconcilable. We will see this in the next chapter, when we explore the account of Judas's death in the book of Acts, which has some striking similarities with the account in Matthew (these are the only two books that mention Judas's death in the New Testament), but important discrepancies as well. Accounts that contain discrepancies cannot both be historically accurate. Is one more accurate than the other? How would we know? What can we say for certain about the life of Judas—what he did and why he did it—based on our few surviving sources? Those are the questions we will ask at the end of the book, after looking at other ways Judas was portrayed, first from other surviving Christian sources such as the book of Acts, the Gospel of John, and several apocryphal works (in the next chapter), and then in the newly discovered Gospel of Judas, a book with its own agenda and distinctive portrayal of this one who betrayed Jesus.

⌘

CHAPTER THREE

Judas in Later Gospel Traditions

The earliest Christians lived in an oral culture. It is hard to establish reliable demographic figures for the ancient world, but the best estimates suggest that at the time of the first Christian centuries, in the Roman Empire, only about 10 percent of the population was literate. That means that nine out of ten people could not read, let alone write. Those who could write—and by that I mean be able to compose entire paragraphs—were a much smaller percentage. The vast majority of people living at the time of Jesus and in the centuries after could not write a sentence if their life depended on it.

Fortunately for them, their lives did not depend upon it. In oral cultures life could be lived and enjoyed without having to read newspapers, office memos, scientific studies, governmental reports, official documents, or literature of any kind. If there was a need for written documentation—for example, for a marriage dowry, a real estate deal, or a tax receipt—there were always scribes around who could provide you with what you needed for a fee. And if you wanted access to literature—if you wanted to enjoy some Homer or Plato, for example, or if you had a taste for drama or fiction, or if you wanted to delve into some religious writings—you could have someone read out loud what someone else had written. As it turns out, that was the most common way to "read" books in the ancient world: you would have someone (the rare educated person) read them to you, along with a group of your friends or family.

You might think that in an oral culture, where so much depended on hearing things by word of mouth, there would be special care taken to make sure that traditions told about important persons or events would be passed along accurately—that every telling and retelling of a story would be exactly the same and that the people telling the tales would be particularly scrupulous not to alter the accounts in any way. As it turns out, that's not true at all. Cultural anthropologists who have studied modern oral societies have shown that just the opposite is the case. In oral culture there is not a concern for what we in written culture might call verbatim accuracy. In oral societies it is recognized that the telling of a story to a different audience or in a different context or for a different reason calls for a different version of the story. Stories are molded to the time and circumstance in which they are told.[1]

We have hard evidence that the same thing was true in ancient oral cultures. This evidence—ironically, I suppose—comes to us in the written sources. Those few written narratives of historical events that we do have from the ancient world were mainly based, of course, on stories that the authors had heard. And we have instances in which the same story is recorded by different authors. In almost every case, the accounts differ from one another.

This is the case with the Gospels of the New Testament. Even when one of the authors used another of the authors as his source for his stories—for example, when Matthew copied some of his stories from Mark—he changed the stories. Why would he do that? Because he lived in an oral society where hardly anyone thought there was a problem with changing the stories. Of course stories were to be changed when the audience, the occasion, or the situation had changed. The widespread notion that stories never should be changed but should be repeated without alteration every time is an innovation of modern written cultures. Before the creation of the printing press, this was not a widely shared view.[2]

Ancient stories about Jesus, which survived principally in an oral culture, were changed in the retelling. That's why there are differences—even discrepancies— in the accounts that eventually were written down. And that's why there are differences—and discrepancies—in our stories about his disciple Judas Iscariot, the one who eventually betrayed him. One of the big discrepancies has to do with the circumstances surrounding Judas's death. We have seen that according to Matthew's Gospel, Judas hanged himself, and that after his death the chief priests used the betrayal money to purchase a field in which to bury strangers in Jerusalem. They called it the Field of Blood, because it was purchased with "blood money." The book of Acts has a different account of Judas's death and its relationship to this field. It is probably impossible to reconcile the details of these two accounts.

The Death of Judas in the Book of Acts

The book of Acts was written by the same author as the Gospel of Luke—on this everyone agrees (compare Luke 1:1–4 with Acts 1:1–4 and you'll see why). Acts, in fact, is simply the second volume of a two-volume work. The first volume, which we know as the Gospel of Luke, has to do with the birth, life, ministry, death, and resurrection of Jesus; the second volume has to do with the mission of his apostles afterward. In it Luke continues the Christian story as he shows how the church spread from its small beginnings among the band of Jesus' followers after his death, throughout the major urban areas of the Roman Empire, until the message of the gospel arrived in the capital city, Rome itself. The main character of the final two-thirds of the book is the apostle Paul, whose conversion is described in chapter 9, and whose mission to take the gospel of Christ afield, especially among the Gentiles (non-Jews), is the subject of most of the rest of the book.

Luke's account of the spread of the Christian mission is not simply a descriptive narrative of facts, which recounts the events as they actually happened. Just as Luke put his own spin on the Gospel traditions about Jesus in volume one, so too he put his spin on the traditions about Jesus' apostles and their mission in volume two. The overriding emphasis of this second volume is that everything that happened in the mission was part of the divine plan, that God was the one who inspired and empowered the Christian missionaries, that the Spirit of God was the one who directed the movement from the beginning, that there were no human obstacles that could not be overcome in bringing it to fruition, that the entire course of early Christian history was under the mighty gaze and directed by the mighty hand of God. Nothing could stop the Christians from gaining numerous converts wherever they went. The enemies of God might imprison, torture, and kill the apostles of Christ, but they could never stop the forward movement of the mission.

This overarching theme of the book can be found in one of its earliest narratives. After the disciples have met with the resurrected Jesus for forty days, and after he has ascended to heaven, they decide that they must remain a body of twelve for the sake of the mission. One of them, though, has obviously "gone over to the dark side." Judas Iscariot has forsaken his place among them. And so they need to elect a new member of the Twelve.

Simon Peter, Jesus' right-hand man during his ministry, is the one who urges this election, in the opening chapter of the account. What is striking in his opening statement to the gathered apostles is that he sees that the betrayal of Judas was itself part of God's ultimate plan, as predicted in the sacred Scriptures. As Peter states:

> Brothers, it was necessary for the Scripture to be fulfilled, which the Holy Spirit spoke in advance through the mouth of David concerning Judas, the one who became the guide to those who arrested Jesus. (Acts 1:16)

In other words, King David—who lived a thousand years earlier and was thought of as the author of the Old Testament book of Psalms—had predicted that Judas would become the betrayer. Peter then quotes the passages that seem to him to predict the event:

> For it is written in the book of Psalms: "Let his place of dwelling be desolate and let no one live in it" [Ps. 69:25]; "and let another receive his place as an overseer" [Ps. 109:8]. (Acts 1:20)

This is a significant passage for understanding the book of Acts. The author of Acts, who has put these words on Peter's lips, sees that everything—even the disastrous events of Jesus' betrayal and execution—was according to plan. In reading back over the Scriptures, he had discovered the key to all that had happened. Despite appearances, God was ultimately in control. Even though Judas had done a wicked thing—had in fact been driven by Satan to do it (remember Luke 22:3)—it was all unfolding as God had ordained in ages past. God had planned for the betrayal to happen, and now his plan was for a replacement for Judas to be elected. The disciples cast lots, and it falls to Matthias, who now replaces Judas as one of the Twelve. Strikingly, Matthias is never mentioned again in the entire book. His job is simply to make sure that the number of the Twelve is complete.

Not only does Peter indicate that the election of a new apostle needs to take place, he makes some parenthetical remarks about why the election is necessary. It is not just that Judas went over to the forces opposed to Christ. If that was all that had happened, then obviously he could repent—as Peter himself had done—and join the apostolic band anew. But this was no longer possible, for Judas had by now died. Peter describes his death in graphic terms:

> Now this one [Judas] purchased a field with the wages of his unrighteous act [the betrayal] and falling headlong he burst forth in the middle and all his intestines spilled out. And this became known to all the inhabitants of Jerusalem, so that this field is called "Akeldamach" in their own dialect, which means "Field of Blood." (Acts 1:18–19)

Interpreters of the New Testament have long been intrigued by this description of Judas's death, both because of its similarities to the account in Matthew and because of its differences. In both accounts Judas's death is connected with a field called the Field of Blood in Jerusalem. But in Matthew, it is called that because it is purchased by the Jewish chief priests with the "blood money" that Judas had returned and thrown down in the Temple precincts. In Luke's version, there is no account of Judas returning the money. He in fact uses the money ("the wages of his unrighteous act") to buy a field. And it is called the Field of Blood not because the money used to purchase it was tainted with the blood of an innocent man (Jesus) but because it was on this field that Judas himself experienced a bloody death. Most striking of all, this is not a death by hanging. Judas somehow falls headlong on this field, and when he does so, his stomach rips open, his intestines gush out, and he makes a bloody mess. It's not clear exactly how Judas falls headlong: Does he jump from a cliff? Does he lurch forward onto some stones? Does he simply fall down and burst open?

Some readers have tried to reconcile these two accounts over the years, for example, by claiming that Judas hanged himself (as in Matthew) but the rope broke (which neither account says) and he fell to the earth (headfirst?), spilling his insides out (as in Acts). Or they claim that he hanged himself but didn't die;

instead he was cut down, and later experienced some kind of internal burst leading to a bloody demise. But most modern critical readers have simply seen that
these accounts are at odds with one another. For not only is the account of his
death different, so too are the questions of who purchased the field (the priests or
Judas?) and why it was called the field of blood (because it was purchased with
blood money or because Judas bled all over it?). This is what happens to traditions as they come to be told and retold in oral cultures. The traditions change as
they circulate. There may have been some connection between the death of Judas
and a potter's field in Jerusalem, but what that connection was seems to have
been lost somewhere during the transmission of the tales.

Judas in the Gospel of John

The Gospel of John was written some ten years or so after Luke and Acts. It
was the last of our canonical Gospels to be written, and it has long been recognized as having a very different portrayal of Jesus from that found in the earlier
accounts of Matthew, Mark, and Luke. Some in the early church called John
the "spiritual Gospel." The three earlier narratives are very similar to one another—
so much so that they are called the Synoptic Gospels. The term *synoptic* comes
from two words that literally mean "seen together." The first three Gospels are
called this because they tell so many of the same stories, often in the same
words, that they can be placed side by side in parallel columns and read together. John by and large tells different stories, and when he does share a story
with any of the others, he tells it in very different ways, using different words.
As a result, most scholars continue to think that John did not make use of
Matthew, Mark, and/or Luke in constructing his account; rather, he based his
narrative on stories that had been in circulation through the oral tradition for
sixty years before he wrote them down.[3]

   The different portrayal of Jesus in the Gospel of John played a significant
role in John's different portrayal of Judas Iscariot, the betrayer. Here again I
don't need to map out all the differences between John and the other Gospels;
I will simply say a few words about some of the differences that can help make
sense of his comments about Judas.

The Distinctiveness of the Gospel of John

What makes the Fourth Gospel so obviously distinct from the others is its portrayal of Jesus himself. In the earlier Gospels Jesus rarely speaks of his own
identity, where he came from, or where he is going. In the Gospel of John, that is
nearly all he talks about. In this Gospel Jesus repeatedly tells his followers, the
crowds, and even his enemies that he is the one who has come down from his
Father in heaven, that he is soon to return there, and that anyone who believes in
him will have eternal life. You look in vain for such teachings in Matthew, Mark,
and Luke. In John, however, they appear in chapter after chapter.

The focus on Jesus' identity can be found in a group of sayings found only in John, where Jesus uses the formula "I am" to describe himself: "I am the bread of heaven," "I am the light of the world," "I am the way, the truth, and the life, no one comes to the Father but by me." Occasionally he simply identifies himself by saying "I am"—in Greek the phrase is *ego eimi*. Interpreters have long seen the significance of this phrase, as it may refer to a well-known and highly significant passage in the Jewish Scriptures. When the lawgiver Moses was talking with God in Exodus 3, he asked what God's name was, and God replied that he could be known as "I am" (in the Greek translation of the Hebrew Bible, *ego eimi*).

Jesus seems to be claiming that name for himself in John. So when he is engaged in controversy with his Jewish opponents, who attempt to mock him for claiming special knowledge about the father of the Jews, Abraham, Jesus replies, "Before Abraham was, I am" (8:58). They realize he is claiming a divine status—which is a blasphemy—and they pick up rocks to stone him.

For John's Gospel, Jesus in fact is divine. He has come from heaven and he is returning to heaven. As a divine being, he knows all things, as seen in some of the early stories in the Gospel, when he can identify his disciples and tell them about their lives, never having known them before (1:47). Among other things, Jesus knows clearly that he is going to die, and spends a good part of the Gospel talking about his death. He knows that it will be a death by crucifixion, which he refers to with a double entendre as the time when he will be "lifted up," that is, he will be lifted up on the cross, but he will also be lifted up to the Father, his exaltation.

Because his death is according to God's plan in this account, Jesus is quite emphatic that no one is taking his life away from him. He is laying it down of his own accord:

> This is why the Father loves me, because I give my life that I might receive it up again. No one takes it from me, but I give it of my own accord. I have the authority to give it and authority to receive it again. This is the commandment I have received from my Father. (10:18)

In John, as in the other accounts, Jesus has enemies. Here again the story is told on two levels. On the divine level, all happens according to God's plan. But on the human level, there are enemies of God and his earthly incarnation, Jesus; they plot against him and try to thwart his purposes. In particular, this Gospel stresses, Jesus' enemies are members of his own race, the Jews. In fact, the term "the Jews" now takes on negative connotations—even though Jesus and his followers themselves are Jews. It is "the Jews" who stand against Christ, who oppose God, who plot to have Jesus killed, and who are responsible for his death.

Because they are his enemies, Jesus says rather nasty things about the Jews in this Gospel, to the point that some modern readers have seen a kind of ancient Christian anti-Semitism in the account. It is easy to understand this view: in this Gospel "the Jews" are the enemies of God and the ones responsible for killing his Christ. More than that, Jesus indicates that they are not descendants of Abraham, let alone children of God. They are children of Satan who do the will of their father, the Devil, in opposing him, the true representative of God.

> They answered him, "Abraham is our Father." Jesus replied, "If you were children of Abraham, you would do the works of Abraham. But now you are trying to kill me a man who has spoken the truth to you which I heard from God. Abraham did not act like this. You do the work of your [real] father. . . . For you are from your father the Devil, and you want to do the desires of your father. That one was a murderer from the beginning, and he did not stand in the truth because there is no truth in him. . . . The one who is from God hears the words of God. For this reason you do not hear them, because you are not from God." (John 8:39–47)

Throughout this Gospel, Jesus the one who comes from God is rejected by his own people, the Jews, who are not from God but from the Devil. As stated early in the Gospel, "[Christ] came to his own home, but his own people did not accept him" (1:11).

As these few quotations show, John's Gospel, more than any of the others, works with a kind of bipolar categorization of people in their relationship to Christ. There are only two kinds of people, reflecting two kinds of reality. There is God on one hand and Satan on the other; there are the children of God and the children of the Devil; people either live in the light or walk in the darkness; they either stand for the truth or propagate error. This stark characterization is stated clearly in one of the early assertions of the Gospel:

> The one who believes in him [Christ] is not judged; but the one who does not believe is judged already, because he has not believed in the name of the unique son of God; and this is the judgment, that the light has come into the world and people loved the darkness rather than the light; for their works were evil. Everyone one who does evil hates the light and does not come to the light. . . . But the one who does the truth comes to the light. (3:18–21)

The Portrayal of Judas in John

Judas is explicitly mentioned more often in John, where his name occurs eight times altogether, than in the other canonical Gospels. But the basic outline of his story is the same: he is one of the twelve disciples chosen by Jesus and who participates with him in the Last Supper before going off to betray him. Many of the things that John says about Judas, however, are reminiscent of the wide-ranging differences between this Gospel and the others.

There is no account of Jesus' choosing of the Twelve in John, but Jesus does refer back to his selection on one occasion, and he mentions Judas in that context. In chapter 6 of John, Jesus has delivered a rather difficult discourse, where he indicates that to have eternal life a person needs to chew his flesh and drink his blood (6:53–54). This image is a turn-off for most of his followers, who decide to leave him. He asks the Twelve whether they too want to leave, and Peter replies that they have nowhere else to go, since "you have the words of eternal life" (6:68). Jesus then replies, referring to an incident not narrated in this Gospel, "Did I not choose you twelve?" But then he adds a comment significant for our purposes here: "And one of you is a devil." The narrator then indicates: "He was speaking about Judas, son of Simon Iscariot. For this is the one who was about to betray him, one of the Twelve" (6:71).

In this case Judas is called "Iscariot" because it is his family name—he inherited it from his father, Simon. But the more striking points are that Jesus already at an early stage of his ministry (not just at the Last Supper) knows he is to be betrayed, and he knows full well the character of his betrayer, who "is a devil."

Both points fit in well with John's account of Jesus, where Jesus knows all things in advance (he is a divine being in this Gospel, so of course he knows everything) and where everything is painted in black and white. You are either for Jesus or against him; you are either in the truth or in error; you are either in light or in darkness; you are either God's or the Devil's. Judas is the Devil's. In fact, he himself is a devil, though not *the* Devil, as later on John will indicate that the Devil "put it into the heart of Judas, son of Simon Iscariot, that he should betray him" (13:2). So Judas is evil—in essence, the son of the Devil— just as, for John, the Jews are. John doesn't explain why Jesus would have chosen an enemy to be his follower, but the reader is probably to assume that it was all according to plan.

The next time Judas is mentioned is during an episode that we have already discussed from the Synoptic Gospels: the account of Jesus being anointed by a woman. In this case, however, it is not in Galilee as in the other Gospels, or in the house of a Pharisee named Simon as in Luke, and the woman is not un- named. Now it takes place in Bethany of Judea (the region south of Galilee) in the house of Jesus' friends Mary, Martha, and Lazarus. And it is Mary of Bethany herself who anoints Jesus with costly ointment. Once again objections are raised, but this time not simply by "some" who were there, as in Mark, or by the "disciples," as in Matthew. In John, it is specifically Judas Iscariot who ob- jects, "Why was this ointment not sold for three hundred denarii and [the money] given to the poor?" (12:5). We're told by the narrator, however, that Judas wasn't actually all that concerned for the poor. He was the treasurer for the apostolic band and a thief. He liked to pilfer their community money box, which he carried around with him (12:6).

John's portrayal of Judas as a devil, the son of the Devil, opposed to Christ from the beginning, and also a money-grubbing thief: does that sound famil- iar? It would to anyone familiar with anti-Semitic slurs leveled against Jews in the Middle Ages—that they were demonically inspired usurers and thieves who opposed and murdered their own Christ. Some scholars have argued that it is not an accident that the "Christ-killer" of the early Christian traditions had a name etymologically related to the term Jew: Judas. In later times, Judas would come to be portrayed as the prototypical Jew.[4]

As in the other Gospels, Judas is present with Jesus at the Last Supper in John (chapter 13). But whereas in the other Gospels Jesus predicts that one of the Twelve would betray him, in the Gospel of John—where Jesus is regularly portrayed as having detailed foreknowledge of all that is to take place—Jesus explicitly informs the one nearest to him that it is specifically Judas who will do the deed (13:26). Satan then enters into Judas, and Jesus tells him, in his famous words, "What you are about to do, do quickly" (13:27). Oddly enough—given Jesus' indication that Judas would be the betrayer—no one at the meal knows what he is talking about. The disciples think that he is telling Judas to go buy some supplies or to give some money to the poor (13:29). But the reader knows the real situation: Judas is to go out to arrange the foul deed. Then comes one of the breathtakingly simple statements of the entire Gospel. "He immediately went out. And it was night."

Yes, indeed—it was night. Judas goes out into the darkness, for in this Gospel he is the agent of darkness. And soon darkness will descend on them all, as Judas performs his foreordained task and leads the enemies to seize his master.

The arrest scene is narrated differently from the other Gospels. There is nothing here about the betrayal with a kiss. Judas comes to the garden, where he knows Jesus will be. With him is a cohort of soldiers, along with servants of the chief priests and of the Pharisees, carrying lanterns, torches, and weapons. Jesus, "knowing everything that is to happen to him" (18:4), asks them whom they are seeking. They answer, "Jesus of Nazareth." This is a strange interchange, since obviously he himself is Jesus, and if they're seeking him with Judas as a guide, presumably they would know. But what happens next is even stranger. Jesus says, "I am he," and all of them, Judas included, involuntarily backtrack and fall to the ground (18:5–6).

From the perspective of the Gospel of John, this reaction is not so strange. In the Greek, Jesus' reply is *"Ego eimi"* ("I am"). He has spoken the Divine name and inferred that it belongs to him. At the name of God, "every knee shall bow and every tongue confess" (Isa. 45:23). The falling of Judas and the soldiers is the natural response to finding a divine being before them.

Jesus again asks whom they seek, they again answer, and this time he allows himself to be arrested. And so the story moves ahead.

In sum, as was the case with Matthew, Mark, Luke, and Acts, the overarching views of the author of John—his views about God, Christ, the divine plan, the disciples—affected the way he told the stories about Judas. Now he is a thieving devil, the son of Satan, whom Jesus knew from the beginning to be on the side of evil, who betrays his own master, but who is compelled, even as his enemy, to fall down before him. Later we will ask if there is anything in this account that can be accepted as historically accurate; for now it is enough to know that when early Christians told stories about the followers of Jesus, even his betrayer, they did so in light of their own views, perspectives, and theological investments.

Judas in Other Gospel Traditions

Christians, of course, did not stop telling stories about Jesus—or about his betrayer, Judas—when the Gospels of the New Testament were completed and placed in circulation. Stories continued to be told, and occasionally to be written down. We don't have as many stories about Judas from the early centuries of the church as we would like, but the ones we have are very interesting. Here I will describe some of the more intriguing ones.

Judas in the Writings of Papias

Papias was an early-second-century Christian writer who claimed that he acquired information about Jesus' words and deeds not only from books but also from interviewing companions of Jesus' own disciples. From the information he garnered, he produced a five-volume work known as the *Expositions of the Sayings of the Lord*. Later Christians chose, for some reason or other, not to preserve this work, so we do not have a copy of it today. But we do have quotations from the work by later church fathers. Two of these quotations have to do with Judas Iscariot.[5]

In the first we are told that Jesus predicted that the future Kingdom of God would be a utopia-like state in which people would enjoy the rich abundance of the earth. The description of this abundance is so bizarre that some scholars have thought it explains why later Christians didn't feel they could trust Papias: he was obviously (they thought) given to extremes. But as the account shows, they weren't the first to think so. Judas Iscariot allegedly had trouble believing that Jesus really could mean such a thing. The full quotation, taken from the writings of the late-second-century church father Irenaeus, is as follows:

> Thus the blessing that is foretold belongs without question to the times of the kingdom, when the righteous will rise from the dead and rule, and the creation that is renewed and set free will bring forth from the dew of heaven and the fertility of the soil an abundance of food of all kinds. Thus the elders who saw John, the disciple of the Lord, remembered hearing him say how the Lord used to teach about those times, saying:
>
> "The days are coming when vines will come forth, each with ten thousand boughs; and on a single bough will be ten thousand branches. And indeed, on a single branch will be ten thousand shoots and on every shoot ten thousand clusters; and in every cluster will be ten thousand grapes, and every grape, when pressed, will yield twenty-five measures of wine. And when any of the saints grabs hold of a cluster, another will cry out, 'I am better, take me; bless the Lord through me.' So too a grain of wheat will produce ten thousand heads and

every head will have ten thousand grains and every grain will yield ten pounds of pure, exceptionally fine flour. So too the remaining fruits and seeds and vegetation will produce in similar proportions. And all the animals who eat this food drawn from the earth will come to be at peace and harmony with one another, yielding in complete submission to humans."

Papias as well, an ancient man—the one who heard John and was a companion of Polycarp—gives a written account of these things in the fourth of his books. For he wrote five books. And in addition he says, "These things can be believed by those who believe. And the betrayer Judas," he said, "did not believe, but asked, 'How then can the Lord bring forth such produce?' The Lord then replied, 'Those who come into those times will see.'"[6]

The implication appears to be that Judas, the betrayer, would not be among those entering into this paradisal state.

The second quotation is more directly related to Judas. It is an account of his death, in which some of the gory details already implicit in the account of Acts are played out to a graphic and lurid extreme. Now Judas does not merely fall and spill out his intestines: the reason he dies is evidently that he has grown so enormous that he literally appears to "blow up."

But Judas went about in this world as a great model of impiety. He became so bloated in the flesh that he could not pass through a place that was easily wide enough for a wagon—not even his swollen head could fit. They say that his eyelids swelled to such an extent that he could not see the light at all; and a doctor could not see his eyes even with an optical device, so deeply sunken they were in the surrounding flesh. And his genitals became more disgusting and larger than anyone's; simply by relieving himself, to his wanton shame, he emitted pus and worms that flowed through his entire body.

And they say that after he suffered numerous torments and punishments, he died on his own land, and that land has been, until now, desolate and uninhabited because of the stench. Indeed, even to this day no one can pass by the place without holding their nose. This was how great an outpouring he made from his flesh on the ground.

Needless to say, this account is like neither Matthew nor Acts. Papias doesn't say so, but he appears to imagine that Judas's bloated state comes about as divine retribution for his sin of betraying Jesus. Throughout ancient sources, it was common to indicate that when God's judgment fell upon a person, she or he was swollen with pus and eaten by worms—even before being placed in the ground. Readers of the New Testament will be familiar with the death of the blasphemous King Herod in Acts 12, who was "eaten by worms and died" (Acts 12:23). A more graphic account of Herod's death is provided by the first-century Jewish historian Josephus, who indicates that a fire began to glow in his belly, so that he was pained from within. This pain created an enormous appetite, which he indulged, leading his entrails to become exulcerated and his colon infected. Then we are told that some kind of transparent liquid settled about his feet and at the bottom of his stomach, and that his genitals became putrefied and filled with worms (Josephus, *Jewish Antiquities,* 17.6.5). Not a pleasant way to go.

But not that uncommon for blasphemers. The fourth-century church historian Eusebius indicates that a similar fate awaited the emperor Galerius, who was largely responsible for the "Great Persecution" that led to widespread torture and martyrdoms among the Christians. God at last punished him for his impiety:

> Without warning, a suppurative inflammation broke out round the middle of his genitals, then a deep-seated fistular ulcer: these ate their way incurably into his inmost bowels. From them came a teeming indescribable mass of worms, and a sickening smell was given off; for the whole of his hulking body, thanks to overeating, had been transformed even before his illness into a huge lump of flabby fat, which then decomposed and presented those who came near with a revolting and horrifying sight. (Eusebius, *Church History,* 8.16.3–5)[7]

His doctors "could not endure the overpowering and extraordinary stench" and so were ordered executed on the spot. Galerius, obviously, died in pain.

Herod and Galerius were not unique. Similar deaths were recorded for others who stood opposed to God and his purposes.[8] Judas stood in a long line of nefarious wrongdoers who in the end, according to our surviving authors, received their just reward.

Judas in the Gospel of Nicodemus

Stories about Judas continued to be told for centuries. One of my favorites comes from a book called the Gospel of Nicodemus—also sometimes known as the Acts of (Pontius) Pilate. This legendary account of Jesus' trial, death, and descent into hell is full of great stories, none of which scholars think is historically reliable but which are highly entertaining nonetheless, and instructive for seeing how Christians were telling tales about Christ in the centuries after his death. The Gospel as a whole appears to stem from a written document of possibly the fourth or fifth century.

Just to give an example of the kind of thing one finds here, in the beginning of the account we find the story of Jesus being brought to Pilate for his trial. Stationed in the room are a number of Roman soldiers who are holding up the standards that bear an image of the divine Caesar. But as soon as Jesus comes into the room, the standard-bearers bow at the waist, so the image of Caesar appears to be doing obeisance to Jesus. The Jewish leaders in the room become incensed and accuse the standard-bearers of doing this themselves. They insist that they couldn't help it, the standards bowed of their own accord.

So Pilate tells the Jewish leaders to find twelve burly men of their own to hold up the standards. They do so, and Jesus leaves the room to enter for a second time. But this time as well, as soon as he crosses the threshold, the standard-bearers bow down before him. The Jews are irate, but the readers get the point. Jesus is the divine being, not Caesar; it is to Jesus that "every knee will bow and every tongue confess that Christ is Lord" (Phil. 2:11).

The story about Judas is not found in every manuscript of the Gospel of Nicodemus—as with all ancient books, this one has come down to us in hand-written copies that all differ from one another.[9] But in one particularly intriguing manuscript we find that after the betrayal, Judas goes home to find some rope in order to hang himself. When he comes into his kitchen, he sees his wife there, roasting a chicken on a spit over a charcoal fire. He tells her to prepare a rope for him to hang himself with. In her perplexity, she asks him why. He tells her that he has handed his teacher Jesus over to evildoers to be killed but that Jesus will rise on the third day, to their woe. His wife tells him to speak and think no such thing: that just as this roasting chicken is unable any longer to speak, so too Jesus will be unable to rise from the dead.

But then, as soon as she stops talking, the chicken roasting on the spit stretches out its wings and crows three times. This is more than enough to convince Judas, who takes the rope and hangs himself.

Judas in the Arabic Infancy Gospel

There were a number of Gospels in the early church, starting in the second century, that narrated the legendary accounts of what Jesus was like as a boy. These are traditionally called infancy Gospels. The earliest of these, probably from the early or mid-second century, is called the Infancy Gospel of Thomas. This account describes the escapades of a rather mischievous but miracle-working Jesus between the ages of five and twelve. Somewhat later a different Gospel appeared that described events that happened even before that; this one is called the Proto-Gospel of James. It is called a proto-Gospel because it narrates events that took place well before the accounts of the New Testament: it is, in fact, concerned principally with the birth, young life, and marriage of Jesus' mother, Mary. Its overarching concern is to show why she was the chosen vessel for the Son of God to make his appearance in the world.

Later infancy Gospel writers often used these two earlier texts as the foundation for their narratives, amplifying, expanding, combining, and modifying them as they saw fit, based on stories the authors had heard about Jesus or on their own imaginations of what must have happened in the years prior to Jesus' adult life. One of these later Gospels, probably from the fifth or sixth century, survives only in an Arabic translation and so is traditionally called the Arabic Infancy Gospel.

This Gospel includes a story of the encounter between the young boy Jesus and his ultimate nemesis, the young Judas. The story comes after an episode about how a woman was liberated from a dragon by one of Jesus' swaddling clothes. That is more or less the tenor of the entire work. The story we are concerned with here, however, is about Jesus and Judas as playmates in Bethlehem. In this Gospel, even at this young age, Judas is often seized by

Satan and driven by him to bite anyone who comes near. When he can't find anyone to bite, he bites his own hands and limbs. His mother brings him to Mary and Jesus, hoping that he can be cured.

Jesus is taken out to play at a stream, and Judas comes up and sits beside him "at his right hand." But just then, as is his wont, Satan intervenes. He enters into Judas, making him want to bite Jesus. He's not able to do so, however—since after all, Jesus is the Son of God—and he ends up only hitting him on his right side, causing him to cry. Satan, though, is driven from the child, fleeing from him in the form of a mad dog. The narrator informs us, however, that the place where Judas struck Jesus was the spot where later, at his crucifixion, "the Jews" pierced his side with a lance (see John 19:34).

Clearly we have here a story that is foreshadowing events to come, in Judas's attempt to harm Jesus. It is striking that Judas again is connected with "the Jews"—portrayed as Jesus' ultimate enemies. I should point out that in the Gospel of John, it is in fact not Jews who pierce Jesus' side but a Roman soldier. For authors such as the one who produced the Arabic Gospel of Judas, these niceties of interpretation were beside the point. The Jews are the enemy, and Judas represents them: children of the Devil determined to do Christ harm.

Judas in the Golden Legend

Throughout the Middle Ages, by far the most popular collection of tales about the disciples of Jesus and about the later Christian saints was a book called the Golden Legend, compiled by the Dominican monk Jacobus of Voragine in 1265. Prior to the Protestant Reformation, this was the most widely read book in all of Christendom, for many people their principal source of "knowledge" about the early medieval church. Most of the stories are about the heroes of the faith, but there is a set of legends told here about Judas Iscariot. It is unlike anything we have seen so far, however, for these are tales modeled in part on the classical story of Oedipus the king, about whom it was prophesied that he would both kill his father and marry his mother. The gripping account of Oedipus is classically told by the Greek tragic playwright Sophocles. Seventeen hundred years later, a similar tale was told of Judas, the greatest tragic figure of Christian drama.[10]

In the Golden Legend, Judas is born to a Jewish woman, Cyborea, who with her husband, Ruben, lives in Jerusalem. Before his birth, Cyborea has a bad dream that her son will "bring ruin on our whole people." Not wanting the dream to come true, they decide to expose the child and leave him to die, casting him adrift in a basket at sea. As (divine) fate would have it, however, he survives and his basket washes up on the island Scariot. (This is what gives him his name, Iscariot.) The queen of the land happens to be walking along the shore when she spots the basket; she has long been wishing to have a son but evidently is unable to do so. And so she hatches a scheme. She takes the child, has him nursed in secret, pretends that she is pregnant, and then when the time is right, claims that she has had a child. She then adopts Judas into her royal line.

But as sometimes happens in these situations, before she knows it she really does become pregnant. She bears a son, and the two boys grow up together. Judas, however, is jealous of his younger "brother" and constantly mistreats him. When he comes to learn that he is in fact not related to the queen, and so is not the royal heir, he kills his brother and flees from the land. As (divine) fate would have it, he ends up in Jerusalem. In some mysterious way, he meets with and impresses the Roman governor of the land, Pontius Pilate, who makes him his head steward.

One day, Pilate is overlooking the yard of his neighbor, who happens to be—big surprise—Judas's real father, Ruben, and sees some delectable apples growing there. He has to have some, and so he sends Judas off to steal them from the garden. But Ruben appears out of nowhere, surprising Judas. This leads to a fight in which Judas kills the older man. Pilate repays Judas's faithful behavior by awarding him all of Ruben's possessions—including his wife, Cyborea. Now Judas is sleeping, unbeknownst to him, with his mother.

But one day Cyborea, overcome with grief over what she and her first husband had done so many years ago, bares her soul to Judas and describes how they had set their infant son afloat in a basket. Judas, who has learned his true history from his adoptive mother, puts two and two together and realizes what has happened. He has committed patricide and is now living in incest.

Out of his guilt and grief, he turns to Christ for forgiveness. Christ accepts him as one of his disciples and entrusts him with the communal purse. But Judas has a bad side that simply won't go away. He regularly pilfers the purse, taking out 10 percent for his own use. Later he becomes angry when Jesus is anointed by a woman who has just wasted three hundred pence worth of ointment for no reason. This is three hundred pence that Judas will never see. As an act of revenge, he agrees with the chief priests to betray Jesus for thirty pence—his share, in his view, of the lost money. He then feels remorse and goes forth to hang himself and bursts forth from the midst (in other words, this story reconciles Matthew and Acts: Judas hanged himself *and* burst open).

Jacobus of Voragine makes a point of stressing that it was appropriate that Judas died by having his intestines pour out of his gut: he could not have died with something coming from the mouth, which had touched the glorious lips of Christ. And it was appropriate that his bowels poured forth, for he conceived of the idea of the betrayal within himself, that is, in his very bowels. Moreover, it was appropriate that the rope injured his throat, since it was with his throat that he uttered his words of betrayal. Jacobus of Voragine, in other words, could see the divinely appointed destiny of Judas in the very mode of his death. What he doesn't need to state is what was obvious to his medieval reader: Judas was rotten to the core, from the very beginning and in every way: fratricide, patricide, incestuous thief, and Christ-killer. Christian readers would understand full well the subtext: this is Judas, the prototypical Jew.[11]

Judas in the Writings of the Church Fathers

Medieval readers would have long been prepared to make this association be-tween Judas and "the Jews" because Christian writers and scholars already had been making it for centuries by the time Jacobus of Voragine undertook his work. I will not give an exhaustive accounting of the theme in early Christian writers, but simply point to a few examples from the fourth and fifth Christian centuries—not long before the original composition of the Gospel of Nicodemus and the Arabic Infancy Gospel.

The first comes from church father Jerome (345–420 CE), famous as one of the great intellectuals of the early centuries and for having produced (at least part of) the Latin Vulgate, which became the Bible of the church down through the Middle Ages. In one of his writings, in talking about a passage in the Psalms that states that "wicked and deceitful mouths are opened against me, speaking against me with lying tongues," Jerome indicates that this is not simply a la-ment of the psalmist about being maligned by his enemies. It is in fact a pro-phetic text, referring to Christ. On one level, it refers to that mouth in particular that mistreated him—that of Judas, who gave him the kiss of betrayal. But on another level the passage refers to "the Jews," for "at that time they were say-ing 'Crucify, crucify this one,' [so that] their mouth was an open passageway of those condemning the Lord."[12]

A similar connection between the traitorous kiss of Judas and the wicked "kiss" of the Jews is found in Jerome's younger contemporary Ambrose, one-time bishop of Milan:

> [Judas] kissed the Lord . . . with his lips, this kiss the Jewish people have, and therefore it is said, "This people honor me with their lips, but their heart is far from me."[13]

So too the famous preacher and bishop of Constantinople, John, who was so eloquent in the pulpit that he earned the sobriquet Chrysostom, which means "golden-mouthed." Like many preachers before him and afterward, Chrysostom maligned Judas for the greed that led him to betray Jesus, and warned his hear-ers not to follow him in the sin of covetousness:

> Hear, you covetous, consider what befell him; how he at the same time lost the money, and committed the sin, and destroyed his own soul. Such is the tyranny of covetousness. He enjoyed not the money neither the present life, nor that to come, but lost all at once, and having got a bad character even with those very men, so hanged himself.[14]

But as is clear from Chrysostom's other writings, this sin of Judas is the sin of all the Jews: "Shall I tell you of their plundering, their covetousness, their abandonment of the poor, their thefts, their cheating in trade? The whole day long will not be enough to give you an account of these things."[15]

A final passage from the writings of Chrysostom deals with the passage in the book of Acts, where Judas spills his intestines on the field he had purchased, so it was afterward called the Field of Blood. According to Chrysostom, that name applied especially to what would happen to the Jews; for about them it could be said what was said about Judas, that "it was better for that man not to have been born." According to Chrysostom:

> We may with propriety apply this same to the Jews likewise; for if he who was guide suffered thus, much more they.

Moreover, when Acts indicates about Judas "let his place become desolate," that applies even more to the Jews, whose city Jerusalem came to be destroyed by the Romans in 70 CE, after a long and horrible siege, because of the Jews' unfaithfulness to God:

> [Judas's] desolation was the prelude to that of the Jews, as will appear on looking closely into the facts. For indeed they destroyed themselves by famine, and killed many, and the city became a burial place of strangers, of soldiers.[16]

Not all of the church fathers who commented on Judas were intent simply to link his act and his fate with those of the Jews. We have some instances in which authors had altogether different agendas—for example, simply expanding the New Testament accounts of Judas with anecdotal legends that had been passed along for decades and even centuries afterward. One particularly peculiar instance comes from the writings of Theophylact, a biblical interpreter living around the year 1200 CE. According to this account, Judas thought he could make some money out of betraying Jesus—but he didn't expect any real harm to come to him. After all, he was the Son of God, and nobody ever before this had been able to lay a hand on him. Overcome with guilt when he saw that Jesus was in fact condemned, he decided to kill himself in order to "get to Hades before Jesus and thus to implore and gain salvation." But when he tried to hang himself, "the tree bent down and he continued to live, since it was God's will that he either be preserved for repentance or for public disgrace and shame." It turned out to be the latter. He developed dropsy and swelled up so large that he could not walk down the street, leading him to burst apart.[17]

Conclusion: Judas as a Disciple to "Think With"

I hope it will be clear from all I've said in both this chapter and the one preceding that I do not think these various and sundry accounts of Judas from the early and medieval church are dispassionate, objectively verifiable descriptions of who he really was, what he really did, and what he really experienced. My thesis has been just the opposite: that the ways these various storytellers have framed their accounts of Judas, and the details of the stories they told about him, are directly related to other views they had about God, Christ, the significance of his death, the way of salvation, how to live in the world, the Jews and the Jewish rejection of Jesus, and so on. As these storytellers told their tales about Judas, they did so in light of their other concerns, perspectives, and theological views, their other loves, hates, likes, dislikes, inclinations, and disinclinations.

It is not merely that they molded their stories about Judas to make them fit their preconceived notions about him, and about everything else on their minds. By telling their stories about Judas they were able to express what they found to be important, not just about him but about everything related to him (and sometimes about things not related to him). In a sense, these storytellers and writers were thinking aloud, molding their understandings of God, Christ, and the world into shape by telling stories that embodied these understandings, affected these understandings, and produced these understandings. Judas, for these storytellers, was one of numerous characters from the life of Jesus that they could "think with."

Another author did just the same thing, although his thoughts were quite different from any of those we have examined so far. This author produced a Gospel about Judas, and his relationship with Jesus, that will sound very strange to modern ears, far stranger than any of the accounts we have read and discussed so far. But in part its strangeness is due to the accidents of history, for this particular Gospel was not regularly copied down through the ages, and the views that it represents were declared off-limits to Christians, dangerous, heretical. This Gospel, as a result, came to be lost sometime after the fourth century. But it has turned up again, and it shows us an intriguing alternative to the various ways of understanding Judas that we have examined so far. All of the accounts we have looked at—despite their wide variety—have agreed on one major point: Judas was the betrayer of Christ, his mortal enemy, the one who stood firmly opposed to the will of God. In this newly discovered Gospel, this is not the case at all. In the Gospel of Judas, he is the closest disciple to Christ, the only one who understands his teaching, and the one who does his will. Needless to say, this is a revolutionary point of view. The discovery of this Gospel marks a turning point in the history of the Christian understanding of Judas.

⌘

CHAPTER FOUR

Before the Discovery:
Our Previous Knowledge of a Gospel of Judas

Thirty years ago, most of the reading public did not know that we have numerous Gospels from early Christianity that did not make it into the New Testament. To some extent that changed when Elaine Pagels published her best-selling study *The Gnostic Gospels,* a book that captivated a wide readership.[1] But even Pagels's book did not reach the masses: it was mainly written for, and read by, highly educated people with an interest in the history of early Christianity.

It was not until the publication of a modern mystery novel that literally millions of people came to be enthralled with the question of other gospels and their hidden messages about Jesus. Dan Brown published *The Da Vinci Code* in 2003, and it has been at or near the top of the *New York Times* best-seller list during the entire three years since. Although the novel is about the mysterious murder of a curator at the Louvre in Paris, not about early Christianity per se, the lost Gospels figure prominently in it. According to the characters in the novel, this curator was murdered because he knew the truth about Jesus revealed in these long-lost texts, that Jesus was married to Mary Magdalene and had a child by her. According to *The Da Vinci Code,* this sacred history is recorded in the eighty or so Gospels that had contended for a place in the New Testament but which came to be excluded when the fourth-century Roman emperor Constantine decided which books would become sacred Scripture.

Despite Dan Brown's claim at the beginning of his novel that all of its "descriptions of documents . . . are accurate," nearly everything he says about the Gospels outside the New Testament is wrong. We don't know if there were eighty Gospels, none of the ones that survive ever mentions Jesus' alleged marriage to Mary Magdalene, and Constantine had nothing to do with deciding which books would be included in the New Testament.[2] Nonetheless, the claim that there were other Gospels that did not become Scripture is one of the "revelations" of *The Da Vinci Code* that has so fascinated its millions of readers.

It is true that these other Gospels portray Jesus in a different light from those of the New Testament. And some of these Gospels have occasionally turned up in spectacular archaeological discoveries of modern times. None of this is news to scholars of early Christianity, of course, but for a lay reader, it can all seem pretty revolutionary.

We don't know how many Gospels were written in early Christianity, but there must have been a lot. Of those that survive, the earliest are those of the New Testament: Matthew, Mark, Luke, and John. These are all from the first century, from within thirty-five to sixty-five years of Jesus' death. Other Gospels had been written earlier still, which no longer survive: one of the New Testament authors, Luke, says that "many" predecessors had written accounts of Jesus' life (Luke 1:1–4). Unfortunately, only one of these earlier accounts survives: the Gospel of Mark, which Luke used as a source.

Other Christian Gospels started appearing in the second century. Some of them are mentioned by church fathers who found their teachings offensive. Every now and then, one of these will turn up—either in an archaeological dig or by pure serendipity. For example, in 1886 a French archaeological team digging in a cemetery near the town of Akhmim, Egypt, uncovered the grave of an eighth-century monk, who happened to be buried with a book. The book contained four fragmentary texts, written in Greek on papyrus. One of these texts was a Gospel composed in the first person, allegedly by the disciple Simon Peter. Before this discovery, scholars knew that a Gospel of Peter once existed: it is mentioned by the fourth-century church father Eusebius, who indicates that the book was banned because it portrayed Christ as a divine being who was not completely human. And in fact, some passages in the fragmentary Gospel discovered in Akhmim might suggest this view of Jesus. Here, then, is a good match between the ancient description of a Gospel and a text that turns up.

On other occasions a Gospel is discovered that does not match its description in an ancient source. In such cases we have to assume either that the church father who describes the text did not know what he was talking about or that there were two Gospels circulating under the same (or a similar) name. For example, the feisty heresy hunter of the fourth century, Epiphanius, wrote an eighty-chapter book attacking Christian heretics and the Gospels they used. In the course of his discussion he mentions a Gospel about Mary Magdalene that sounds very bizarre indeed. In this account, Epiphanius alleges, Jesus took Mary to the top of a mountain and then in her presence pulled a woman out from his side (much as Eve came forth from Adam) and began having sexual intercourse with her. When he reached his climax, he pulled out from her and consumed his own semen, telling Mary: "Thus must we do, that we may live." Mary, as one might understand, was shocked into unconsciousness.

Epiphanius calls this alleged book *The Greater Questions of Mary*. It would be terrific if this Gospel would turn up, but so far we have no evidence of its existence outside of Epiphanius's vivid description. But another Gospel of Mary has been discovered, which is very different indeed. This book was found in Egypt in 1896 and made its way to Berlin where, due to a number of highly unfortunate circumstances, including two world wars, it languished before being published in 1955. This text has nothing lewd or immoral at all in it; it is a revelation to Mary Magdalene by Jesus after his resurrection in which he explains how the human soul can ascend from this inferior material world through the heavens to return to God. Here an ancient description (Epiphanius's *Questions of Mary*) and a modern discovery (the Gospel of Mary) do not match, so we are dealing with a different Gospel altogether.[3]

There are other Gospels that have been discovered in modern times which we knew nothing about until they were found. This was the case with the most famous of all archaeological discoveries of early Christian texts, the cache of documents unearthed in 1945 by a group of Egyptian farmhands digging for fertilizer next to a cliff face near the town of Nag Hammadi. Sealed inside an earthenware jar were thirteen books that contained fifty-two different tractates. The books had been produced in the fourth Christian century—as became clear when scholars examined them closely: some of the books had leather covers that had been strengthened at the spine with scrap paper, including dated receipts. Whereas some of the documents discovered in this cache were known before (there was a fragment from Plato's *Republic,* for example), most of them had been completely unknown before this time, including Gospels allegedly by Judas Thomas and Philip, and another one simply called the Gospel of Truth.[4]

Whenever a new Gospel is discovered, one has to ask whether this is a Gospel that is mentioned by an early church father or not. If it has the same title as one mentioned by a church father, one still has to ask whether the contents of the Gospel coincide with the description he gives. If they do coincide, then there is a clear match. If they do not, then either the church father knew about the document but didn't know what was in it (and so gave a false description) or it is a different document that simply has the same title.[5]

This brings us now to the Gospel of Judas. In this case we are lucky to have a description of just such a Gospel in the works of an early church author, Irenaeus, who wrote a five-volume attack on Christian heretics around the year 180 CE. If his description of the Gospel matches the contents of the recently discovered Gospel, then we are dealing with a very early Gospel indeed, one that could have been written no later than the mid-second century, prior to Irenaeus's writing.

Irenaeus's Mission and Message

To help make sense of Irenaeus's comments about the Gospel of Judas, I need to provide some background information on Irenaeus himself and on the book that he produced, in which he attacks "heretical" groups of Christians as nefarious enemies of the truth.

Irenaeus was the Christian bishop of Lyons in Gaul (modern France), living at a time when the church was under severe attack externally—by non-Christian mobs and the local Roman authorities—and was experiencing serious turmoil and divisions internally. We know about the persecution of the Christians in Gaul not so much from Irenaeus's own books as from other writings produced at about the same time. In particular, we have a letter written by members of Irenaeus's community sent to another church in which they describe a horrific persecution in 177 CE, when Marcus Aurelius was the Roman emperor. This letter is preserved for us in the writings of the church historian Eusebius, who was living 150 years later but who managed to procure a copy and quoted from it at considerable length. In the letter, the Christians of Lyons indicate that the mobs turned against them, forbade their participation in the life of the community, and eventually subjected them to physical violence. The Roman authorities intervened—not to protect the Christians but rather to force them to abandon their faith in Christ and worship the gods of the state.

In graphic and lurid detail the letter describes the tortures endured by the Christians who had been arrested for the faith. They were imprisoned, starved, put in stocks, thrown to wild beasts, roasted alive on iron seats set over raging fires, tortured on the rack, and so on. Most of them died, either in prison or in the public spectacles in the arena, where the pagan crowds came to watch and enjoy the public humiliation, torment, and dismemberment of these recalcitrant Christians who would have been let off the hook if they simply had denied their faith.[6]

Some Christians did recant under torture. Others died, including a number of the leaders of the church. Yet other Christians were evidently—and for unknown reasons—spared arrest, torture, and execution altogether. Irenaeus appears to have belonged to the latter group. Obviously those who survived the persecution, whether battered or unscathed, would take their religious commitments with the utmost seriousness. These were commitments that were worth suffering and dying for.

Irenaeus is nothing if not serious. But his surviving writings are not designed to exhort Christians to remain true to their faith in the face of imperial opposition. His concern instead is with the internal health of the church, for there were massive divisions within the Christian community. As Irenaeus describes it, large numbers of heretical teachers had infiltrated its ranks, proclaiming versions of the Christian message that Irenaeus and others like him considered absolutely false, inspired by the Devil, and mortally dangerous—at least as dangerous as the instruments of torture wielded by the ruling authorities. If one needs to die for one's faith, one had better know what that faith is, and not die for a heretical or false version of it.

Irenaeus was particularly distressed about the widespread presence of Gnostic Christians in the midst of the church. He viewed Gnostics as false believers propagating a false gospel, sowing weeds among the pure wheat of the true people of God. These heretics needed to be rooted out and destroyed—not by torture and execution but by invective and argument. For the church to be pure, it had to embrace the true teaching about Christ and his apostles. And so Irenaeus wrote a long attack on Gnostic heretics in which he detailed their nefarious views, described their insidious writings, attacked their heretical perspectives, maligned their immoral teachers, and generally tried to set the record straight so that his readers would know the "truth" about the Christian religion they claimed to profess.

Who were these Gnostics that Irenaeus found so threatening to the unity and message of the Christian church? It is an important question for our inquiries here, because Irenaeus claimed that the Gospel of Judas was in fact a Gnostic book, written to propound a false view of the world in the name of Jesus' betrayer, Judas Iscariot.

The Gnostics

For centuries scholars knew about the Gnostics principally from what Irenaeus had said about them in his five-volume work *Against Heresies,* the more complete title of which is *On the Refutation and Overthrow of Gnosis, Falsely So-called.* Other church fathers, such as the wildly imaginative Epiphanius of the fourth century, also attacked Gnostics—but many of their views appeared to derive from Irenaeus.

In modern times scholars have learned much more about Gnosticism from other sources, as such discoveries as the Nag Hammadi library have provided us with firsthand accounts of what the Gnostics believed and taught. These discoveries include books written by Gnostics for Gnostics; as such, they set out the Gnostics' own views, not simply their views as attacked by enemies such as Irenaeus. For this reason they allow us to compare what Irenaeus has to say about Gnostics with what the Gnostics say about themselves. In broad terms, Irenaeus appears to give us a general sense of what Gnostics stood for, even if he is completely off base in numerous details and wrong in many of the allegations he levels.[7]

Based on a reading of Gnostics' own writings, combined with a critical reading of Irenaeus, what can we say about the Gnostics? The first thing to note is that some scholars have been so impressed with the enormous range of beliefs and practices labeled "Gnostic" that they think we should abandon the term altogether. For them, it is an umbrella term that has grown too large to be of any real use for describing the views that it allegedly covers.[8]

My own opinion is that this is taking the matter too far. It is true that scholars (and even Irenaeus) have sometimes inappropriately applied the term *Gnostic* to groups that do not fit any recognizable Gnostic pattern, and it is true that many of the things Irenaeus and others say about Gnostic groups appear to have been made up in the heat of battle. But in my judgment there were groups that broadly held to views that we can call Gnostic. If we abandon the term *Gnostic,* we may as well abandon the terms *Christian* and *Jewish*—these too are very broad umbrella terms that cover a range of religious groups, both in antiquity and today.

In its broadest terms, *Gnosticism* refers to a number of religious groups from the early centuries of Christianity that emphasized the importance of secret knowledge to escape the trappings of this material world. The name *Gnostic* itself comes from the Greek word for "knowledge," *gnosis.* Gnostics, then, are ones who are in the know. And what do they know? They know the truth that can set them free from this world of matter, which was created not by the one true God but by lower, inferior, and often ignorant deities who designed this world as a place of entrapment for elements of the divine. Gnostic religions indicate that some of us have a spark of divinity within us, a spark that longs to be set free from the prison of our bodies. These religions provide the secret knowledge that allows us to transcend our mortal, material bodies to return to the heavenly realm whence we originally came, where we will once again live with the gods.

This may not sound particularly Christian—and in fact there were Gnostic groups (Irenaeus apparently didn't realize this) that were not connected with Christianity. One of the debates that rages among scholars today is the relationship of Gnostic groups to other forms of Christianity. Did Gnostic religions begin independently—and possibly prior to—Christianity, and eventually come to interact with communities of Christian believers so as to influence them, and to be influenced by them? Or is Gnosticism (as Irenaeus thought) a perversion of Christianity (and therefore later in origin), which sometimes took its views to such an extreme that it no longer looked like traditional Christianity? However one resolves these issues, it is clear that most Gnostic texts known today show some connection with Christian thought, in that it is usually Christ himself who brings the knowledge necessary for liberation from this world. As Jesus himself is recorded as saying in the Gospel of John: "You shall know the truth, and the truth shall make you free" (John 8:32).

Many Gnostics loved the Gospel of John: here Jesus is portrayed as a divine being come to earth from the realm above in order to lead people home by revealing the truth needed to transcend this world. But Gnostics had lots of other texts as well. Some of them explain at greater length how this world came into being in the first place, how some sparks of the divine (some of us) came to be entrapped here, and how we can escape.

Some of these texts—a number of them found at Nag Hammadi—express these teachings in highly mystical terms, narrating a set of myths to explain our existence in this world. There are different myths told in different texts, and they cannot all be reconciled in their many details. Still, most of these myths start before the beginning described in the book of Genesis, when there existed just one transcendent, completely unknown and unknowable divine being who was exclusively spirit, with nothing material about him. In eternity past, this divine being generated other divine beings out of himself as personifications of his own characteristics. He was eternal, and so Eternalness itself came into existence as its own divine entity; he thought (about himself), and so his Thought came into existence as a distinct being; he was alive, and so Life came into being; he was all light, no darkness, and so Light came into existence; he was wise, and so Wisdom became a divine being. Some of these divine beings themselves, in pairs, generated yet other divine beings. Eventually the heavenly realm was filled with such divine beings, often called "aeons." Together the aeons make up the entire divine realm, known as the Pleroma, which literally means "the fullness."

All of this took place before there was any universe. There was only a divine realm. But a cosmic disaster occurred. One of the aeons for some reason fell from the divine realm, leading to the generation of a different kind of divine being, one who was generated not within the Pleroma but outside it. This misshapen and imperfect being is called by different names—most commonly Yaldabaoth, which may be related to the name of God in the Old Testament, Yahweh, Lord of Sabbaths. This divine miscarriage is, in fact, the creator god of the Jews, who ignorantly proclaimed, "I am God and there is no other." He simply didn't know that there were other gods, far superior to him in power and knowledge. They dwelt where he had never been, in the divine realm of the Pleroma.

Yaldabaoth generated yet other imperfect divinities, and together they became the creator(s) of the material world, which they made as a place for imprisonment for that aeon that had fallen from the Pleroma (sometimes known as Sophia, the Greek word for "wisdom"). Human bodies were created in order to house sparks of this divine being, Sophia.

That brings us to the state of the world today. Why is it a place of such misery, pain, and suffering? Because it is not the good creation of the ultimate true God. It is a faulty creation of a lower, inferior, ignorant, and (sometimes) evil deity. The goal of salvation, therefore, is not to create a paradise on earth, a Kingdom of God in this realm. The goal is to allow the divine sparks scattered among humanity to escape this material world, to become reunited, and to return to the realm whence they came.

How can that happen? Only when those of us who have divine sparks within us learn the truth about who we are, where we came from, how we got here, and how we can return. Saving knowledge, in other words, is self-knowledge. This knowledge cannot come to us through natural means—for example, by looking around at the world and thinking hard about it. This material world is the creation of an inferior deity, and nothing in it can tell us what we need to know to escape it. No, the knowledge for salvation must come to us from above. A divine being—an aeon from the Pleroma—must come down to tell us what we need to know.

But how can an aeon come into this material world without itself partaking of the realm of matter? Gnostics had different ways of solving that problem. Those Gnostics who were Christian insisted that Christ was this aeon. And they had two different ways of explaining how he could reveal the truth of salvation without becoming entrapped himself in matter. According to one explanation, Christ came into the world in the "appearance" of human flesh— that is, Christ was a phantasm who only seemed to be a real man. He was completely spirit, human in appearance only. The other explanation, found more commonly in Gnostic texts, is that Christ was an aeon who was tempo- rarily housed in the body of the man Jesus. In this view, Jesus was the human shell that provided Christ with the medium he needed in order to reveal the truth to his followers. When the shell was killed, or perhaps before, Christ was released to return to the Pleroma, whence he came.

Irenaeus and the Gnostics

One can see why Irenaeus would find the Gnostics dangerous. They claimed to have the "true" knowledge about God, the world, Christ, and salvation. But what they said stood fundamentally at odds with the Christian message as Irenaeus and others like him—the Christians who eventually established the "orthodox" view of the faith—understood it. For Irenaeus, there was only one God; according to the Gnostics, there were numerous divine beings. For Irenaeus, the one God had created this world; according to the Gnostics, the world was created by a lower, inferior, or even evil deity. For Irenaeus, the God of this world was God the Father of Jesus; according to the Gnostics, the God of this world was the enemy of Jesus. For Irenaeus, the world was inherently good (even if sin had corrupted it); according to the Gnostics, the world was a wicked place of entrapment. For Irenaeus, Christ was both human and divine, at one and the same time, the preincarnate divine being who became fully and com- pletely man; according to the Gnostics, Christ was a divine aeon who either only appeared to be human or temporarily inhabited the mortal shell of the man Jesus. For Irenaeus, salvation came by having faith in the death and bodily resurrection of Jesus; according to the Gnostics, salvation came by learning the secret truths that Christ taught concerning how to escape this world of the body.

I should stress that these truths were not available to just anybody. Only those who had the spark of the divine within could receive them. Others— those without the spark—belonged to the god of this world, the creator who made matter and all the misery and suffering connected with it. These others could not know the truth because they were not from above. This made it ex- ceedingly difficult to argue with Gnostics. If you claimed they were wrong, they could simply point out that you didn't "know." If you interpreted a pas- sage of Scripture to counter their claims, they could smugly assure you that

you misunderstood the passage. If you claimed that their interpretation vio-
lated that natural meaning of the text, they could say that the real meaning lies
beneath the surface, there only for those with eyes to see.

It may have been his frustration with dealing with Gnostics head-on that led
Irenaeus to write the kind of attack we find in his five-volume work *Against
Heresies*. Here he is writing not for the Gnostic insiders but for other, non-
Gnostic Christians, to warn them away from the Gnostics and to keep them
aligned with the "true" faith—that is, with the faith as Irenaeus saw it. His
mode of attack is ridicule and slander. Irenaeus goes to great lengths to describe the Gnostic myths in detail, principally so he can show how absurdly
complicated and convoluted they are—as opposed to the true Gospel, which he
sees as very simple. Some modern scholars have thought that in fact Irenaeus
either misrepresented or misunderstood the Gnostics when he detailed their
myths.[9] In fact, these myths were not meant to be propositional truths about
things that happened in the past, historically accurate sketches of what really
transpired when the world was created. They are *myths*—stories conveying the
Gnostic understanding of the truth of the world and our relationship to it. No
one would take a metaphysical poem and argue that it can't be true because the
metaphors and imagery that it uses are not literally correct; no one would ma-
lign a meteorologist for saying that sunrise will be at 6:34 a.m. when we all
know that in fact the sun doesn't rise at all, but the earth rotates.

Irenaeus and his successors took the Gnostics' mysterious, mythical texts,
passed them off as containing propositional claims, and so successfully managed to mock them. But it wasn't a laughing matter for Gnostics, who saw in
these myths a statement of the reality that they encountered every day in this
material world, which needed to be transcended for one to find peace.

The other thing that Irenaeus seems to have misunderstood about Gnostics
has to do with their ethical relations to one another. Irenaeus realized that
Gnostics opposed this material existence and thought that, at the end of the
day, the body was to be transcended in order to find salvation. The body, in
other words, did not matter. Irenaeus drew the conclusion that if the Gnostics
thought that the body didn't matter, then it didn't matter what they did with
their bodies. Throughout his assault he charges Gnostics with leading highly
immoral, promiscuous lives—especially in their communal services of worship, where they allegedly engaged in all sorts of orgiastic practices.

The discovery of the Nag Hammadi library has shown how this view—as
sensible as it may have seemed to Irenaeus—was in fact dead wrong. It was
precisely because the Gnostics devalued the body that they thought that a person should not be enslaved to the body or its desires. Rather than being promiscuous, Gnostics were highly ascetic, urging their followers not to cave in to
the lusts of the flesh, but to fast and abstain from good food and fine wine and
even from sex. Bodily pleasure ties one to the body, but Gnostic religions urged
people to escape from their bodies.

Irenaeus, the Cainites,
and the Gospel of Judas

Not every Gnostic writing recounts the Gnostic myths, just as modern Marxist writings do not always reprint the Communist Manifesto. Most Gnostic texts simply presuppose the mythical basis of the religion and talk about other things. That is why some scholars, wrongly in my view, have thought that a text such as the Gospel of Thomas, discovered at Nag Hammadi, or the Gospel of Mary, discovered fifty years earlier, are not actually Gnostic—because they do not lay out the Gnostic myth. But these books do appear to presuppose some form of the myth. I tell my students that to read these books you have to understand the mythological basis without having the author spell it out for you—just as reading the sports page requires you to understand the rules and history of basketball without the sportswriter telling you all about them before describing what happened in the fourth quarter of last night's game.

In any event, there were lots of Gnostic groups with lots of different myths. One of the groups that Irenaeus mentions is especially germane to our main interest in this book. It is a group known as the Cainites.[10] They are important because they allegedly had a Gospel of Judas. Judging from what Irenaeus says about this book, we appear now to have it in hand in the newly discovered Gospel.

The Cainites

Irenaeus mentions the Cainites near the end of book 1 of *Against Heresies*. They were allegedly named this because they understood themselves to be related to Cain, the first son of Adam and Eve. In the annals of biblical history, Cain has always been understood to be one of the "bad guys." He did not get along with his younger brother, Abel, and when God showed a preference for Abel—because his animal sacrifices were superior to Cain's sacrifices of grain— Cain took Abel out into a field and murdered him. Cain, in other words, was the first fratricide, and God punished him by casting him out of his land and laying a curse on him (Gen. 4:1–16).

Why would any group of religious believers identify themselves with Cain, of all people? It must be remembered that these Cainites were Gnostics, who believed that the creator god of this world—the one who punished Cain for disobeying him—was not the true God but a lesser, inferior divine being. The Cainites evidently believed that in order to worship the true God you needed to oppose the god of this world. And if this god was against Cain, then Cain must have been on the side of the true God.

So too with other biblical figures who have traditionally been seen as standing opposed to God. According to Irenaeus, the Cainites saw Korah as one of the heroes of the faith. This is a figure who opposed Moses and urged a rebellion against him; in response, God caused the earth to open up and Korah and all his family were swallowed alive (Num. 16). More striking still, the Cainites revered the men of Sodom and Gomorrah, infamous in the annals of the Judeo-

Christian tradition as completely godless and immoral, whom God punished by destroying their cities with fire and brimstone (Gen. 19).

Thus, according to Irenaeus, the Cainites saw themselves standing in line with those who had been outspoken in their opposition to the god of the Jews, the creator of the world. And they believed that they themselves "were attacked by the Maker" (*Against Heresies* 1.31.1).[11] But none of them suffered any real harm, because their protector, the aeon Sophia, intervened on their behalf.

After giving us these few details, Irenaeus goes on to describe one other hero of the Cainites' faith:

> Also Judas, the traitor, they say, had exact knowledge of these things, and since he alone knew the truth better than the other apostles, he accomplished the mystery of the betrayal. Through him all things in heaven and on earth were destroyed. This fiction they adduce and call it the Gospel of Judas. (*Against Heresies,* 1.31.1)

This, then, is our first reference in any ancient text to a Gospel of Judas. Irenaeus does not indicate that he himself had read the book, making it impossible to know whether he is describing it from firsthand knowledge or from hearsay, or if instead he is simply surmising what must have been in a book of this sort.[12]

The Gospel of Judas

What Irenaeus says about the book appears to coincide closely with the fragmentary document now at our disposal, the full contents of which I will be discussing in chapter 6.[13] But for now the following points may be noted about the newly discovered Gospel of Judas, in anticipation of that fuller discussion:

1. This Gospel has the same title as the one mentioned by Irenaeus.
2. It is a Gnostic Gospel obviously written by and for Gnostics.
3. Judas is portrayed as the "hero" of the account.
4. He alone is said to understand Jesus and his message; the other apostles worship the god of this world, who is not the God of Jesus.
5. The betrayal is characterized as a good deed done by Judas for Jesus; as Jesus states: "You will exceed all the others (i.e., the other apostles), for you will sacrifice the man that clothes me" (in other words, the betrayal is what allows Jesus to escape the trappings of his material body).
6. Judas's act will eventually cause the material world to be overcome, as others follow Jesus back to their heavenly home (so that he "destroys" all that is in heaven and earth).

We appear to have a match between the description of the Gospel of Judas in the writings of Irenaeus and the text that now has turned up in an amazing archaeological discovery of the twentieth century.

Other Writers on the Cainites

Irenaeus makes a couple of other comments about the Cainites, and they are not nice. In fact, they are so much like what he says about other groups, and so nasty in their intent, that some modern scholars have concluded that the Cainites never actually existed as a social group but were a figment of Irenaeus's imagination.[14]

In particular, Irenaeus indicates that the Cainites were like other Gnostics who took their opposition to the creator god to an extreme. Since this god called Israel to be his people and then gave them his law through Moses, the Cainites allegedly maintained that the best way to demonstrate independence from the god of this world was by disobeying his commandments. And so, for example, if the Jewish god commands his people to observe the sabbath, not to eat pork, and not to commit adultery, the best way to show that you belong to the one true God, as opposed to the Jewish god, is to work on the sabbath, eat pork, and commit adultery. Irenaeus indicates that for the Cainites, perfect "knowledge" led them into acts of immorality too gross to mention. I think we can rest assured that even if Irenaeus didn't want to mention these acts, he was at least thinking of them.

Two other church writers after Irenaeus discuss the Cainites: the early-third-century author of a book called *Against All Heresies,* sometimes wrongly thought to have been the famous Tertullian, and the feisty fourth-century Epiphanius, whom I have already mentioned. It does not appear, however, that either author had any independent knowledge of the group, if indeed the group existed. Instead, they simply expanded what Irenaeus himself said, adding lurid details of their own as they saw fit. The first author (Pseudo-Tertullian) does not mention the fact that the Cainites used a Gospel of Judas. Epiphanius does so, but he appears to have derived this information from Irenaeus.

Questions About the Cainites
and the Gospel of Judas

There are several remaining issues to address before moving on, in the next chapter, to an account of the discovery of the Gospel of Judas. One has to do with whether this is really the book used by the Cainites. One problem with thinking so is that this newly discovered Gospel contains no reference to the Cainites themselves.

As it turns out, this is not really a problem. Gospels—like most other books—almost never mention the groups that use them. Still, wouldn't we expect some extensive discussion of Cain in a book used by the Cainites? To that I think there are three main responses: (1) The Gospel of Judas that we have is missing portions of its text, as we will see. It is possible, at least, that Cain did figure more prominently in the text in its complete form. (2) Irenaeus never says that the Gospel of Judas was actually *written* by the Cainites, only that they used it.

By analogy, the Gospel of John was used by Irenaeus, but Irenaeus is obviously never mentioned by the Gospel of John. (3) As I've indicated, there are some scholars with serious doubts about whether the Cainites actually existed.

But doesn't the existence of the Gospel of Judas mentioned by Irenaeus hinge on the existence of the group that he claims used it? Actually, this is not the case at all. The church fathers who attacked heretics are well known for their propensity to expand on what little knowledge they had in order to provide a fuller, more well-rounded picture for their readers. Sometimes these expansions had historical grounding, but sometimes they were just details that the heresy hunters made up.

In the present case, one could imagine a scenario such as the following. Suppose Irenaeus knew of a Gospel based on the perspective of Jesus' betrayer, Judas. Whether or not he actually had read the book, he realized that it was one of those nefarious Gnostic Gospels that portrayed the Jewish god not as the one true God but as a lesser divinity. The creator of this world was not the Father of Christ but a god whom Christ and his followers were to escape. Even more, this Gospel made the betrayer of Christ his one true disciple, the one who understood his message, the one who faithfully did his will. This is a Gospel that turned the truth upside down, celebrating what was true as false.

If Irenaeus knew of (or read) such a Gospel, it is not at all implausible to envisage that he came up with a viable social context within which it would have been written, read, and revered. If so, he may have imagined a group whom he associated with Cain and provided some explanation of their nefarious beliefs, based on what he had found in this Gospel. Another option is that there really was a Gnostic group that cherished the memory of Cain, the men of Sodom, and Judas, and that this was their Gospel.

In either event, we have in the witness of Irenaeus, from around 180 CE, the first attestation of this Gospel of Judas. This was not a Gospel written many centuries after the days of Jesus. It was written soon after the Gospels of the New Testament. They were all produced in the second half of the first century, from possibly 65 to 95 CE. This one must have appeared fifty years later, in the mid-second century, if not before. It came into being in a completely different context from the Gospels of the New Testament. It was written in different circumstances to address different needs. It was written by someone with a completely different perspective. Its author was a Gnostic, and he wanted his Gnostic understanding of the truth to be embodied in a Gospel with apostolic authority. The apostle in whose name it was written was none other than the betrayer of Jesus. For this author, the betrayer was the one who had gotten it right. Judas in this Gospel is Jesus' closest disciple, to whom alone he revealed the truths necessary for salvation. He acted upon the knowledge Christ had given him and fulfilled his destiny by performing the deed that Christ set out for him. He turned Jesus over to the ruling authorities so that he could be executed, to allow his soul to escape its entrapment in the body, to return to its heavenly home. For this Gospel, Judas was not the enemy of Christ; he was his dearest friend.

⌘

CHAPTER FIVE

The Discovery of the Gospel of Judas

I n chapter 1 I described my trip to Geneva in December 2004. There I laid
eyes on the Gospel of Judas for the first time. I was obviously elated by the
possibilities. But as I returned from my trip I had more questions than answers.
I had looked over some pages of the Coptic text but had no opportunity to
study and translate them. What could be found in the pages I had seen? Was
this an earth-shattering discovery that would make the cover story of major
magazines, a discovery that would interest everyone in the Christian world? Or
would it be interesting only to a small group of scholars who study Coptic and
the ancient texts preserved in it?

It depended entirely on the kind of document it was. If it was a Gnostic
revelation similar to the dozens of other Gnostic revelations that have been
discovered, scholars would be intrigued. But a text such as that would not
carry the enormous significance of, say, the discovery of the Dead Sea Scrolls.
If, on the other hand, the Gospel contained ancient views about the relationship of Jesus and his betrayer, Judas Iscariot, told from Judas's own perspective, that would be a different matter altogether.[1]

At no point did I think that a second-century Gospel about Jesus and Judas
would force us to rewrite everything we knew about Judas. I had no hope that
this would be a Gospel Judas himself had written, or that its second-century
author would somehow have had access to the historical truths of what happened between Judas and his teacher a hundred years earlier. But to have a
Gospel that was potentially this early—from before the time of Irenaeus, before the writing of most of our other Gospels from the ancient world—that
gave an alternative view of Judas, celebrating him as the one who truly understood his master . . . well, a Gospel such as *that,* in my opinion, would be very
big news indeed. It would open up new vistas of understanding about early

Christianity and show us just how wildly diverse this religion was in its early centuries. If there was a group of Christians who revered Judas Iscariot, of all people, how strange would *that* be?

My Initial Disappointment

While still thrilled by the prospects, I found a discussion on the Internet that made my heart sink.

There is a Dutch blogger named Michel van Rijn who runs a very peculiar Web site that specializes in debunking claims about modern art and ancient artifacts. Van Rijn had gotten wind of the Gospel of Judas story, tracked down some leads, and learned that National Geographic was planning to spend considerable time and effort promoting the release of the document and its translation—and presumably would make a lot of money off it. Van Rijn decided to explode the entire operation by publishing all the surviving materials before National Geographic itself had a chance to do so.

Van Rijn had found an American scholar, Charlie Hedrick—a New Testament scholar I have known and liked for years—who claimed to have photographs of the Gospel of Judas and to have already made preliminary translations of them. In order to squash any speculation about the Gospel, and to beat National Geographic to the punch, van Rijn published the photographs and the translations. When I read them, I was massively disappointed.

The text appeared to have nothing to do with Judas and Jesus. It was a Gnostic document whose main figure was someone called Allogenes, who prays to God and hears God's answer. The text had Gnostic characteristics, and it would be of some limited interest to scholars of Gnosticism. But as far as Judas and Jesus were concerned, it was a complete bust.

It is amazing how even those of us who teach for a living fail to practice what we preach. Every semester in my undergraduate courses at Chapel Hill I have to tell my students not to trust everything they find on the Internet, since anyone can publish anything there, and there is often no way of knowing if the source is credible or bogus. In this particular case, not having followed my own advice, I was completely taken in.

What I didn't know at the time, but eventually came to realize, is that Hedrick had translated the wrong text.

My first indication that something was amiss came on July 1, 2005. I was in New York on other business and had set up a lunch date at the Harvard Club with Herb Krosney, whom I mentioned earlier as the investigative journalist who had originally tracked down the Gospel of Judas, found that it was owned now by the Maecenas Foundation in Geneva, interested National Geographic in the story, and more or less single-handedly pushed the story forward—leading eventually to my hurried trip to Geneva six months before. Over lunch in July I expressed my real frustration that the whole story was soon to collapse on itself, that there was not in fact much of a story at all, because I had read the Hedrick translation and frankly couldn't understand why National Geographic was still interested in pursuing the matter.

Herb knew what was actually in the text, but he was not at liberty to give me all the details. With a twinkle in his eye, he suggested that I not believe everything I read on the Internet (the advice I give students just about every week). But I persisted: I had seen the photographs of the Coptic pages, they looked similar in quality to the pages I had seen in Geneva, I had seen Hedrick's transcription of the pages, and I had checked his translation. There just wasn't much there. All Herb could do was throw out a tantalizing hint: maybe Hedrick was translating a different part of the book.

It was only later that I realized what had happened. As we will see in this chapter, when scholars first gained access to this manuscript and were able to determine its contents, they believed it contained fragmentary copies of three texts, two of which were already known from earlier archaeological discoveries: the Letter of Peter to Philip and the First Apocalypse of James, copies of which had been discovered among the writings of the Nag Hammadi library in 1945. The third text was the gold mine: the Gospel of Judas. But it was not until Florence Darbre, the expert in manuscript restoration, and Rodolphe Kasser, the eminent Coptologist responsible for editing and translating the text, had worked on the manuscript for three years that they realized what no one—including van Rijn and Hedrick—had before suspected. The final part of the manuscript contained not just one document—the Gospel of Judas—but two. The other one is a fragmentary copy of an otherwise unknown Gnostic treatise about this figure Allogenes. Hedrick had assumed that his photographs were from the Gospel of Judas. They weren't. They were from a different text. This changed things drastically.

As it turns out, whereas the pages about Allogenes are of some interest, the Gospel of Judas itself is endlessly fascinating. It too, like the other three texts found in this manuscript, is Gnostic, and a good portion of it contains a rather difficult-to-understand Gnostic revelation concerning how the world came into being and how humans were created (*not* by the one true God). It also contains previously unrecorded dialogues between Jesus and Judas, and portrays Judas as the hero of the apostolic band, the one who both understood and obeyed his Lord.

Before describing the full contents of this Gospel—the subject of the next chapter—I want to go back to the beginning, back before the time I first laid eyes on the text in December 2004, before the time it was placed in the capable hands of Florence Darbre and Rodolphe Kasser, before it was even known to any scholar living in the Western world. How was this document discovered, and how did it finally make its way into the possession of the Maecenas Foundation? In order to give credit where credit is due—and in this case it is richly deserved—I need to acknowledge that our understanding of the history of the discovery and circulation of this Gospel are because of the relentless energies of Herb Krosney, whose book *The Lost Gospel: The Quest for the Gospel of Judas Iscariot* is, to date, the authoritative account. I have drawn the sketch of this chapter from his narrative, supplemented by private conversations with him and others involved, and by comments by the editor and translator of the text, Rodolphe Kasser. I should add that there remain large gaps in our knowledge about the discovery and postdiscovery fortunes of the Gospel, in no small measure because some of the principal figures are either unknown or no longer living.

The Discovery

One of the strangest facts about archaeological discoveries of early Jewish and Christian manuscripts is that the most spectacular finds are almost never made by trained archaeologists. Most of them are the result of pure serendipity. Moreover, they are typically discovered by people who have no idea what it is they have discovered and no sense of their real worth. In 1945, the Nag Hammadi library of early Gnostic texts was discovered by a group of *fellahin,* or peasants, digging for fertilizer near a cliff face in the wilderness of Egypt, just north of the Nile. The *fellahin* were illiterate and had no use for the thirteen volumes they found inside a sealed earthenware jar. A year and a half later, in 1947, a shepherd boy discovered a number of documents in a cave in the wilderness just west of the Dead Sea; other caves were eventually searched (by both Bedouin and archaeologists), and eleven would yield their treasures—known today as the Dead Sea Scrolls.[2]

So too with the Gospel of Judas and the other documents connected with it. These were discovered by illiterate peasants who had stumbled upon a cave that had centuries before been used as a burial site. They rummaged among the cave's contents looking for trinkets they might sell, and landed upon some manuscripts.

The year was evidently 1978. The place was the Al Minya province of Middle Egypt, some 120 miles south of Cairo, next to a set of cliffs called Jebel Qarara, not far from the town of Maghagha (pronounced "mu-rair-a"). We don't know the names of the individuals who made the discovery.

Inside the cave were some baskets filled with ancient Roman glass flasks; there were also a number of human remains. Next to one of these were two limestone boxes. Opening the boxes, the peasants found several ancient manuscripts.

This was not the first time that important early Christian documents were found beside skeletal remains—presumably of the documents' onetime owner. I mentioned earlier that this is how the Gospel of Peter was discovered in 1886 —in one of those rare instances, by archaeologists actually looking for antiquities—buried with a monk, possibly because this was his favorite book or because he was the scribe who had copied it. So too the Nag Hammadi library: before the *fellahin* found the earthenware jar containing the thirteen books, they had uncovered a skeleton. Presumably (though this is not absolutely certain), the Nag Hammadi books were connected in some way to the man buried next to them. Were they his books? Was he off in the wilderness trying to hide them? Was his death an accident? Did he die of natural causes? Was he murdered? We have no way of knowing. The scholars who pieced the story together came along twenty years later and the skeleton was never recovered.

So too in the present case. Later rumors about the find indicate that it was made next to human remains, but the remains are no longer there.

The limestone box contained four different manuscripts in codex form (that is, they were books, not scrolls). Later scholars would identify these ancient codices as follows. None of them, except for the Gospel of Judas codex, has yet been published or otherwise made public:

1. A mathematical treatise, written in Greek
2. A fragmentary copy of the Old Testament book of Exodus, also in Greek
3. A fragmentary copy of some of the New Testament letters of the apostle Paul, written in Coptic
4. The codex containing the Gospel of Judas (as I will explain later, we have the complete beginning and end of the Gospel, and much of the middle, but some portions have now been lost because of the rough handling of the manuscript after its discovery; about 10–15 percent of the text is now unrecoverable), along with three other fragmentary texts, all of them in Coptic: the Letter of Peter to Philip (in a version slightly different from the one discovered at Nag Hammadi), the First Apocalypse of James (also different from the Nag Hammadi version), and the Gnostic treatise on Allogenes (which is a different work from the Nag Hammadi tractate that is entitled "Allogenes")

These manuscripts had evidently resided in this limestone box for over sixteen hundred years, completely undisturbed. They could survive that long because of their location. Manuscripts will last for enormous lengths of time in a dry environment such as the wilderness of Egypt, where there is never much change in the humidity. Unfortunately, as we'll see, once they were taken from their resting place and circulated in other climes—sixteen years in a bank vault in a strip mall on Long Island, of all places—they quickly began to deteriorate, and portions of them are now beyond recovery.

In any event, the nameless *fellahin* who found the books sold them as booty to a man called Am Samiah (a pseudonym), a local dealer in trinkets, beads, and ancient textiles. Samiah was a small-time trader in antiquities; if someone in town found something that looked ancient, he was the one who would buy it up and then sell it to a dealer who could put it on the market in Cairo or Alexandria. Samiah himself was strictly a middleman; like the people with whom he did business, he was illiterate, and he supported himself principally by farming, especially the local specialty, garlic.[3]

In the Hands of Hanna

Am Samiah had connections with better-placed antiquities dealers, to whom he would sell whatever came to him (with a markup, of course), who would then market them in the large cities (with an additional markup) or sometimes, for the really important finds, to international traders who would sell them to museums and private investors (usually with a very large markup; the antiquities trade, from top to bottom, is unfortunately driven far more by the profit motive than by real concern for antiquarian finds).[4] In any event, Am Samiah sold the books (either directly or through a middleman) to a rather small-time antiquities dealer in Cairo called Hanna Asabil (another pseudonym). Evidently the price was relatively low: according to later reports, Samiah received something like 8,000 Egyptian pounds, which was at that time worth maybe $2,000. For him, this would have been a big sale. We don't know more about the actual transaction, in part because Samiah died about ten years later, in the late 1980s.

Hanna was not an urbane, sophisticated, multilingual international dealer in antiquities. But he was on the lookout for that unexpected find that could make his fortune. He was known to specialize in ancient papyrus in the Cairo markets. We aren't sure how, but somehow or other he got it into his head that these manuscripts could be worth a fantastic sum. Those who have been involved in tracking down the story have suggested that he had the manuscripts appraised by a scholar of antiquity visiting in Cairo, although the names normally mentioned— for example, Ludwig Koenen, a German professor of classics at the University of Michigan—are Greek scholars, and the most valuable parts of the collection were in Coptic.[5] In any event, Hanna let potential buyers know that he would be interested in parting with the documents in his possession for a cool $3 million.

This was obviously a princely sum, especially given the circumstance that Hanna had no idea what was actually in his codices—he simply knew that they were very old and that someone had told him they could be worth a fortune. The real problem was that with the kind of trading Hanna normally did, he didn't have the big-name clients needed to pull off such a deal. And so he contacted someone else who did, a powerful international antiquities dealer who had the necessary connections and clout to fetch a high price for the find, Nicolas Koutoulakis of Geneva, sometimes considered the most successful buyer and seller of antiquities in the modern age. Hanna had previously dealt with Koutoulakis, selling him items that had come to him, which Koutoulakis then turned around to sell for large profits. Born in Crete, Koutoulakis was multilingual and comfortable in high-powered circles; he did not have a formal education, but he was famously shrewd and regularly traded in goods worth millions.

Hanna did not want to sell his prize manuscripts to Koutoulakis, however. He wanted Koutoulakis to assist him to find a buyer. In the course of their negotiations, Hanna did sell Koutoulakis other items he had acquired, and this ended up leading to some tragic circumstances. Hanna had a statue of the Egyptian pharaoh Amenemhat II, of the Middle Kingdom, and sold it to Koutoulakis.

But when Koutoulakis went to have it appraised, he learned that it was a fake. Naturally he wanted his money back, but Hanna refused. This did not set a good tone.

Somewhat later, in 1979, Hanna evidently crossed the powerful Koutoulakis a second time, trying to negotiate a deal for his manuscripts not through the international antiquities dealer himself but on the sly, through one of his business associates. What happened next may have been a complete coincidence, but Hanna never thought so: there was a break-in at Hanna's apartment in Heliopolis (a suburb of Cairo). The burglars took everything he had: gold pieces, statues, jewelry, textiles, coins—and the papyrus manuscripts. This was an enormous haul: Hanna estimated the losses, even apart from the manuscripts, in the millions. He always suspected that Koutoulakis was behind the break-in. But it was never proven.

Hanna had no way to recoup the loss, and he considered the papyrus manuscripts to be the biggest loss of all. If only he could recover them, he could find a buyer, make a quick sale, and retire from the business a wealthy man. But these manuscripts had not yet been examined by a scholar to see what they contained. And now they appeared to be lost for good.

In an act of humility, Hanna pleaded with Koutoulakis to help him retrieve the manuscripts (an act that made a certain amount of sense, since he suspected Koutoulakis had them in his possession). Koutoulakis never made any concessions, never admitted that he had had anything to do with the break-in, never allowed that he had direct connections that could set to rights this great wrong. But he did promise to make inquiries and to do what he could do. Three years later, in 1982, Koutoulakis had the manuscripts returned to Hanna, in an exchange set up by middlemen in Geneva. For safekeeping, Hanna deposited the manuscripts in a safe deposit box in a bank there in Switzerland.

Looking for a Buyer

In 1983, Hanna located a potential buyer of the manuscripts. Ludwig Koenen was often in Cairo and other places in the Middle East, trying to buy Greek papyri for the University of Michigan's famous papyrus collection. Although he was born and raised in Germany, with a Ph.D. in classics from Cologne, Koenen had taught at Michigan since 1975.

Koenen must have been given a chance to look over the manuscripts briefly, because he informed Hanna that he would like to assemble a small team of experts from America to examine what was there and possibly negotiate a purchase. Since one of the texts was evidently a copy of the book of Exodus, Koenen asked David Noel Freedman, an Old Testament scholar who was his colleague at the University of Michigan. Since there were Coptic texts, he asked James M. Robinson, professor of Christian antiquity at Claremont Graduate University, in California; Robinson had served as head of the UNESCO team that put together the edition and translation of the Nag Hammadi library, and he was clearly a leading expert in the field. Unfortunately, Robinson had other commitments, and in his stead he sent a young but promising Ph.D. candidate from Yale, Stephen Emmel, who was already a rising star in the field of Coptic studies.

And so Koenen, Freedman, and Emmel agreed to meet with Hanna in Geneva to examine the manuscripts and to negotiate a price. They had no idea that Hanna was thinking in the millions. They were thinking $50,000.

The meeting took place on May 15, 1983, in Hanna's room at the Hotel de l'Union in Geneva. Later, reflecting on the meeting, Emmel explained the ground rules:

> We would be allowed to examine the papyri for a few minutes. No photographs would be permitted, and we weren't allowed to write anything. We were also told that we would not be able to take any notes so we had no paper, no writing implements of any kind.[6]

Once they had looked over what Hanna had, they would try to negotiate a deal.

Emmel's examination of the manuscripts is what matters most to us here, as he was allowed to look at the codex that contained what was later identified as the Gospel of Judas. But at the time, he didn't know what he was looking at. The manuscripts were being stored, rather carelessly, in three cardboard containers the size of shoe boxes, lined with newspapers. To avoid further damage to the already manhandled manuscripts, Emmel reached down into the box and carefully lifted pages with a special pair of tweezers he had brought along for the occasion. In even the short time he had, he was quickly able to recognize most of the contents of the codex. As he indicted in a written report produced afterward, he found that it contained the First Apocalypse of James, the Letter of Peter to Philip, and, as he said, "a dialogue between Jesus and his disciples (at least 'Judas' [i.e., presumably, Judas Thomas]) is involved, similar in genre to 'The Dialogue of the Savior' and 'The Wisdom of Jesus Christ.'"[7]

This was an extremely perceptive comment. What Emmel could detect, quickly reading the Coptic on pages that he noticed had already been rather badly treated, was that this "third" text was a discussion of Jesus with his disciples that seemed similar to two of the tractates discovered among the Nag Hammadi library but was different in content. As it was "Judas" with whom Jesus was talking, Emmel naturally assumed this was the figure known from other early Christian texts as Judas Thomas, the alleged author of the Gospel of Thomas. Had he been given more time, he would no doubt have discovered that in fact this was not Judas Thomas but Judas Iscariot. What Emmel had under his gaze was the long-lost Gospel of Judas.

But their time was quickly up. Hanna wanted to know if he could strike a deal with them, but when he stated his asking price, it floored the Americans, who had no access to that kind of funding. As a perfunctory gesture, Freedman suggested 10 percent of the price, $300,000 instead of the $3 million—even though they had nowhere near even that amount at their disposal. Hanna took the counteroffer as an insult and broke off the negotiations. The Americans left empty-handed, and the manuscript remained in the hands of an antiquities dealer who still did not know what he had.

The next year, 1984, Hanna came to the United States, hoping to sell the manuscripts here, possibly through the local community of Coptic Christians (there are twenty thousand in New Jersey alone), who could make contacts with dealers in rare books and antiquities. In April of that year, he contacted a rare book dealer in Manhattan, an Austrian Holocaust survivor named Hans P. Kraus Jr., who had become an eminent figure in his field and who had significant contacts with major American university resources. He was especially well connected with Yale, and over the years he had both purchased books and manuscripts for the university's Beinecke Rare Book and Manuscript Library and made a number of donations himself. Out of some frustration, Hanna had dropped his asking price to $1 million. But that was still a lot of money—especially for unidentified texts.

Kraus brought in an illustrious classicist from Columbia University, Roger Bagnall, to help him determine when the manuscripts were produced and what they contained. After giving the matter some thought, he turned down the sale. The price was too high, and there would be significant costs in restoring the manuscript to a useable state: the pages had already deteriorated significantly.

At his wits' end, Hanna decided simply to put the manuscripts in safekeeping for the time being. One of his American contacts had a friend who worked for a branch of Citibank in a strip mall in Hicksville, Long Island. And so, in spring 1984, Hanna rented a safe deposit box there and committed his precious manuscripts to it. He returned to Cairo. He stayed away for sixteen years. During those years, the manuscripts quietly deteriorated in the humid conditions of the New York suburb.

The Recovery of the Manuscripts

The next character in this involved plot is the eventual owner of the manuscript of the Gospel of Judas—who continues to own it to this day—Frieda Tchacos Nussberger. Born in Egypt, she is of Greek descent. From an early age, she had an international life. She studied at the Ecole de Traduction et d'Interprétation in Geneva, and then went to the Ecole du Louvre in Paris, where she studied Egyptology. In the early 1980s she married Werner Nussberger, a Swiss jeweler and artist.

With her international contacts and her interest in Egypt, Greece, and other ancient civilizations, Nussberger was a natural for the antiquities world, and was involved as a dealer since the 1970s. She had heard about Hanna's manuscripts in 1982, when someone showed her a photograph of what later came to be identified as manuscript page 5/19. It is called this because at a later point in the story, as we will see, the manuscript eventually tore (or was torn) into two parts, an upper portion of about a third of each page and a lower portion of about two-thirds. After the pages had been torn, an antiquities dealer who briefly acquired the codex evidently shuffled the pages around, to put the most impressive ones on the top and the bottom (in case someone looked just at the beginning and the end to get a sense of the state of the manuscript). And so tops were rearranged with bottoms. No wonder people like van Rijn and Hedrick had trouble knowing what was what from photographs.

In any event, Nussberger had seen a photograph of a page and knew that at the time Hanna was asking $3 million for the entire set of manuscripts. She wasn't interested. Now, some eighteen years later, in 2000, in an unrelated deal, she had purchased several pages of Coptic writing, and wondered if these could have come from the same manuscript(s) that Hanna had been selling before. She suspected that Hanna hadn't sold the manuscripts yet—if he had, she certainly would have heard of it. She decided to see if he would be willing to come down significantly in the asking price. He was much older now, of course. Moreover, he had settled down with a family and had long since lost hope of making an enormous fortune off his prized possession. What neither Nussberger nor Hanna knew was that the manuscripts were rotting away in the vault.

Nussberger agreed to buy the manuscripts, sight unseen—at a price that to this day she won't disclose. (Antiquities dealers can be funny that way.) In any event, she had to collect the goods, and that required her to meet up with Hanna in New York. He was not at all eager to go—he spoke no English and hated flying—but money speaks louder than words, and eventually they made the trip. It was April 3, 2000. After all these years, the bank had changed the locks on its safe deposit boxes—good thing the bank was still standing—but eventually they had a locksmith do the necessary work. When they opened the box, they experienced a profound shock: the manuscripts were in nowhere near the state they had been in when last seen. Ancient papyrus doesn't do well in humidity, even when not handled. It wasn't clear what would be salvageable.

But Nussberger didn't completely lose heart. She boxed the manuscripts and headed straight to Yale University, to leave them with someone she could trust, the chief curator of the Beinecke Rare Book and Manuscript Library, Robert Babcock, an eminent scholar of antiquity. It was there, at the Beinecke, that someone finally recognized the most precious document of this manuscript find for what it was. A professor of Coptology at Yale, Bentley Layton, examined the manuscripts and identified the third text as the Gospel of Judas.

The manuscripts stayed at Yale for some months while Nussberger tried to convince the Beinecke Library to purchase them. But in the end, the library had to decline. Money, once again, appears to have been the issue: it was not certain that Nussberger owned the legal rights to the manuscripts, since they evidently had been smuggled out of Egypt (Hanna had not declared them upon leaving, sixteen years earlier).[8] If the library publicized its possession of the

Gospel of Judas, as it would obviously want and need to do, there could well be an international incident, and it might lose the codices—along with all the money it had spent on purchasing them. Babcock returned the manuscripts to Nussberger, who still needed to find a buyer for them. But now she knew what she had in her possession: the one and only surviving copy of an infamous Gospel from Christian antiquity that took Judas's side of the Gospel story of the betrayal of Jesus. This was enormously important. More than that, it was valuable. But how to find a buyer?

Through her connections she located one. There was a manuscript dealer in Cleveland, Ohio, named Bruce Ferrini, who was reputed to have access to billionaire collectors, including, allegedly, Bill Gates. Nussberger flew to Cleveland to show him what she had; he immediately became enthralled at the prospect of what he could do with the manuscripts—not just sell them but also put on an international exposition. On the spot he agreed to purchase them for $2.5 million. On September 8, 2000, Ferrini wrote Nussberger two checks for the total, one postdated to January 15, 2001, the other to February 15, 2001. For some reason, Nussberger trusted him completely: maybe she was simply glad to be rid of the manuscripts at last. But in any event, she left the manuscripts with him and did not even get a receipt. That was a big mistake.

Ferrini thought that he would have an immediate buyer for the manuscripts in one of his faithful clients, a multimillionaire antiquities collector named James Ferrell, owner of a leading propane gas company in America, Ferrellgas. Ferrell was, in fact, initially interested in making the purchase and pursuing the idea of the exposition. Before the deal could close, he recommended to Ferrini that he try to preserve the manuscripts from further decomposition by putting them in a deep freeze. Ferrini did so. It was a very stupid thing to do. The manuscripts had by now absorbed a good deal of moisture from the humid American environment. Freezing them did incalculable damage. As their later editor and translator and associate restorer, Rodolphe Kasser, explains:

> After a calamitous sojourn in the moistness of numerous American summers, this inauspicious freezing apparently produced the partial destruction of the sap holding the fibers of the papyrus together, making it ten times more fragile—and susceptible to crumbling, producing the weakest folios of papyrus that professional papyrologists had ever seen, a fragility that is a true nightmare for the restorer. Furthermore, this freezing made all the water in the fibers migrate toward the surface of the papyrus before evaporation, bringing with it quantities of pigment from inside the fibers, which darkened many pages of the papyrus, and therefore made the writing extremely difficult to read.[9]

The manuscripts were not the only things falling apart; so too was Ferrini's relationship with his would-be buyer. Ferrell had for some reason come to suspect that Ferrini's financial dealings were not being handled well, and he began cutting off his connection with him. He was not prepared to make any more large purchases, just when Ferrini needed the cash to cover the checks he had written Nussberger.

Nussberger sniffed out the problems and began to wonder if in fact the checks might bounce. This would have been an enormous problem, not simply because of the money but also because she no longer had the manuscripts that the checks had been used to buy. Torn with anxiety, she turned to a lawyer friend whom we met in an earlier chapter, Mario Roberty, an urbane Geneva lawyer who was well connected to the European trade in art and antiquities and who in 1994 had personally established the Maecenas Foundation, an organization devoted to the preservation of ancient discoveries and to returning them to their lands of origin.

Roberty wisely advised Nussberger to get the manuscripts back immediately and return the worthless checks. Ferrini, however, was reluctant to back out of the deal, hoping still to be able to salvage it. Roberty suspected that he would be able to do no such thing, and when Ferrini proved recalcitrant, Roberty decided to force his hand.

At the beginning of the chapter I mentioned Michel van Rijn, the Dutch blogger who maintains a scandal-seeking arts and antiquities site on the Internet. Roberty contacted van Rijn in the hope that he could publicize Ferrini's underhanded dealings and compel him, on pain of a ruined reputation and no prospect of the respectability required to work in the field, to return the manuscripts. Once van Rijn was put on the job, he went at it with a vengeance, attacking Ferrini on his Web site, informing the reading public about Ferrini's shady dealings, and maligning his character, citing instances of bounced checks, financial failures, and personal issues.

Ferrini finally caved in under pressure, and on February 15, 2001, Nussberger and Roberty flew to Cleveland to collect the manuscripts. Ferrini agreed as well to hand over all photographs, and copies of photographs, that he had taken of the manuscripts while in his possession. This exchange itself was an enormous problem: since Nussberger could not read Coptic and had not previously counted the pages of the manuscripts or known exactly what their contents were at a glance, she had no way of knowing if Ferrini was genuinely keeping his end of the bargain. Was he holding anything back? Any manuscript pages? Any photographs?

As it turns out, he was. That is how Charlie Hedrick got photographs of a number of pages of the treatise on Allogenes (and the final page of the Gospel of Judas) that later made their way to van Rijn, who published them on his Web site. Ferrini evidently gave him the photos. He may also have kept some pages of the manuscripts.

Nussberger did allow Ferrini to purchase one of the texts in the collection, the mathematical treatise written in Greek. The rest (well, most of the rest) she took away with her. But that landed her in the situation she had been in before the Ferrini fiasco: she had the manuscript but no buyer. Plus the manuscript was now in far worse shape than before, having been frozen and thawed, and evidently manhandled by Ferrini. The pages were broken and had been shuffled together largely in random order. And there were hundreds of small to tiny pieces that had broken off, with no way of telling which pages they had originally belonged to.

Nussberger decided to hand the problem over to Roberty's Maecenas Foundation for Ancient Art. The manuscripts were sent to Switzerland, where they are still today. On Roberty's advice, Nussberger decided to secure the services of one of the world's leading Coptologists, whom we have met before, Rodolphe Kasser, a professor emeritus from the University of Geneva who happened to live just outside of Geneva in the town of Yverdon-les-Bains. They arranged a meeting, which took place on July 24, 2001.

Kasser's initial impression on seeing the remains of the manuscript on this occasion are worth quoting in full:

> [The manuscript] was so precious but so badly mistreated, broken up to the extreme, partially pulverized, infinitely fragile, crumbling at the least contact; the "ancient book" . . . was that evening a poor small thing pitifully packed at the bottom of a cardboard box.[10]

> During my long career, I have had before my eyes many Coptic or Greek documents on papyrus, sometimes very "sick," but damaged to this point, never! In many places the papyrus was so blackened that reading had become practically impossible. The papyrus had become so weakened that it didn't tolerate the least touching; nearly all contact, as light as it was, threatened to leave it in dust. In brief, it was a case apparently without hope.[11]

Kasser immediately contacted Florence Darbre, one of Europe's premier experts in manuscript conservation, who lives in Nyon, a small city on Lake Geneva. Darbre had herself taken degrees at the University of Geneva and at an art institute in Bern. She was in principle agreeable to working on the project, and a deal was eventually struck that the first stage in the publication and dissemination of the manuscript would occur: the manuscript would be restored and preserved.

Darbre was unusually talented at this kind of work. Kasser says of her that "with her fairy's fingers, she made largely possible what, at first glance, appeared doomed to failure."[12] Their first step was to place every folio (that is, a page written on front and back), and every fragment, no matter how small, under protective glass, and then to photograph the entire lot. Afterward could begin the arduous task of reassembling the manuscript, folio by folio, and then determining where the fragments fit in relationship to the folios. This was not easy work. Sometimes they could see how the ink from a page matched the ink on one of the fragments, so if the fragment was inserted where there was a gap, a word was formed that made sense. Sometimes they had to match up fragments based on the pattern of the fibers of the papyrus. Many times they simply had to throw up their hands in despair and come back to this piece of it later. It took an exceedingly long time to come to a reasonably complete reconstruction of what had probably been at its initial discovery a relatively intact codex.

In their work they were eventually joined by Gregor Wurst, the right-hand man of Stephen Emmel, who had himself gone on to be the distinguished professor of Coptology at the University of Münster, in Germany. Wurst was able to use digitized photos of the fragments to make tentative connections between the pieces on the computer. Work went on apace. It was nearly three years before they realized that the codex containing the Gospel of Judas had not three separate works in it but four, that the passage known to Hedrick via Ferrini in fact came from a separate tractate altogether.

Today Kasser thinks that something like 10 to 15 percent of the manuscript has been lost through its mishandling since discovery. The restoration is now nearly complete, but while I was working on this chapter I received an e-mail from Marvin Meyer, who has produced the fine English translation of the text for the National Geographic Society, that another fragment has been successfully placed, one that affects the translation at a crucial point. It is hoped, in any event, that all the work will be completed soon.

The Public Announcement and the Involvement of National Geographic

Having worked three years on the restoration, conservation, transcription, and translation of the manuscript containing the Gospel of Judas, Kasser decided, in close consultation with Frieda Tchacos Nussberger and Mario Roberty, that it was time to announce to the world that the Gospel of Judas, lost to human sight for centuries, had now been found. It was an auspicious moment but not a well-publicized one. The occasion was the Eighth International Congress of Coptic Studies in Paris, a small scholarly meeting attended only by Coptic specialists from around the world, principally Europe and North America. This is not the kind of gathering covered by *Time* magazine.

But the leading scholars of Coptic were there, including Bentley Layton of Yale, James Robinson of Claremont, and Stephen Emmel of Münster, names that have cropped up time and again in this narrative. To the frustration of many in the audience, in making his announcement Kasser did not divulge the contents of the Gospel—the matter of greatest importance to most people. He instead made a bold, and tantalizing, declaration of the discovery itself, giving some attention to the details of the manuscript, indicating steps that had been taken in its conservation, and stating when the text would become public, with suitable translations.

Facing page   The opening page of the Gospel of Judas; notice the gaps, where fragments have broken off or been destroyed.

In addition, he handed out a kind of fact sheet with the following information:

1. The manuscript is in the form of a codex that was originally bound in leather. It consists of thirty-one folios [i.e., sixty-two pages], which measure approximately 16 by 29 centimeters [roughly the size of a regular 8½-by-11 sheet of paper].
2. Preserved still are parts of the leather binding and about sixty pages, which have been torn about three-fifths of the way up from the bottom. Most pages are in a highly fragmentary and fragile state, but they have all been placed under glass. About two-thirds of the text can still be read. The manuscript appears to be missing at least one folio and a number of fragments.
3. The codex contains three treatises [note that this announcement was made before Kasser realized that the pages on Allogenes came from a different tractate]:
   a. The Letter of Peter to Philip [also known in different form from the Nag Hammadi library]
   b. The First Apocalypse of James [also known in a different form from Nag Hammadi]
   c. The Gospel of Judas [completely unknown until now]
4. The text is written in a dialect of Coptic known as Sahidic, with some regional variations that suggest its composition in Middle Egypt. Linguistic considerations show that this is a translation of texts originally written in Greek.
5. The date of the manuscript can be estimated, based on its style of writing, as fourth or fifth century. [The carbon-14 dating done later suggested late third or early fourth century.]
6. It was found in the Al Minya province of Middle Egypt.
7. The whereabouts of the manuscript can be well documented since 1982.
8. The manuscript is owned by a Swiss foundation that prefers for the time being to remain anonymous [later identified as the Maecenas Foundation]. It is concerned to restore and publish the manuscript and then return it to a public institution of Egypt, where it was originally found.
9. The restoration is being undertaken in Switzerland.
10. The publication of the manuscript has been entrusted to Rodolphe Kasser and is expected to occur in 2005. [It actually came out in 2006.]

Word of the discovery slowly filtered through the academic community. I have to admit, I didn't hear of it until National Geographic got involved and asked me if I would help them provide the verification they needed of the manuscript's antiquity and to tell them something about its potential historical significance. Neither did anyone else that I knew in the field. Coptologists were aware of it, but no one else.

National Geographic came to be interested in the manuscript not because they knew about the Eighth International Congress of Coptic Studies but because Herb Krosney, whom we've met before, got wind of the find and put them onto the story. Krosney has been involved with a number of TV, documentary, and writing projects and had been contacted by Bruce Ferrini when the latter had "purchased" (more or less) the manuscript and was thinking about setting up an international exposition. He wanted to know if Krosney would be interested in developing a TV special about it. But after an initial meeting, that was all Krosney heard from him. After that, Ferrini returned the manuscript to Nussberger, so the TV idea was dead in the water.

Then in 2004 Krosney heard something again about the manuscript—this time that it was back in Switzerland, as Kasser had publicly announced. That sparked Krosney's interest, and he started poking around and asking questions. He eventually learned of the Maecenas Foundation, and he was on the trail of what for him was a fascinating and important story.

Krosney was already in contact with National Geographic at the time, discussing with them the possibility of doing a TV special based on the Old Testament. But his interest completely shifted once he realized just how big this new story could be. He got National Geographic interested in it, and once they saw what they were sitting on, they needed no more encouragement. They contacted me to help them put together a team of specialists, we flew to Geneva, and we saw the Gospel with our own eyes.

But it wasn't until later that I could read a translation of the text. It is a rare moment in a scholar's life—a moment that many scholars never have—when they read a newly discovered, not-yet-published text for the first time. The anticipation of what happens from one sentence to the next is scintillating. You read and reread the sentences, making sure you understand them. You compare them with the original language, in this case Coptic, that they were translated from. You ponder their meaning, you think about how they connect with other texts you're familiar with from the same time period, and you wonder how they might change your understanding about your field—in this case, the field of early Christianity and the many Gospels that were used by the early Christians to promote their own understandings of Jesus. It was a special moment for me, a moment of wonder and discovery. In the next several chapters, I'll explain what it is I found.

⌘

CHAPTER SIX

The Gospel of Judas: An Overview

B ecause of the vicissitudes of survival, some of the ancient Gospels that have been rediscovered in modern times are highly fragmentary—missing their beginnings and/or conclusions. This is the case, for example, with the Gospel of Peter, discovered in 1886. It begins in the middle of a sentence discussing the trial of Jesus before Pilate:

> . . . but none of the Jews washed his hands, nor did Herod or any of his judges. Since they did not wish to wash, Pilate stood up.

In this case we are relatively fortunate, because we can at least determine fairly easily what happened just before the fragment begins: Pilate has just washed his hands of the "innocent blood" of Jesus, a scene that we know otherwise from the Gospel of Matthew (27:24). What we don't know is how much of the beginning of the Gospel is lost. Did this Gospel contain an entire narrative of Jesus' life, beginning with his birth (like Matthew and Luke) or his baptism (like Mark and John)? Or was it an account of just his trial, death, and resurrection?[1]

We do have some idea how the Gospel of Peter concluded, even though the surviving portion also ends in midsentence. After Jesus' crucifixion and resurrection, we are told:

> But I, Simon Peter, and my brother Andrew, took our nets and went off to the sea. And with us was Levi, the son of Alphaeus, whom the Lord

That's where it ends. Evidently the resurrected Jesus is about to appear to the fishermen at the Sea of Galilee, as he does in John 21. But is that where the

Gospel concluded, or were there other resurrection appearances? We probably will never know.

We are better situated with other Gospels that have been discovered in modern times. The most famous is the Gospel of Thomas, one of the books of the Nag Hammadi library discovered in 1945. In this case we have both the beginning and the ending of the Gospel. The text starts right at the beginning with an introduction, which scholars call an incipit:

> These are the secret sayings which the living Jesus spoke, and Didymus Judas Thomas wrote them down.

There then follows a series of sayings of Jesus, 114 of them altogether, given one after the other, until the final saying and the conclusion of the text—the title: "The Gospel According to Thomas" (titles were usually given at the end of books in the ancient world, instead of at the beginning). Not only the beginning and end but also most of what comes in between is preserved in this one, relatively complete copy of the Gospel of Thomas. There are a few words missing here and there (and an odd blank page in the middle of the text), but otherwise it is reasonably intact.

The newly discovered Gospel of Judas is more like Thomas in this respect. We have the beginning and we have the end, and we have most of what is in the middle. But not everything. Because the manuscript was so badly handled during the twenty-three years between its discovery and its scientific restoration, there are lots of words, sentences, lines, and partial pages now lost. Its editor, Rodolphe Kasser, estimates that we are missing something like 10 to 15 percent of the contents. But at least the incipit and conclusion are intact, and most (if not all) of the pages are now restored to their original location (having been at one time reshuffled and mangled), so it is possible to study this text and get a relatively complete sense of what it was about. In this chapter I will give an overview of the document, from beginning to end, explaining how it is structured and what it says. In the two chapters that follow I will take up specific aspects of its message, trying to unpack the Gnostic teaching it represents and discussing in greater depth its portrayal of the two main characters, Jesus himself and Judas, who alone among the disciples understood Jesus' teaching and performed his master's will.

The Gospel of Judas at a Glance

Before going through the text of the Gospel of Judas in detail, I can sketch the basic flow of its narrative. The Gospel consists of a number of conversations between Jesus and his disciples, principally Judas Iscariot, during the days before his arrest at the Passover feast in Jerusalem. It begins with an incipit, which indicates that it is

> The secret account of the revelation that Jesus spoke in conversation with Judas
> Iscariot during a week three days before he celebrated Passover. (33:1–6)[2]

This statement is not entirely accurate: in this Gospel Jesus speaks not only
with Judas Iscariot but at times with all the twelve disciples—although in many
instances these discussions with the entire group function to show their ignorance and inferiority to Judas. The phrase translated "during a week" may also
be translated as "during eight days"—a reference to Jesus' last days on earth,
before his crucifixion. The crucifixion itself, however, is not presented in this
Gospel. The narrative ends with the betrayal of Judas, the denouement, for this
author, of the story of Jesus (and, of course, of Judas). In any event, this is not a
Gospel about Jesus' entire life or ministry, in the way Matthew, Mark, Luke, and
John are. It is about his last days on earth and the conversations he held then.

After the incipit there is a very brief summary of the rest of Jesus' life—just
four sentences in Marvin Meyer's English translation. These indicate that when
Jesus "appeared on earth" he performed many miracles "for the salvation of
humanity." Moreover, "since some [people walked] in the way of righteousness while others walked in their transgressions," he called twelve to be his
disciples (33:10–15). It is not clear why the presence of human saints and sinners
required Jesus to call the Twelve.

Next we are told that Jesus spoke with his disciples "about the mysteries beyond [or "on"?—BE] the world, and what would take place at the end." And finally, this summary indicates that he often appeared to the disciples not in his own,
bodily form, but sometimes "was found among them as a child" (33:19–20).[3]

Following this summary of Jesus' public ministry comes a series of encounters and conversations that he has with his disciples, especially with Judas Iscariot,
the one disciple in the text who is mentioned by name.

In his first encounter, Jesus finds the disciples at a ritual meal (literally a
"eucharist"), giving thanks for their bread (the Greek word for giving thanks is
eucharisto—a loan word used here in the Coptic text). To their chagrin, he
laughs, and this leads into a discussion about "their" god and Jesus' intimation
that his God is different from theirs, and that they have misunderstood who
Jesus really is. This makes them angry, but Judas stands up and confesses the
truth about Jesus, that in fact he comes from another realm, that of Barbelo—
a divine being known from other Gnostic texts as the mother of all creation,
who resided in the Pleroma, far above the realm of the creator God of this
world. This confession of who Jesus is leads to a private conversation between
Jesus and Judas. But before Jesus explains very much, he suddenly departs.

The next day Jesus returns to his disciples, who ask him where he has been.
He has spent the night in another realm, and they want to know about it. Jesus
informs them that mere mortals cannot go there. He apparently then leaves again.

When he comes back, the disciples want him to explain a vision they have had
of priests offering sacrifices in the Temple. Jesus interprets their vision by indicating that it was about them, the disciples themselves, and that their sacrifice of
animals on the altar represents the way they are misleading their followers. This

leads Judas to ask about the different kinds of human beings—those who will attain ultimate salvation and those who won't. Much of Jesus' reply is hard to reconstruct, because the manuscript of the Gospel is badly damaged at this point.

Judas then tells Jesus that he too has had a vision that needs to be interpreted. He saw himself being stoned by the other members of the twelve apostles; he then saw a great house with many people in and around it. He wants to enter that house. Jesus explains that Judas has seen a vision of his own fate—he will be hated by the others and persecuted. But no one who is mortal is able to enter that great house, "for that place is reserved for the holy" (45:18–20).

Jesus then takes Judas aside to teach him the mysterious truths that "no one has ever seen." This mysterious revelation takes up most of the rest of the narrative. It is a bizarre and difficult revelation to understand, a version of the Gnostic myth that explains how the divine realm of the aeons (i.e., divine beings) that make up the Pleroma (the "fullness" of the divine realm) came into existence, and how the world and humans were then created. I will try to explain this lengthy revelation in greater detail later. For now it is enough to stress its major point: this world is not the creation of the one true and great God. It is the creation of much lesser divine beings who are inferior, foolish, and bloodthirsty. The implication is clear: humans who declare their devotion to the god(s) who created this world have been fooled into worshiping the wrong god(s). The goal of salvation is to transcend this creation and the divine beings that brought it into existence.

In response to this vision, Judas wants to know whether it is possible for humans to exist in the afterlife when this world ends. Jesus replies that some humans have only a temporary existence in this life, but others have a divine spirit that will transcend this world and have eternal life in the great realm above this world, even after this creation and the gods who made it are destroyed.

Judas in particular will be prominent among those who are saved, because he is the one who understands these mysteries and does what is required of him. In the key line of the text, Jesus tells Judas: "You will exceed all of them. For you will sacrifice the man that clothes me" (56:17–21). In other words, Judas's act of "betrayal" is in fact his faithful obedience to Jesus' will. Jesus needs to die so that he can escape the material trappings of his body and return to the divine Pleroma from which he has come. And Judas will make it happen.

Judas next has a vision of his own exaltation and glorification. That brings us to the concluding scene of the Gospel, an account of Judas handing Jesus over to the Jewish authorities. The title then is given: "The Gospel of Judas."

Key Moments in the Gospel of Judas

Having sketched the narrative in broad strokes, I now return and discuss some of the key passages in more detail.

The Opening of the Narrative

As we will see in the next chapter, the Gnostic character of this Gospel is evident in all its parts. The very beginning is no exception. The narrator indicates that he is writing "the secret account of the revelation" (33:1–2) that Jesus delivered to Judas. Gnostic texts are filled with the secret knowledge (gnosis) that is given by the divine revealer to his faithful followers. Often these revelations are hard for readers to understand, and that's no accident. The entire point of the secret knowledge, or the mysteries of salvation, is that they are not easily accessible or intelligible to the normal person. They are reserved only for the Gnostics, for those in the know.

The incipit mentions Judas Iscariot explicitly as the recipient of this secret revelation because he alone of the disciples understands who Jesus is and where he has come from. This becomes clear in the opening narrative, where Jesus finds his disciples gathered for a eucharistic meal, in which they thank God— the creator God, of course—for their bread. The narrator indicates that the disciples are "seated in pious observance," a phrase that could also be translated less elegantly as "seated engaged in practices with respect to divinity" (33:24–26). That is, they were worshiping their God while partaking of their sacred meal. When Jesus sees them giving thanks, he laughs. This will be the first of four times in the Gospel that he does so—a striking feature of the text, especially given the circumstance that in the canonical Gospels of the New Testament, Jesus is *never* portrayed as laughing. But he laughs here, regularly. In this particular instance, the disciples find Jesus' reaction puzzling at the least: "Why are you laughing at our prayer of thanksgiving [or "at our eucharist"—BE]? We are doing what is right!" (34:2–6).

Jesus' reply might seem a bit disingenuous: "I am not laughing at you." Well, he may not be laughing at *them,* but he is certainly laughing at what they are doing. And why? Because, he says, "you are not doing this because of your own will but because it is through this that your god [will be] praised" (34:6–11).[4] Jesus finds it laughable that the god who provides bread—the material creator of this material world—should be praised. For as we learn later in the text, this god is an inferior, ignorant deity. The disciples, naturally, don't understand. "But you are the son of our God" (34:1–13), they say. As it turns out, however, he is not. They don't know who he really is. In fact, as he tells them, "no generation of the people that are among you will know me" (34:13–17).

Throughout this Gospel, Jesus will differentiate between "this" generation— the mortals who live their lives in ignorance—and "that" generation, the people of the true God, who know the truth about the world, the divine realm, and their own identity. The disciples, strikingly, are not members of the elect— with the exception of Judas.

Even though they don't understand what he's talking about, the disciples know that he doesn't think highly of them, and so they react by "getting angry and infuriated," and they begin to blaspheme against him. This leads Jesus to issue a challenge, that any of them who is strong enough should "bring out the perfect human and stand before my face" (35:3–6). What he appears to be implying is that within them there may be a spark of the divine, the "perfect human." If they have this spark, they will be the equal of Jesus, the one who comes from above—they will stand their ground before him. With some bravado the disciples reply, "We have the strength" (35:6–7). But none of them is able to stand—except Judas Iscariot, who stands alone before Jesus. Yet even he has to avert his eyes.

This must mean that Judas has the spark of divinity within him (making him equal with the divine Jesus), but he does not yet have the full revelation from above, and so he cannot yet look Jesus in the eyes. Later in the text, however, Judas will be exalted, and presumably then he too will enjoy the full measure of divinity that is his by nature.

To show that he has some understanding of the truth, Judas does make a confession to Jesus:

> I know who you are and where you have come from. You are from the immortal realm of Barbelo. And I am not worthy to utter the name of the one who has sent you. (35:15–21)

Barbelo, as I have mentioned, is one of the superior aeons in other Gnostic texts, the one who is the mother of all there is. Judas, then, alone among the disciples, knows the truth. And so Jesus separates him from the others, to teach him "the mysteries of the kingdom" (35:23–25). He tells Judas that he will be able "to reach it," but that doing so will involve some grief, as he will be replaced among the Twelve once he departs from them. This appears to be a reference to the episode recorded in the New Testament book of Acts that we examined in chapter 3, where after Judas's death the remaining eleven disciples elected Matthias to take Judas's place so that they could remain twelve in number. As Jesus puts it here, the Twelve do so in order that they "may again come to completion with their god" (36:3–4). Clearly their god is not the God of Jesus, and of Judas.

Judas asks when he will receive the revelation necessary for these things, but instead of replying, Jesus leaves him.

A Second Encounter: The Generation of Immortals and the Vision of the Temple

The next morning Jesus reappears to his disciples, who want to know where he went. He tells them that he went "to another great and holy generation" (36:15–17)—that is, he left the realm of the mortals to visit those in the spiritual realm. The disciples want to know about this realm "that is superior to us and holier than us" (36:19–21). For the second time, Jesus laughs. Once again, his mirth is directed at their ignorance. He tells them that no one from this mortal world can see or visit that realm—in fact, that realm is not ruled even by the "angels of the stars." His response leaves the disciples speechless.

The next day Jesus comes to them again, and this time they have a question for him. They have seen a vision that needs to be interpreted. The account that follows is roughly similar to an episode from the Gospels of the New Testament. According to Matthew, Mark, and Luke, Jesus and his disciples traveled to Jerusalem for the Passover feast, the last week of Jesus' life. The disciples, who were rural peasants from the backwaters of Galilee, were overawed by the impressive sights of the big city, especially the amazing Temple: they tell Jesus, "Look at these wonderful stones and wonderful buildings!" (Mark 13:1). Jesus predicts that as impressive as these all are, they will be destroyed by the judgment of God: "not one stone will be left upon another, but all will be destroyed" (Mark 13:2).

In the Gospel of Judas the disciples have a vision not of the Temple building itself but of what was happening inside of it, as twelve priests slaughter the sacrificial animals brought to them at the altar, with people surrounding them looking on. But in their vision, the disciples see that the priests, who seem to be performing their holy duty, are in fact acting in most unholy ways. Some of them

> sacrifice their own children, others their wives . . . ; some sleep with men; some are involved in [slaughter]; some commit a multitude of sins and deeds of lawlessness. And the men who stand [before] the altar invoke your [name], and in all the deeds of their deficiency the sacrifices are brought to completion. (38:16–39:3)

Some of this slightly fragmentary passage is hard to understand, but the basic gist is not. The Jewish priests in the Temple are understood to be violating every standard of decency and morality, all the while invoking the name of Jesus. Their sacrifices are therefore described as completely deficient.

The disciples may well have been expecting an explanation from Jesus that maligned the Jewish religion and its sacrifices. But Jesus' explanation is not at all what they expected. He acknowledges that the priests of the vision are the ones who invoke his name. But who does that mean they are? They are none other than the disciples themselves, Jesus' own followers:

> Those you have seen performing religious duties at the altar—that is who you are. That is the god you serve, and you are those twelve men you have seen. (39:18–25)

So the twelve priests who commit flagrant acts of immorality are the disciples; and the god that they serve is obviously not the true God, as this is what the religion in their god's name leads to. But what do the sacrificial animals represent? They are "the many people you lead astray" (39:27–28). Those being sacrificed, in other words, are the followers of the disciples—that is, the Christians of later generations who think that the twelve disciples represent the truth (as opposed to Judas, who later in this text will be described as the "thirteenth"). This interpretation of the vision, in other words, is a disparagement of the traditional Christian church that came to be declared "orthodox" when Gnostics, in the time this book was written, were declared "heretics." According to the Gospel of Judas, this judgment is precisely wrong. It is the Gnostics who understand Jesus' revelation; Judas and people like him are the ones who have it right. The members of the orthodox churches, on the other hand, are worshiping the wrong god and are involved in crass acts of immorality: they are slayers of children, sexually immoral, and "people of pollution and lawlessness and error." As leaders of these churches, the "priests" are "ministers of error."

Much of the rest of Jesus' reply is unfortunately lost, as the manuscript is fragmentary at this point. When it becomes readable again, some lines later, Judas is asking Jesus a question about the generation of mortals, wondering "what kind of fruit does this generation produce" (43:13–14). Jesus replies that there are two kinds of people. Those who belong to the "human generation" have souls that will die—that is, when their bodies die, they cease to exist. But others will live on after death: "their bodies die but their souls will be alive, and they will be taken up" (43:20–23). Those of the former group do not have immortal souls—that is, sparks of the divine within—for "it is impossible to sow seed on [rock] and harvest its fruit" (43:25–44:2). Without the makings of fruit, the trees of mere mortals remain barren.

Again, a good deal of what follows has been lost from the manuscript. But Jesus does refer to "corruptible Sophia," who has evidently been responsible for bestowing immortal souls among some people (44:3–4). As I have already mentioned, Sophia was understood by some Gnostic groups to be the fallen aeon whose disastrous action led to the creation of this world and the entrapments of sparks of the divine with it. Much of what Jesus has to say about her, unfortunately, is lost. After his speech, Jesus again departs.

A Third Encounter: The Vision of Judas and Jesus' Account of Creation

Judas approaches Jesus and says that now that Jesus has interpreted a vision of the Twelve, he too has had a vision that needs to be explained. For the third time Jesus laughs. Once again it appears to be directed at the ignorance of his interlocutor. In this case it is not because Judas is lacking a spark of the divine, as is evidently the case with the others, but because he has not yet understood all the mysteries that Jesus is to reveal. Jesus gives him a mild rebuke: "You thirteenth spirit, why do you try so hard?" (44:20–21). This passage is difficult to translate into English. Judas is called a "spirit." The literal reading is *daimon,* a Greek loanword in this Coptic text. The word *daimon* does not carry the same connotations as its English counterpart *demon,* which refers to an evil spirit. A daimon is a spiritual being that is superior to mere mortals. Judas is the thirteenth of the (twelve) disciples—that is, he stands outside their number; but he has (or is) a daimon, a ruling spirit. When Jesus asks, "Why do you try so hard?" he uses the same word found earlier when the disciples were "practicing" their piety in the first encounter. Paraphrased, Jesus is asking why

Judas is exercising his religion with such diligence. It is not diligence that is required but knowledge.

JUDAS'S VISION

But knowledge is exactly what Judas is seeking, and so Jesus explains to him his vision. Judas saw the twelve disciples stoning him to death; then he saw a great house with a large crowd, and he wants to know if Jesus can take him there.

Parts of Jesus' response are easy to follow; others require some unpacking. To begin with, he tells Judas that "your star has led you astray" (45:13–14). This comment is premised on the notion that everyone has a guiding angel and that each angel is connected with a star. The stars in the sky in fact are angelic beings, and each of these beings has oversight of a person here on earth, being connected to the person's soul.[5] Just as we today might speak about our "guiding light," so ancient people—especially those influenced by the teachings of the Greek philosopher Plato, as were the Gnostics—could speak about their guiding star.[6] In this case—as opposed to later in the text—Judas's star has misled him. Or rather Judas has fallen out of step with his star. In either case, he has made a mistake thinking that he can go to this great house he has seen. No one "of mortal birth is worthy to enter the house . . . for that place is reserved for the holy" (45:15–19). The holy ones will live there forever, in the eternal realm outside of this world, where there will no longer be "sun nor moon."

The next bit of the conversation is hard to follow, because there are holes in the manuscript. Jesus begins to talk about Judas's persecution by the Twelve. As Jesus indicates, "You will become the thirteenth, and you will be cursed by the other generations" (46:17–21). That, as it turns out, is not a bad thing. Judas will transcend the Twelve, who continue to think the creator god of this world is the true God, and he will enter into the truth. Upon his death (when they stone him), he will ascend "to the holy [generation]" (46:23–47:1).

Jesus then explains the real mysteries that lie at the heart of this Gospel, the mysteries of how the divine realm (the Pleroma) came into being and how this (inferior) world came to be created. This is a sacred revelation that "no one has ever seen." And for good reason: it is told in highly symbolic and complicated language, designed to make us mere mortals scratch our heads or throw up our hands in despair of understanding. In that, it is like a lot of other Gnostic myths that have come down to us in texts from antiquity.

THE MYSTERIES OF CREATION

The revelation begins with "a great and boundless realm, whose extent no generation of angels has seen, [in which] there is a great invisible [Spirit],

> which no eye of angel has ever seen,
> no thought of the heart has ever comprehended,
> and it was never called by any name. (47:9–13)

That is, before there was a beginning, there was only the one true spiritual God who has never been known—even by the angels—and who is in fact beyond knowing, the Great Invisible Spirit from whom all else ultimately derives.

Within the vast realm of this originating divine being, a "luminous cloud" appears. This is the invisible God's self-manifestation, in which other beings will appear. The Great Spirit says, "Let an angel come into being as my attendant" (47:16–18). An angel appears, who is called the Self-Generated (literally the name is Autogenes). He is self-generated because he is an offshoot of the Great Spirit, who has used nothing in order to make him come into being except his own will and command. There then appear four other angels to serve as the attendants to the Self-Generated.

Then the Self-Generated begins his own act of creation. He creates four great aeons, each of whom is given a luminary ("great light") to rule over him, along with countless thousands of angels—"myriads without number"—to serve them.

We are then told that in the original luminous cloud—that is, the self-manifestation of the Great Invisible Spirit—there appears a being called Adamas. (You will see that the name of this being resembles that of Adam, the first man, who is not yet created.) This Adamas is the divine counterpart for the first human, after whose image humans are ultimately to be created.

But first there are creations of other divine beings, including the "incorruptible [generation] of Seth" (49:5–6). This represents a group of spiritual beings who will eventually make an appearance on earth, only to escape their entrapment in matter to return to this heavenly home where they originated.

At this point the narration gets even more confusing and a bit numerical. Twelve aeons are created, along with six luminaries (shining beings, like stars) for each of them; each of these seventy-two luminaries has a heaven, so there are also seventy-two heavens. They also each have five "firmaments," so altogether there are 360 firmaments. These numbers are not accidental, of course. The text doesn't explain them, but they appear to be astronomical references: there are twelve months of the year and twelve signs of the zodiac; in Egyptian lore there are seventy-two "pentads" (stars) that reside over the days of the week, and so seventy-two luminaries; and there are 360 degrees in the zodiac (and 360 days in some calendars of the year) and so 360 firmaments.[7]

Altogether, all of these divine creations make up the cosmos, or universe. We are told that the cosmos is "perdition" (50:14)—the word used could also be translated as "corruption." This is because it is the realm, ultimately outside the luminous cloud representing the realm of God, in which our world will appear, a realm of destruction or corruption.

From this baffling description of the creation of the divine realm, Jesus moves to an almost equally baffling description of the creation of the world and humans. In this realm of corruption the first human appears. This is not Adam but a heavenly image of what will be the first man on earth. Before this earthling appears, we need the creation of our world, the world below, and so the account now introduces a new divine being called El. As students of the Bible know, El is one of the names of God in the Old Testament. Here El is said to have created twelve angels to rule over the realm of chaos and the underworld.

Then, finally, there appear the divine beings who will create the world. First there is Nebro, a divinity "whose face flashed with fire and whose appearance was defiled with blood" (51:8–11) and whose name means "rebel"; he is also called Yaldabaoth, a name familiar from a number of other Gnostic texts that describe him as the maker, or demiurge—that is, the creator of our heavens and earth. Yaldabaoth has a number of angelic assistants, including one named Saklas, a word that means "fool" in the Aramaic tongue. Yaldabaoth's assistants, with Saklas at their head, produce twelve angels to rule the heavens and five to rule the underworld.

And then Saklas, the fool, is the one who says to his angels, "Let us create a human being after the likeness and after the image" (52:16–17). So they form Adam and Eve, and tell Adam, "You shall live long."

Even though the details of this complex myth are almost impenetrable in places, the overall point is clear. This world was not created by the one true God. Not even close. The divine beings responsible for creation are far removed from the ultimate realm of divinity. The god of the Old Testament, El, is nowhere near the top of the divine hierarchy; this world was created by a wrathful, bloodthirsty rebel, and humans were created by a fool. The other disciples—and, of course, their followers in the "orthodox" Christian tradition—are so far wrong in what they think about this god that it is hard even to know where to start in explaining their error. They are hopelessly lost. Only those who receive this "secret revelation," Judas and those like him, will come to realize how we came to be here, who Jesus really is, and how we can return to our heavenly home.

It is this latter matter that Judas wants Jesus to clarify for him: "Does the human spirit die?" (53:16–17). Jesus replies that there are two sorts of humans. On one hand, there are those with spirits that eventually die, who have been granted only a brief existence: "God ordered (the angel) Michael to give spirits to them as a loan, so that they might offer service" (53:17–22). On the other hand, there are those who will live on: "but the Great One ordered (the angel) Gabriel to grant spirits to the great generation with no ruler over it—that is, the spirit and the soul" (53:22–25). Again, this requires a little bit of explaining. In the understanding of this text, a "true" human being has three components. There is the body, which is the material part; there is the spirit, which is what animates the body and gives it life; and there is the soul, which lives on once the human spirit has departed, causing the body to die. Some people have spirits "so that they might offer service"—in other words, these can worship the creator god in the time they have to live. Others have both "the spirit and the soul"—in other words, these have a divine spark within them that will live forever once the spirit departs and the body dies.

Or as Jesus goes on to explain, some people—"Adam and those with him"—have been given knowledge, gnosis; those who have this gnosis, that is, the Gnostics, are superior even to the rulers of this world, "so that the kings of chaos and the underworld might not lord it over them" (54:9–12). This state of affairs will continue to the end, until "Saklas completes the span of time assigned for him" (54:18–21). Then, at the end of time, chaos will erupt on the earth, until the final consummation.

After Jesus explains all this, he laughs again, for the fourth and last time. Now he is laughing not at the ignorance of the disciples but at the ignorance of the rulers of this world, who do not understand that "they all will be destroyed along with their creatures" (55:19–20).

Judas wants to know the fate of those baptized in Jesus' name, but unfortunately the lines of Jesus' answer are missing from the manuscript. When the text resumes, however, it does so in an auspicious place. How lucky we are that the key passage of the entire text is preserved intact. For Jesus moves from talking about those baptized in his name to Judas himself, informing him of his superiority to all others: "But you will exceed all of them. For you will sacrifice the man that clothes me" (56:17–21).

Judas is above all other humans. He has received Jesus' mysterious revelation and is about to do Jesus' mysterious will. This material body that clothes us is to die. But those of us who escape the material trappings of this world, who know the truth that Jesus has revealed, will transcend this world and return to that luminous cloud whence, ultimately, we have come. Judas will make this possible for Jesus himself, who is a divine being temporarily entrapped in a body of flesh. At his death, Jesus will be released; Judas will make it possible. Far from being Jesus' enemy, he is his most intimate confidant and faithful disciple. He will enable Jesus to return to his heavenly home.

Jesus begins to sing a paean of praise to his beloved disciple:

Already your horn has been raised,
Your wrath has been kindled,
your star has shown brightly
and your heart has (56:21–24)

There the text breaks off. When it resumes, Jesus is continuing to praise Judas. He points out that "the great generation of Adam will be exalted" (57:10–11)—that is, those who are true humans, who have been made after the likeness of the prototypical man in the heavens. That generation, which is "from the eternal realms," exists "prior to heaven, earth, and the angels." Judas is at the head of that generation. As Jesus tells him:

Lift up your eyes and look at the cloud and the light within it and the stars surrounding it. The star that leads the way is your star. (57:18–20)

In other words, the soul of Judas is the guiding star for all those who will be saved once they transcend this life. Judas then has a vision of his own reentrance to the realm of the blessed: "Judas lifted up his eyes and saw the luminous cloud, and he entered in."

The Final Scene: The Betrayal of Judas

Now that the reader knows that Judas is the only one among the disciples who has understood the mysterious teachings of his master, the act of his betrayal takes on a completely different character. This is not a malicious act, as it is portrayed in the earlier Gospels of Matthew, Mark, Luke, and John. Judas is not acting out of greed; he is not being driven by Satan; he is not himself a wicked man acting out the evil machinations of his heart. He is doing Jesus the greatest favor possible. He is enabling him to escape this wicked world to return to his heavenly home.

The story of the betrayal is told in straightforward, nearly stark terms. There are similarities to the accounts of the New Testament Gospels but some differences as well. Here as in the canonical texts it is the Jewish leaders who have Jesus arrested, and Judas hands him over to them. But it is not in the garden, it is in a guest room in a house, and the leaders appear to be alone, not accompanied by a mob.

We are told that Jewish high priests are murmuring because Jesus has gone into the guest room to pray. Why this is upsetting to them, we are not told. Some of the scribes are keeping a watch, wanting to arrest him while he is still praying by himself, not when other people are around, "for they were afraid of the people, since he was regarded by all as a prophet" (58:17–19).

The leaders find Judas there and are a bit taken aback; they ask him, "What are you doing here? You are Jesus' disciple" (58:20–22). Evidently Judas is alone, all the others having fled. This may be a final hint from the author that Judas is the only one to remain faithful to his master until the end. The others have run for their lives, not understanding that life in this material world is not real life, that salvation comes precisely at death, when the soul can escape the entrapment of this material prison and return to its heavenly home. That is what Jesus himself is about to do, thanks to the act of Judas.

Judas gives his interlocutors the reply they wish, but we're not told what that was—presumably he told them where to find Jesus in the house. He then receives some money from them, "and handed him over to them" (58:25–26).

And that's where the Gospel of Judas ends. Later we will explore the intriguing implications of this ending. There is no account of Jesus' death here; that is almost an afterthought. And there is certainly no account of his resurrection. That would violate the entire point of the Gospel: that Jesus was to be saved—as all of us are—not *in* the flesh but *from* the flesh.

It is worth noting the precise phrasing of the title of the Gospel, given here at the end. The titles of our Gospels of the New Testament are given in various forms in our various manuscripts (we don't have the original copies of any of these books, only copies made later—in most instances many centuries later—and these manuscript copies all differ from one another, including in their titles), but the most common way that Matthew, Mark, Luke, and John are designated in the surviving manuscripts is as Gospels "according to" these people. The same is true of other Gospels—for example, Thomas, whose title, at the end, is given as "The Gospel According to Thomas." In other words, in these books, it is not the Gospel *about* Matthew, Mark, Luke, et cetera, but the Gospel *as told by* these people.

Maybe too much should not be made of the point, but that is not how the Gospel of Judas is entitled. Here it is not the Gospel according to Judas—that is, his version of the Gospel story. It is the Gospel *of* Judas, that is, the good news about Judas himself.[8] Judas, even more than Jesus, is the hero of this account. To be sure, Jesus is the divine revealer who alone knows the mysterious truths that can lead to salvation. But the Gospel is about Judas: how he received these revelations; his superiority to all the other disciples, who continued to worship the false god(s) who created this material world; and how he would ultimately transcend this world, as at the end of his life he would enter into that "luminous cloud," in which dwells the ultimate and true God himself.

⌘

CHAPTER SEVEN

The Gospel of Judas and Early Christian Gnosticism

As a scholar of early Christianity, I give a lot of lectures on Gnosticism. Over the years I have found that people—regular lay audiences—like to hear and talk about Gnostics in broad terms, because they can relate to the Gnostics' basic idea of the world and our place in it. But people are not so interested in the details of the Gnostic texts, which are nothing if not detailed. The complexities of these texts can be a real turn-off, with their aeons, luminaries, archons, firmaments, Pleromas, and oddly named divine beings: Autogenes, Barbelo, Yaldabaoth, Saklas, Nebruel, and on and on. Reading these texts takes you into a different world, and without a map, it is nearly impossible to navigate your way through it. People tend to be more interested in the map than in the world it describes. The world of Gnosticism is complex and virtually impenetrable. But the map makes sense.

The map shows that behind all the divine beings, layers of the cosmos, and mythological tropes, Gnosticism involves a sense of alienation in the world and our need to escape the material trappings of this life to return to our spiritual roots in another world. Gnostics realized that this world was foreign territory. Many modern people can relate to this sense of alienation. Some of us look around this world and just don't understand it. We feel like we are alien here; the world doesn't make sense; we just don't belong.

Gnostics insisted that we feel alienated from this world because we *are* alienated from it. This is not our home. We have come to be entrapped here, and we need to learn how to escape. Once we receive the knowledge (Greek: *gnosis*) necessary for salvation, we will be able to transcend these mortal bodies, these prisons that confine our souls in a world of misery and suffering, to return to the divine realm whence we came.

In broad terms, then, the Gnostic view of the world makes sense to many of us. The Devil is in the details.

Even though regular lay people are not so keen on the details of the Gnostic texts, for scholars of Gnosticism they are like the fruits of paradise. Scholars puzzle over these details in their ancient languages (usually Coptic), discuss them, debate them, dispute them, research them, teach them, and write about them. Give Gnostic scholars a new Gnostic text filled with aeons and cosmic mysteries and they think they're in hog heaven.

Eventually there will be hundreds of scholarly books and articles written about the Gospel of Judas. Many of these works of scholarship will be impenetrable to mere mortals. Most of them in one way or another will be about the Gnostic character of the text, as this Gospel will contribute to the numerous heated and ongoing debates about Gnosticism. I have merely alluded to these debates to this point in my discussion. But I will now say something more concrete about them and explain why they matter for our understanding of early Christian Gnosticism in general and for our interpretation of the Gospel of Judas in particular.

There is nothing unusual in scholars having disagreements over important historical phenomena such as Gnosticism. Disagreement is simply something that scholars *do*. But the debates over Gnosticism have grown in extent and intensity over the past decade or so. It is probably ironic that the discovery of new texts—that is, new sources of information, additional pieces of data— have not resolved the debates but rather have exacerbated them. There was much less debate concerning what Gnosticism was *before* the discovery of a cache of primary Gnostic documents at Nag Hammadi. It may seem strange that the more information you have, the less you realize you know, or the more you disagree with others about what you think you know. But that's how scholarship works sometimes.

At present nearly every aspect of Gnosticism is hotly contested. Scholars disagree on such basic issues as the following:

1. Where did Gnosticism come from? Did it originate as a Christian heresy? Did it come from non-Christian Judaism as a sister religion to Christianity? Did it originate in Platonic theological circles and only secondarily come to be influenced by, and to influence, Christianity (and Judaism)? Did it come from somewhere else?
2. When did it come into existence? Was it an offshoot of Christianity, a heretical movement of the second Christian century? Did it sprout at the same time as Christianity? Did it begin before Christianity and affect Christian theology from the very outset?
3. Were there well-defined groups of Gnostics with different sets of beliefs? Were there distinct groups who identified with Seth, the son of Adam and Eve (the Sethian Gnostics)? With Jesus' disciple Thomas (the

Thomasine Gnostics)? With the teacher and leader Valentinus (the Valentinian Gnostics)? With others?

4. Which texts should be associated with which of these groups? Are some texts Gnostic but not clearly defined as belonging to any particular Gnostic group? Should some of the texts traditionally thought of as Gnostic—such as the Gospel of Thomas and the Gospel of Mary—no longer be called Gnostic because they lack important features found in other Gnostic texts?

5. Since the term *Gnostic* has been used to define such an enormous range of religious beliefs and practices from antiquity, should we abandon the term altogether (or find a different term)? In other words, if this is an umbrella term that covers a disparate set of texts and groups, has it become an umbrella that is too large to be of any use?

Every scholar in this field has opinions about these and related issues.[1] I do not need to go into all the ins and outs of these various debates, but I will lay out the perspectives on them that I personally find to be the most persuasive. Then I will try to show how these perspectives affect our understanding of the newly discovered Gospel of Judas.

First, I am not one of those scholars who thinks we should come up with another name for Gnosticism or abandon the term altogether. Some of the alternative names that have been proposed for Gnosticism are not, frankly, particularly catchy or self-evidently superior to the term *Gnosticism* itself —for example, "biblical demiurgic religions."[2] Moreover, I've never been persuaded that we should stop using umbrella terms because too many phenomena get placed under the umbrella. Instead, we should decide more carefully what the term will cover and what it won't. I have earlier noted the irony that scholars who feel the term *Gnosticism* covers too broad a territory have not also argued that we should jettison such terms as *Christianity* and *Judaism,* let alone even more problematic terms such as *Hinduism* or even *religion.* All terms are difficult, and the question is always whether there is any utility in using them.[3]

In my opinion, there is utility in using the term *Gnosticism* to refer to a range of ancient religious groups and texts that teach that liberation from this material world comes through secret gnosis (knowledge). These groups typically understood that souls have become entrapped in the world of matter, and they used myths to explain how it happened. These myths show how the divine realm (of the aeons) derived from one ultimate completely spiritual divine being, and they explain how the material world came into being as the result of a cosmic disaster. The goal of these Gnostic religions is to learn the truth of these matters, which ultimately is the truth about ourselves—that we have come from the divine realm and are to return to it. This truth can come to us only from above.

I should stress that, in my opinion, a text does not have to lay out the myths themselves in order to be classified as Gnostic. Some texts do so—for example, some of the books discovered at Nag Hammadi, such as the Secret

Book of John, or the Gospel of the Egyptians, or Eugnostos the Blessed, or On the Origin of the World. But many others do not: they simply presuppose the myths. In such an instance, readers can make best sense of the text when they understand key aspects of the mythology that lies behind it. This is the case, for example, with the Gospel of Thomas. Many scholars have come to dispute that the Gospel of Thomas is Gnostic, in large measure because there is no (or little) trace of the Gnostic myth in it. But to my mind that is a completely misguided notion. The Gospel of Thomas does not *describe* a Gnostic myth, but many of its sayings appear to *presuppose* the myth and to make sense only if you read them in light of the myth. This was a Gnostic text written for Gnostics presupposing a Gnostic system.[4]

In the case of the Gospel of Judas, there will be, I think (and hope), less dispute over whether it is genuinely Gnostic (at least for those who continue to use the term *Gnostic*), since a good portion of this text lays out the Gnostic myth of how the divine realm (the aeons, luminaries, firmaments, angels, etc.) came into being and how the world was created by a lower, inferior set of deities.

Some scholars have already begun to claim that the Gospel of Judas shows a relatively early or primitive stage of the Gnostic movement because its mythology is not as highly developed as in other texts—such as the Secret Book of John and the others I mentioned above. This too I think is probably a mistake. No one today would take a modern treatise on ordinary-language philosophy and claim that it must predate Wittgenstein's work because it is less complex and nuanced, or claim that a modern novel must have been written before George Eliot's *Middlemarch* because its characters are less developed and its plot less intricate.

About the only chronological claims we can make about the kind of Gnosticism found in the Gospel of Judas is that it postdates the New Testament writings, since it seems to presuppose the story of the book of Acts, in which a new disciple was added to the apostolic band to replace Judas after his death, and that it predates Irenaeus, who appears to mention it. So this kind of Gnosticism, and this particular text, probably dates from between 90 and 180. My hunch is that most scholars will date it to about the middle of that period, around 140–150 CE or so.

As such, it will not tell us much about whether Gnosticism predated Christianity, sprang up as a sister religion at about the same time, or postdated Christianity as a heretical version of the Christian religion. At the same time, this text may lend some support to the view that Gnosticism—at least the form embodied here—probably did not begin as a reaction to Christianity—or as an offshoot—but that it had its beginnings in non-Christian Judaism. I will discuss the evidence for this view later in the chapter.

Before getting to a discussion of the kind of Gnosticism in the Gospel of Judas, I should say something generally about kinds of Gnosticism. I agree with scholars who think that there probably were well-defined Gnostic groups in the ancient world. But I also think that the situation with Gnosticism was much messier than is sometimes allowed by scholars who study these texts for a living. The idea that there were several clearly demarcated branches of related phenomena that we might call "brands" of Gnosticism—Sethian Gnosticism, Thomasine Gnosticism, Valentinian Gnosticism—may be right, but it is also inadequate. There are lots of texts that don't fit neatly into this kind of taxonomy, and other texts that share characteristics of more than one of these groups. The way I see it is this: there were lots of groups of Christians in the ancient world, and lots of cross-fertilization among groups. Trying to pigeonhole every text into one of the groups is a bit like taking a Christian in the modern world and asking whether she is Baptist, Mormon, or Roman Catholic. The answer, obviously, may be "none of the above." That doesn't mean, however, that we should abandon the label *Christian,* any more than we should abandon the label *Gnostic.* It simply means that historical reality is much messier than the categories we use to understand it, that there can be both broader and narrower categories, and that sometimes there is considerable overlap among them.

The Gospel of Judas as a Sethian Gnostic Text

Here in the early months of our knowledge of the Gospel of Judas, the most sophisticated treatment of its relationship to Gnosticism is by Marvin Meyer. Meyer is the translator of the text into English (he was assisted by the Swiss editor of the manuscript, Rodolphe Kasser, and Kasser's German assistant, Gregor Wurst). In the notes accompanying Meyer's translation and in the essay that he included as part of the commentary to the text, he argues that the Gospel of Judas is best seen as an example of Sethian Gnosticism.[5]

Meyer is an impeccable authority. His earlier work was largely on the Nag Hammadi library, which he helped translate as well. He has published widely in the field of early Christian Gnosticism and is by all accounts one of the premier scholars in the field in North America. In my opinion, there is much to agree with in Meyer's views, and readers owe him a considerable debt for making the Sethian features of the text clear.

To explain these features I should first say a word about how Sethian Gnosticism is usually characterized by modern scholars.[6] This version of Gnosticism is named after Seth, the righteous son of Adam and Eve, born after their son Abel was murdered by their other son, Cain. Seth took on mythological proportions for this Gnostic group. He was not merely a mortal but a preexistent divine being who was both the one from whom the Gnostics themselves descended and the one who came to earth to reveal the gnosis that is necessary for salvation. Sometimes the Sethian Gnostics called themselves "the generation of Seth" (which corresponds, Meyer argues, to "that generation" mentioned in the Gospel of Judas, over against "this generation" made up of humans without the spark of the divine within).

In the Sethian version of the Gnostic myth, there is a kind of divine triad that stands at the head of all the aeons of the Pleroma: the Great Invisible Spirit (the Father), Barbelo (the Mother), and the Self-Generated (Autogenes, the Son).[7] All these terms figure in the myth of creation found in the Gospel of Judas. Moreover, what is said about these figures in the Gospel of Judas corresponds to what can be found in some of the other, more complex Sethian mythological texts, such as the Secret Book of John.

For example, at the very outset of Jesus' explanation of how the divine realm came about, he mentions the Great Invisible Spirit. Much more is said about this ultimate divine being in the Secret Book of John:

> He is the invisible Spirit of whom it is not right to think of him as a god or something similar. For he is more than a god, since there is nothing above him, for no one lords it over him. For he does not exist in something inferior to him, since everything exists in him. . . . He is eternal since he does not need anything. For he is total perfection. He did not lack anything that he might be completed by it. He is always completely perfect in light. . . . He is unsearchable since there exists no one prior to him. . . . He is not corporeal nor is he incorporeal. He is neither large nor is he small. There is no way to say "What is his quantity?" or "What is his quality?" for no one can know him. He is not someone among other beings, rather he is far superior. Not that he is simply superior, but his essence does not partake in the aeons nor time. (Secret Book of John II, 3–4)[8]

In addition, in the Gospel of Judas, Judas confesses to Jesus that Jesus comes from the realm of Barbelo. She too figures prominently in Sethian texts. Again, from the Secret Book of John, it is clear she is the first to come forth from the Great Invisible Spirit:

> And his thought performed a deed and she came forth, namely she who had appeared before him, in the shine of his light. This is the first power which was before all of them. . . . She is the perfect power which is the image of the invisible, virginal Spirit who is perfect: the first power, the glory of Barbelo, the perfect glory in the aeons. (II, 4–5)

In the account of the Gospel of Judas, it is the Self-Generated (Autogenes) who creates the aeons and luminaries. So too in the Secret Book of John:

> And the holy Spirit completed the divine Autogenes, his son, together with Barbelo, that he may attend the mighty and invisible, virginal Spirit as the divine Autogenes, the Christ whom he had honored. . . . From the light, which is the Christ, and the indestructibility, through Secret the gift of the Spirit, the four lights appeared from the divine Autogenes. (II, 7)

Other parts of the Gospel of Judas resemble yet other Sethian texts, as Meyer notes. For example, in another treatise discovered at Nag Hammadi, called the Gospel of the Egyptians, we also find reference to the Great Invisible Spirit,

Barbelo, and Autogenes (III, 40–41), as well as the great luminaries and the incorruptible man Adamas (III, 51). In addition, the foolish, bloodthirsty creator gods Sakla and Nebruel (in the Gospel of Judas the latter is called Nebro) are here:

> Then Sakla, the great angel, saw the great demon who is with him, Nebruel. And they became together a begetting spirit of the earth. They begot assisting angels. Sakla said to the great demon Nebruel, Let the twelve aeons come into being in the world. (Gospel of the Egyptians III, 57)[9]

For the Gospel of the Egyptians, Sakla (also called Yaldabaoth in the Gospel of Judas and other Gnostic texts) is clearly the God of the Old Testament: "After the founding of the world Sakla said to his angels, 'I, I am a jealous god, and apart from me nothing has come into being.'" As in the Gospel of Judas, here too he is a fool.

We could go on for a very long time looking at similarities between the Gospel of Judas and other Gnostic texts that scholars have labeled Sethian. These other texts do help us to provide a kind of interpretive context for the Gospel: its mythology may seem in passing strange to a first-time reader, but to someone immersed in the other Gnostic works discovered in modern times, they will not seem strange at all.

At the same time, I think it would be a mistake to conclude that the Gospel of Judas is a Sethian text without remainder. Even though there are very close parallels to Sethian documents, there are also some differences. Maybe these differences are due to the fact that we don't have the entire text of the Gospel of Judas (as I've noted, we're missing 10 to 15 percent of it, due to its being mishandled over the years), or to the circumstance I alluded to earlier, that some Gnostic texts (such as the Gospel of Thomas) appear to presuppose mythological views that they don't explicitly narrate. Even so, it is worth noting that the name Seth plays only a minor role in the Gospel of Judas. In a fragmentary section, Seth *may* be referred to as the ultimate head of "that generation" (49). But otherwise his name occurs just once, as one of the five inferior divine beings who rule the underworld and who will be destroyed at the end of time (54). Probably not too much should be made of the fact that the actual course of creation in the Gospel of Judas differs from other Sethian texts—these disagree widely with one another as well. But it is striking that many of the closest parallels to the Gospel's creation of the divine realm can also be found in texts that are *not* usually considered Sethian.

As Meyer notes, the heavily numeric description of the divine aeons, luminaries, and firmaments in the Gospel of Judas 49–50, for example, is very close to a description in a Nag Hammadi Gnostic text that has no Christian imprint on it, the non-Sethian book called Eugnostos the Blessed:[10]

> All-begetter, their Father, very soon created twelve aeons for retinue for the twelve angels. And in each aeon there were six [heavens], so there are seventy-two

heavens of the seventy-two powers who appeared from him. And in each of the heavens there were five firmaments, so there are altogether three hundred sixty firmaments of the three hundred sixty powers that appeared from them. (III, 84–85)[11]

This close similarity—some of these Gnostics just loved numbers—leads me to consider additional connections with other non-Sethian texts.

Themes Found in Non-Sethian Texts

It is relatively simple to make some basic comparisons with some of the best known non-Sethian writings, just to give a sense of how broad-ranging the comparisons can be.

The Basic Revelatory Trope

A large number of Gnostic writings involve a revelation that Jesus gives to one or more of his followers, often (but not always) after his resurrection. These are sometimes called revelation dialogues, and they come in a range of patterns and present a range of teachings. The Gospel of Judas is obviously that sort of book. Unlike most of the others, it consists of revelations given before Jesus' death. But what makes it most unusual is that the revelation is given not to one who is usually considered an intimate of Jesus but to one who is outside their band. The revelation, in fact, is given to his alleged betrayer.

We don't have anything else exactly like that among the other surviving Gnostic texts, but we do have something comparable. As I mentioned earlier, the Gospel of Mary was discovered in 1896, although it was not published until fifty-nine years later. This Gospel has recently struck a vibrant chord among some scholars and lots of lay people, because in it Mary Magdalene, not one of the twelve (male) disciples, is given pride of place.[12]

The Gospel of Mary is built on this very theme that Christ's revelation can come to one who stands outside the band of the eleven faithful disciples. We are missing the first six pages of the text, but where the fragment begins, Jesus is giving instructions to his disciples, telling them that the material world is not what matters since it will eventually dissipate. He then leaves them, and they are distraught, fearful for their lives ("if they did not spare him, how will they spare us")—overlooking everything Jesus has just taught them about the unimportance of the material existence. Mary comes and comforts them, leading Peter to ask her to tell them what Jesus had revealed to her privately. Mary begins to narrate a vision she had of Christ. Unfortunately, we are missing four pages at just this point, but when the text resumes, Mary is describing how the human soul, equipped with knowledge, can transcend this material realm of ignorance and desire to return to its heavenly home. When she finishes describing this revelation, an argument breaks out among the male apostles, some of whom (including the hotheaded Peter) can't believe that the Savior would give such an important revelation to Mary, of all people—a *woman*. Wouldn't he reveal it to them, the men? Eventually the apostle Levi intervenes and urges them to take Mary's words to heart and go forth to preach the gospel, which they then do.

Here, as in the Gospel of Judas, a Gnostic revelation is given to one who is outside the apostolic band (as normally understood), to one of the last persons you would expect—not to the betrayer, but to a woman.

Jesus' Earthly Appearance

One of the first things said about Jesus in the Gospel of Judas is that "often he did not appear to his disciples as himself, but he was found among them as a child" (33:19–20). This last word is difficult to translate. The Coptic term is very rare, and it may mean "phantom" rather than "child."[13] Either way, it is clear that Jesus is able to change his appearance at will, according to this text—an idea found in a number of other early Christian writings. One of the places from which it is best known is not a Gnostic writing found at Nag Hammadi but a fictitious account of the missionary escapades of the apostle John, known as the Acts of John.

The Acts of John is an interesting book in that it relates numerous miracles that John performs while spreading the Gospel of Christ after his death. In particular, John appears to have the remarkable ability to raise the dead. There is one section of the Acts of John, however, that does not fit in well with the rest. Scholars have often thought this section originated from a different book and was inserted into the Acts of John by some unknown scribe for some unknown reason. In this section John describes his relationship with Jesus and indicates that Jesus was polymorphous: he could change his outward appearances because he was not, in fact, a normal flesh-and-blood human being. In one of his appearances, he is a child.

John indicates that he was in a boat with his brother James along with Peter and Andrew, when he saw someone (Jesus) beckoning to them from the shore:

> And my brother said, "John, this child on the shore, who called to us, what does he want?" And I said, "What child?" He replied, "The one who is beckoning to us." And I answered, "Because of our long watch that we kept at sea you are not seeing straight, brother James; but do you not see the man who stands there, fair and comely and of cheerful countenance?" (Acts of John 88)[14]

They go ashore and see the one who had been beckoning to them, but his appearance has changed once more:

> He again appeared to me bald-headed but with a thick and flowing beard; but to James he appeared as a youth whose beard was just starting. (Acts of John 89)

John goes on to describe Jesus' remarkable body and its outward appearances:

I tried to see him as he was, and I never at any time saw his eyes closing but only open. And sometimes he appeared to me as a small man and unattractive, and then again as one reaching to heaven. Also there was in him another marvel; when I sat at table he would take me upon his breast and I held him; and sometimes his breast felt to me to be smooth and tender, and sometimes hard, like stone, so that I was perplexed in myself and said, "What does this mean?" (Acts of John 89)

The wonders just kept coming. As John later says:

Another glory I will tell you, brethren, sometimes when I meant to touch him, I met a material and solid body; and at other times again when I felt him, the substance was immaterial and bodiless and as if it were not existing at all. . . . And often when I was walking with him I wished to see whether the print of his foot appeared upon the earth—for I saw him raising himself from the earth—but I never saw it. (Acts of John 93)

So too in the Gospel of Judas: Jesus appears to be polymorphous, able to change his appearance at will, not a real flesh-and-blood human.

Christ Merely Clothed in the Flesh

As I mentioned in an earlier chapter, this view that Jesus was not really human is called docetism, from the Greek word *dokeo,* which means "to seem" or "to appear." For docetists, such as the author of this section of the Acts of John and the Gospel of Judas, Jesus was not really human but only appeared to be.

A different kind of docetic view held by other Gnostics was that Jesus himself was a man in whom the divine aeon, Christ, made his temporary residence. This understanding also claimed that Christ himself did not really suffer. In this case, however, it was not because he was a phantasm; it was because Christ had departed from the man Jesus prior to his death.

Logically speaking, these two kinds of docetism—the phantasmal kind and the separationist kind—are different. The reality, however, is that *both* views were sometimes presented in one and the same Gnostic text. This appears to be what happens in the Gospel of Judas, for at the end of the book comes that striking line in which Jesus praises Judas as the one who will exceed all the other apostles, "for you will sacrifice the man that clothes me." In this understanding, the body Jesus inhabits is simply a temporary dwelling that must be taken out of the way for his spirit to return to the heavenly realm.

Another Gnostic text that combines the two docetic views is named after Seth, even though it does not have extensive parallels with Sethian Gnostic texts otherwise: the Second Treatise of the Great Seth (the name Seth never

Facing page   Page 44 of the manuscript, where Judas begins to describe his vision to Jesus.

occurs in the book after the title). Here too there are passages that sound like Jesus' body is merely the temporary dwelling for the Christ. At the beginning of the treatise Christ says, "I visited a bodily dwelling. I cast out the one who was in it previously, and I went in. And the whole multitude of the archons was disturbed" (Second Treatise, 51).[15]

On the other hand, other passages suggest that Jesus' body was a phantasm:

> I did not give in to them as they devised. And I was not afflicted at all. These there punished me, yet I did not die in solid reality but in what appears, in order that I not be put to shame by them. (Second Treatise, 55)

Here too, as in the Acts of John, Jesus has the ability to change the appearance of his body: "I kept changing my forms above, transforming from appearance to appearance" (Second Treatise, 56). This ability to change forms led to a very bizarre situation at Jesus' crucifixion:

> As for me, on the one hand they saw me; they punished me. [But] another, their father, was the one who drank the gall and the vinegar; it was not I. They were hitting me with the reed; another was the one who lifted up the cross on his shoulder, who was Simon. Another was the one on whom they put the crown of thorns. But I was rejoicing in the height over all the riches of the archons and the offspring of their error and their conceit, and I was laughing at their ignorance. (Second Treatise, 56)

As in the Gospel of Judas, we see a laughing Jesus. I'll have more to say about that in a moment. For now, though, what does it mean that Christ was not the one who was tormented and crucified? This passage is reminiscent of the teachings of an early-second-century Gnostic teacher named Basilides, mentioned by the heresy hunter Irenaeus. According to Irenaeus, Basilides also taught that Jesus could change appearances at will, so that when Simon of Cyrene carried his cross for him to the place of crucifixion (see Mark 15:21), Jesus pulled an identity switch: he made himself look like Simon of Cyrene and made Simon look like him, Jesus. And so the Romans crucified the wrong man. Jesus stood by the cross, in the image of Simon, laughing at his little stunt (Irenaeus, *Against Heresies* 1, 24, 3).

So too here in the Second Treatise of the Great Seth: Jesus changes appearance, and it is Simon who gets crucified in his stead, to Jesus' great merriment.

Christ Laughing at the Ignorant

What is one to make of all this laughter? Closely related in many ways to the Second Treatise of the Great Seth is another Nag Hammadi tractate called the (Coptic) Apocalypse of Peter.[16] Here too Jesus laughs at his crucifixion, not because he has pulled an identity switch but because those who think they are harming him do not realize that he is a divine being beyond pain and suffering. He can't be killed; only his mortal shell can be.

In this account the apostle Peter is talking with Christ when suddenly he sees, in the distance, Christ being seized and crucified. And then he sees yet a third Christ above the cross of the second one, laughing. Needless to say, Peter is completely confused:

> When he had said those things I saw him seemingly being seized by them. And I said, "What do I see, O Lord, that it is you yourself whom they take, and that you are grasping me? Or who is this one, glad and laughing on the tree? And is it another one whose feet and hands they are striking?" (Apoc. Pet. 81)[17]

Jesus explains that the one above the cross laughing is "the living Jesus." But the one being crucified is merely "his physical part, which is the substitute. The are putting to shame that which is in his likeness" (81). Later the laughing Jesus from above the cross comes to Peter and tells him:

> Be strong, for you are the one to whom these mysteries have been given, to know through revelation that he whom they crucified is the firstborn, and the home of demons, and the stone vessel in which they dwell, belonging to Elohim. . . . But he who stands near him is the living Savior, the first in him, whom they seized and released. . . . Therefore he laughs at their lack of perception. . . . So then the one susceptible to suffering shall come, since the body is the substitute. But what they released was my incorporeal body.

In the Gospel of Judas, one of the creator gods was called El; here he is called Elohim—the plural of the word, which is the form more commonly found in the Hebrew Bible. This creator is the one to whom the body belongs. But the inner person, the divine element, is incorporeal and cannot suffer. When the body—the "substitute" for the real person—is killed, the inner self is released. This, then, is very close to the Gospel of Judas.

And notice again that Jesus is laughing. His laughter is directed against the ignorance of the world, which thinks it knows him. Those in this world, who know him "in the flesh," don't know him at all—any more than the disciples know him in the Gospel of Judas, where they are subject to Jesus' laughter when they assume he is the Son of the God who created this world.

The Polemic Against the Emerging Orthodox Church

Still more can be said about Jesus' laughter. In the Gospel of Judas and both the Nag Hammadi treatises I have just mentioned, the Second Treatise of the Great Seth and the Coptic Apocalypse of Peter, Jesus' laughter appears to be directed against those who misunderstand him. Strikingly, the ones who misunderstand him the most are not the Roman soldiers who attempt to crucify him but his own followers, who think they have a firm handle on who he is. At the time of the writing of these works, no one thought they understood Christ better than the leaders of the orthodox Christian churches. But according to Gnostic writings, these Christians were badly mistaken. They had mistaken his outward appearance for his inward reality.

This is especially clear in the Coptic Apocalypse of Peter, where the Savior begins by telling Peter:

> These people are blind and deaf. Now then, listen to the things which they are telling you in a mystery and guard them. Do not tell them to the children of this age. For they will despise you in these ages. . . . But they will praise you in knowledge. (Apoc. Pet. 73)

Just as Judas was to experience serious grief, according to the Gospel of Judas, so too will Peter be despised in the Apocalypse that bears his name. But Judas in one text and Peter in the other are in fact on the side of knowledge; it is to them that the true mysteries are revealed; it is they who will exceed all the others. The others "are without perception" (Apoc. Pet. 74).

The Coptic Apocalypse of Peter goes further to explain what it is the ignorant misunderstand. They think that Jesus' death is what brings salvation: "They praise the men of the propagation of falsehood, who will come after you [i.e., the orthodox leaders of the churches]. And they will cleave to the name of a dead man [i.e., they think that Jesus' death is salvific]." Later we're told that these false leaders are none other than the bishop and deacons of the churches. But they are not sources of vibrant teaching of the truth: "those people are dry canals."

We saw in the Gospel of Judas that the leaders of the orthodox churches were maligned for their false understandings of Christ. In making that charge, the Gospel of Judas is standing in a tradition known from these other two (non-Sethian) Gnostic writings discovered at Nag Hammadi.

Similarities to the Gospel of Thomas

The first time I read the Gospel of Judas, I was particularly struck by how many similarities there seemed to be with another of the Nag Hammadi tractates, the most famous of them all, the Gospel of Thomas. The Gospel of Thomas, as I have indicated, is a collection of 114 sayings of Jesus. There are no narratives here, no accounts of what Jesus did, no miracles or exorcisms, no transfiguration or Last Supper, no description of the Passion, no arrest, trial, death, or resurrection. The book consists of one saying after the other. The only narrative elements come when the disciples ask Jesus a question, which he then answers.

The Gospel of Judas is a different genre, of course. There we find a narrative framework, as Jesus comes to the disciples and leaves them. Moreover, his sayings are given in the form of discourses, instead of principally a series of one-liners. But the overarching theology of the Gospel is very similar, as I will discuss further in the next chapter. What really matters to both authors is not what Jesus did (e.g., his miracles, which get only the briefest mention in the

Gospel of Judas and none at all in the Gospel of Thomas), and it is not his death and resurrection (which again are not described in either account). What matters is what he said. Eternal life comes to the one who understands his teaching.

This is stated explicitly at the outset of the Gospel of Thomas, which begins as follows:

> These are the secret words which the living Jesus spoke, and Didymus Judas Thomas wrote them down. And he said, "The one who finds the meaning of these words will not taste death."[18]

Just as the Gospel of Judas begins by stating that it is "the secret account of the revelation that Jesus spoke," so too Thomas begins by speaking of "the secret words of the living Jesus." These are similar accounts in many ways, with a similar theology of salvation.

Not only the overall theological understanding of the two texts but also individual episodes are very similar to one another. Here I cite just a handful of examples:

1. When Jesus introduces his revelation of the creation to Judas, he speaks of that "which no eye of an angel has ever seen, no thought of the heart has ever comprehended, and it was never called by any name." This sounds like a reference to what the apostle Paul says in 1 Corinthians 2:9, when he speaks of "what no eye has seen, nor ear heard, nor the human heart conceived." But also similar is the Gospel of Thomas 17: "Jesus said, 'I will give you what no eye has seen and what no ear has heard and no hand has touched and what has not come into the heart of a human.'"

2. When Judas alone of the disciples has the strength to stand before Jesus in the Gospel of Judas, he cannot look him in the face but averts his eyes. This sounds very much like what is said in the Gospel of Thomas 46, where no one can go eye to eye with John the Baptist, who is greater than everyone "born of women."

3. In the Gospel of Judas, it is Judas alone who receives the mysteries; in Thomas, it is Thomas alone. In both, the other disciples show they don't understand Jesus. In the Gospel of Judas, they wrongly think he is the son of their own god (i.e., the creator); Judas, however, states that Jesus comes from the realm of Barbelo and that "I am not worthy to utter the name of the one who has sent you." So too in Thomas, other disciples such as Simon Peter and Matthew misconceive Jesus' identity, but Thomas says, "Master, my mouth will not be able to say what you are like" (Gospel of Thomas 13). In both cases Jesus then takes his closest disciples aside to reveal to him the secret mysteries. In neither case are we told what those mysteries are. But in both instances Jesus' faithful disciple is set over against the others. In the Gospel of Thomas, Thomas

indicates to the others that if he were to reveal what Jesus had told him, they would "pick up stones and throw them at me." In the Gospel of Judas we're told that Judas is to be replaced, so that "the twelve [disciples] may again come to completion with their god."

4. This vision in the Gospel of Thomas of Thomas being stoned by the others is similar to the vision in the Gospel of Judas, where Judas has to ask Jesus what his vision of the other disciples stoning him means.

5. In the Gospel of Judas the disciples have a vision of the sacrifices being performed in the Temple, and want to know what the vision means. Jesus interprets it in such a way as to show that this traditional form of Jewish piety is in fact opposed to God, that what is being sacrificed there in his name are the people who follow the disciples, the false teachers. In the Gospel of Thomas too, traditional forms of Jewish piety are attacked as being opposed to God: "Jesus said to them, 'If you fast, you will bring sin upon yourselves and, if you pray, you will be condemned and, if you give alms, you will do evil to your spirit'" (Gospel of Thomas 14).

More similarities could be added, but these are enough to make the basic point. The Gospel of Judas is similar not only to works of Sethian Gnosticism, especially in its specific mythology, but to non-Sethian Gnostic texts as well. What is more, it has yet other striking similarities to religious movements of the time that were not Gnostic at all.

Similarities to the Teachings of Marcion

Marcion was a second-century teacher-theologian who was thriving at just the time the Gospel of Judas must have been written—mid-second century. He was not a Gnostic: he did not believe that there was a Pleroma filled with numerous divine aeons, luminaries, firmaments, and so on, nor did he think that salvation came by receiving secret knowledge from on high. But he had some views that were similar to those of Gnostics.

Marcion's starting point for his theology were the letters of the apostle Paul, who claimed that salvation came to all—Jew and non-Jew alike—through his gospel about the death and resurrection of Christ. For Paul, it was the gospel, not the law of the Jews, that made a person right with God. Marcion pressed this distinction between the law and the gospel to what seemed to him a natural conclusion. The god who gave the (harsh) Jewish law could not be the same God who gave the (merciful) Christian gospel. The Old Testament god is different from the God of Jesus and his follower Paul.

According to Marcion, the god of the Old Testament is the one who created this world, chose Israel to be his people, gave them his law, and then punished them, and everyone else, for not keeping this law. The God of Jesus, on the other hand, had never had any involvement with this world prior to Jesus' appearance in it. This God was superior to the Old Testament god and sent Jesus in the likeness of human flesh (i.e., as a phantasm) in order to save people from the harsh justice of the god of the Jews. This Jesus did by apparently dying on the cross. People could believe in this death and be saved, evidently because the just god who created this world considered this death to be salvific for others (since Jesus did not die for his own sins).

According to Marcion, Jesus' disciples never did understand that he was not himself the son of the creator god. They continued in their Jewish ways after his death, and so the God of Jesus had to make a second intervention in order to show people the true way of salvation. Jesus appeared to Paul on the road to Damascus, told him the gospel truth, and sent him on a mission to convert others to believe in his gospel apart from the law.

Even this brief summary of Marcion's teaching shows a number of key similarities with the teachings of the Gospel of Judas:

1. The god who created this world is not the true God and is not the Father of Jesus; Jesus represents another God.
2. Jesus is not a real flesh-and-blood human being (e.g., in the Gospel of Judas he can change appearances at will).
3. Those who worship the creator god of the Jews have gone astray from the truth of salvation.
4. The disciples of Jesus never do understand the truth but assume that they are to continue following the Jewish religion (cf. the vision of the Temple sacrifices in the Gospel of Judas).
5. It is only someone outside the Twelve who understands the truth of Jesus (either the outcast Judas or the latecomer Paul).

I certainly do not want to claim that the Gospel of Judas is Marcionite (as opposed to Gnostic). But I do want to claim that there were lots of religious points of view floating around in the second century, and that religious groups, and their views, affected each other in lots of ways. Discoveries of new texts simply show us how murky, rather than clearly delineated, the religious world of the Christian second century actually was.

Similarities to Jewish and Christian Apocalyptic Thought

As I have read and reread the Gospel of Judas, there is one other feature of the text that has continued to strike me. This is not something that will be as obvious to a first-time reader. It certainly wasn't obvious to me at first. But the more I read, the more I started to see it. Not too far beneath the surface of this Gnostic text there appear to be remnants of what we might call apocalyptic thought. Seeing these remnants and recognizing them for what they are may help us make sense of where a Gospel such as this (and even Gnosticism itself, some might argue) might have come from.

First I need to make some introductory remarks about the ancient religious phenomenon that scholars have called apocalypticism. The word comes from the Greek term *apokalypsis,* which means "a revealing" or "an unveiling." Jewish apocalypticists believed that God had revealed to them the heavenly secrets that could make sense of our earthly realities.

Jewish apocalypticism can be firmly dated to the second century before Christ.[19] It appears to have arisen as a kind of intellectual movement among Jews who were trying to explain the suffering of God's people in the midst of a world allegedly controlled by God. For centuries Jewish prophets had claimed that people suffered because they were being punished by God, and that if people would return to God and his ways, he would relinquish the punishment and allow his people to prosper.

But what was one to say when the *righteous* were the ones who suffered? How can one explain that some people suffer precisely because they do what God commands—sometimes suffer horribly, through illness, torture, or execution? How does one explain that when the people of God—Israel—returned to God in national repentance, they continued to suffer painful setbacks: plague, drought, famine, military defeat, humiliation at the hands of their enemy? How can one explain ongoing suffering for those who side with God?

About 150 years before Jesus, some Jewish thinkers moved away from the claims of the prophets and said that suffering did not come as a punishment for sin. Suffering, for these thinkers, was not from God. On the contrary, suffering was caused by God's enemy, the Devil. Those who side with God suffer in this world because there are forces of evil aligned against God who are bound and determined to eradicate God's people from the face of the earth. These forces of evil are willing to use any form of pain and suffering necessary to accomplish their nefarious task.

Jewish apocalypticists, in short, developed a dualistic view of the world. There was God and the Devil. Each side had its supernatural forces: just as God had his angels, the Devil had his demons. Moreover, just as God gave life, the Devil brought death. Just as righteousness was on the side of God, sin was on the side of the Devil. Sin and death, in fact, were themselves cosmic powers, demonic forces opposed to God. Sin enslaved people and removed them from God's presence; when it completed its work, it handed people over to the power of death, and they were annihilated.

This dualism of good and evil was worked out in a historical scenario in which the present age was evil, controlled by the Devil and his minions. But a future age was coming that was good, in which God would overthrow all the forces of evil and bring in his good Kingdom. Apocalypticists did not believe that we could improve our lot in this world by our own efforts. Evil was in control of this world, and it would increase its stranglehold until the very end, when literally all hell would break out.

But then, at the end, God would intervene. He would enter into history, overthrow the forces of evil, and bring in his Kingdom on earth, in which there would be no more evil, pain, or suffering, no more famine or drought, no more epidemics or war, no more misery or death. Moreover, this utopian Kingdom was not reserved only for those who happen to be alive when the end comes; it would be for all people who have ever sided with God, for at the end of this age, God would raise people from the dead, to live forever. Those who had sided with God (and suffered as a result) would be given an eternal reward. Those who had opposed God would be sent to eternal damnation.

When would this happen? Very soon. Jewish apocalypticists maintained that the end was imminent, right around the corner. They insisted that suffering had reached its height, and people needed to hold on just a little while longer, for God was soon to intervene in history and destroy all that is opposed to him and bring in his Kingdom. "Truly I tell you, some of those standing here will not taste death before they see that the Kingdom of God has come in power." These are the words of Jesus (Mark 9:1), some of many in which he embraces the apocalyptic view of the world. I will be arguing in a later chapter that Jesus and his followers, along with Judas Iscariot, were in fact Jewish apocalypticists, believing they were living at the end of the age.

Now, what has this to do with the Gospel of Judas? As it turns out, there are passages scattered throughout the Gospel that appear to contain remnants of Jewish apocalyptic thought. Near the beginning of the Gospel we are told that Jesus' revelation involved the mysteries in the world and "what would take place at the end" (33:17–18). This is apocalyptic language; its concern is with what happens at the end of this age.

Later in the text Judas wants to know from Jesus: "When will you tell me these things, and when will the great day of light dawn for the generation?" (36:5–8). This is very similar to what we find in our earliest Gospel, Mark 13:1, where the disciples ask Jesus what the signs will be for the coming of the end. Jesus, in Mark, proceeds to deliver his "apocalyptic discourse," in which he describes the disasters about to transpire at the end of the world.

When the disciples have a vision of the sacrifices being performed in the Temple in the Gospel of Judas, we learn that the priests making those sacrifices are actually slaying their own children and their wives, sleeping with men, and committing "a multitude of sins and deeds of lawlessness" (38:22–23), all in Jesus' name. This sounds like an apocalyptic vision of the "desolating sacrilege" in the Temple—a desecration of the holy precincts of God (Mark 13:14), which is possibly referred to in one of the Pauline letters as well, where we learn of a kind of Antichrist figure who "takes his seat in the temple of God" (2 Thess. 2:4) and commits all sorts of lawless acts through the power of Satan.

Later Judas has a vision of a great house, which evidently represents the heavenly realm to which liberated souls go upon death. In his interpretation of the vision Jesus says that in this place "there will be no need for sun or moon; but the holy will abide there always, in the eternal realm with the holy angels"

(45:22–24). This is highly reminiscent of the description of the destination of the saints in the apocalyptic vision of the book of Revelation in the New Testament, who will dwell in the new city of God, the new Jerusalem, a city that "has no need of sun or moon to shine on it, for the glory of God will be its light." Into that city, we are told "nothing unclean will enter, nor anyone who practices abomination or falsehood, but only those who are written in the Lamb's book of Life" (Rev. 22:23, 27).

Another apocalyptic fragment appears in the Gospel of Judas near the end of Jesus' revelation of the mysteries of creation, where he indicates that the creator god Saklas will "complete the span of time assigned for him"—suggesting that even the wickedness of this material world has an allotted amount of time, as in apocalyptic texts. Chaos will then break out: "they will fornicate in my name and slay their children" (54:24–26). Jesus goes on to laugh at those divine beings who think they control matters here on earth, as he indicates to Judas: "I am not laughing at you but at the error of the stars, because these six stars wander about with these five combatants, and they all will be destroyed along with their creatures" (55:14–20).

The end will bring not only destruction for the evil in the world but exaltation for those among the saved: "The image of the great generation of Adam will be exalted, for prior to heaven, earth, and the angels, that generation, which is from the eternal realms, exists" (57:10–14).

What is one to make of these passages in the Gospel of Judas that appear to embrace an apocalyptic perspective within a Gnostic document? On the surface, they might seem a bit anomalous. Gnostic Christians had deeply rooted disagreements with Jewish and Christian apocalypticists. Apocalypticists believed in one God who created the world; Gnostic Christians insisted that the god who created this world was not the only god and was certainly not the true God. The true God had nothing to do with this world. Apocalypticists believed that the material world had become sinful but that it was inherently good, a creation of God. Gnostics maintained that the material world was a cosmic mistake at best, the root of all evil at worst. Apocalypticists claimed that eternal life would be a material existence in the body, when God redeemed this world (and human flesh) by removing evil from it; Gnostics argued that eternal life would be a nonmaterial existence and that the goal of salvation was not to redeem the body but to escape it.

If these two ways of thought are so opposed, why do we find apocalyptic traces within a Gnostic text such as the Gospel of Judas? As it turns out, there are other Gnostic texts that also have apocalyptically oriented passages. Sethian Gnostic texts, in fact, typically have an apocalyptic element in them.[20] But how can that be, given the starkly different assumptions about God and the world between apocalypticists and Gnostics?

It helps to put this question in a broader context, for the apocalyptic character of some Gnostic texts is not their only puzzling feature. Many of these texts, of course, seem to be completely anti-Jewish. The Jewish god, after all, is portrayed either as a fool or as a bloodthirsty maniac, and the goal of the religion is to escape his domination. But why are Gnostic texts obsessed with the Jewish god at all? Why not some other god?

It is striking that many Gnostic texts seem to be rooted in some kind of Jewish thought. A large number of them represent creative readings of the book of Genesis, for example. Not only that, some of the words and names that typically occur in these Gnostic texts appear to have Jewish roots. Just within the Gospel of Judas, for example, there is the god El (the name of the God of the Old Testament), the god Sakla (an Aramaic word in an originally Greek text), Yaldabaoth (which is reminiscent of Yahweh, Lord of Sabbaoth), and so on.[21]

As I indicated at the beginning of this chapter, scholars have long debated the origins of Gnosticism. My own view is that Gnosticism—or at least some forms of Gnosticism—originated as a Jewish reaction against an apocalyptic vision that never materialized.[22]

Gnosticism as Failed Jewish Apocalypticism

As I pointed out earlier, Jewish apocalypticism itself came from failed prophecy. The prophets had said that suffering came as a punishment for sin; they urged the people of Israel to return to God's ways so that their suffering would end. But the suffering didn't end, even when the people of God repented. This led to a radical shift in thinking: maybe God wasn't really in control. Maybe his personal enemy was. Thus begins apocalyptic thinking, which insisted that even though God was ultimately in control, he had relinquished control for the time being. In this view, God didn't cause suffering; the Devil and his forces did. But God would soon intervene, overthrow these forces of evil, and bring in a good Kingdom on earth.

What happens to Jewish apocalypticists when the end they proclaim as imminent does not, in fact, ever come? What happens when suffering continues, even intensifies, and there is no end in sight? What happens when the forces in control of this world appear to be completely, not just temporarily, in control, and the material world we live in itself seems to be the root of our suffering? One of the things that happens is a radical rethinking of apocalyptic theology.

In this still newer way of thinking, God is not ultimately in control of this world. God is far removed from this world and has never had anything to do with it. This world is material, but the true God, since he is unconnected with this world, must be completely spirit. Matter comes to be seen not as the creation of the true God. Matter is itself a cosmic disaster. It is the problem. It is what causes us pain. It must have been formed into existence by maleficent, or at least fantastically ignorant, divine beings. We have been trapped here by those beings, and we need to learn how to escape. Salvation will not come in some future moment, when the true God reasserts his power over this creation. This is not his creation and he is not going to redeem it. Salvation will come when he removes us from this world of matter. That can happen only when we learn how we got here in the first place and what we can do to escape.

Various Gnostic systems—at least some of them—were grounded in this radical new way of looking at the world. They had their roots in Jewish apocalyptic thinking. That's why so many Gnostics were obsessed with the first book of the Jewish Bible, Genesis, which recounted the "creation" of the material world. That's why so many of the names for the divine beings in Gnostic texts are Aramaic (the language of Palestinian Jews) or derive from the Old Testament. And that's why there are so many apocalyptic remnants in some of our Gnostic texts. These texts originated among people who had turned their back on their roots in Jewish apocalyptic traditions.

But as always happens when people take a trip into new and uncharted territory, they bring along some baggage. For those thinkers who adopted a Gnostic worldview, this baggage included fragments of their earlier apocalyptic views, such as those still embedded in the Gospel of Judas.

CHAPTER EIGHT

Jesus, Judas, and the Twelve in the Gospel of Judas

When scholars talk to nonscholars, they often tell them what they ought to be interested in. That's not necessarily bad—in fact, it can be very good. Enormous chunks of a scholar's time are devoted to research into matters that most other people can think about only in passing, in the evenings or on the weekends. But one result is that scholars tend to have different perspectives from others and to emphasize different things. Most scholars coming to the Gospel of Judas, for example, will be interested in recondite questions concerning the relationship of this text to other documents from Christian antiquity and to the precise character of its form of Christian Gnosticism. Regular readers are more likely to be interested in what the book has to say about its main characters: Jesus, the twelve disciples, and Judas. Both sets of concerns are completely legitimate.

I've already said something about the Gospel's relationship to Gnosticism. What more can we say about the way it depicts its main characters, an issue of interest to an even broader group of people? How does this text portray Jesus and the others?

Jesus in the Gospels

In Mark, our earliest surviving Gospel, Jesus asks his disciples: "Who do people say that I am?" (Mark 8:27). That question has been asked time and again through the centuries. Scholars who spend their entire lives studying the ancient records of Jesus in their original languages (Greek, Coptic, Latin, Syriac, and so on) have given remarkably different answers. Some have claimed that Jesus was a political revolutionary intent on overthrowing the Roman oppressors of the

Promised Land. Others have insisted that he was interested in starting a social revolution, changing the values and priorities of people's lives. Some have argued that his social concerns involved a noticeably modern agenda, that he was a kind of proto-Marxist or protofeminist. Others have argued that he was uninterested in political and social change and was merely a peace-seeking Jewish rabbi whose principal concern was that his followers love one another. Others have claimed that he was a Jewish holy man who did miracles to demonstrate his closeness with God, a closeness his followers also could share. Others have maintained that he was like a Cynic philosopher, mainly committed to teaching his followers to be concerned not about the material things of this life but with the spiritual realm. Probably the majority of scholars of the past hundred years or so have been convinced that he is best understood as an apocalyptic prophet who anticipated that God would overthrow the forces of evil in this world to bring in a Kingdom on earth in which there would be no more pain, misery, or suffering.[1]

Just as modern scholars have their own views, so too did ancient Christian writers. And just as many of these modern views appear to conflict with one another, so too do the views found in our earliest sources. I won't give the full panoply of perspectives here—that would take an entire book of its own—but I will mention a couple of ancient views that stand at opposite ends of the theological spectrum, to help contextualize the views found in the Gospel of Judas.

Jesus in the Writings of Paul

The apostle Paul was not one of Jesus' followers during Jesus' lifetime. According to the book of Acts and Paul's own writings, he was in fact the major opponent and persecutor of Jesus' followers soon after the crucifixion. But in probably the most significant turnaround in Christian history, Paul converted from being the enemy of Christ to being his greatest missionary and proponent. The persecutor became a preacher, and it was Paul's efforts to spread the Christian gospel among non-Jews (Gentiles) that largely accounted for the dissemination of the religion in its early decades. Paul established churches by converting former pagans to believe in the one God of the Jews and in Jesus his son, who died for the sins of the world and was raised from the dead. After starting a church in one locale, he would leave to go to another, and start again. Invariably he would receive word about the congregation he had left behind, and he wrote letters to address problems that had arisen. The Pauline epistles of the New Testament are some of those letters. These are actual pieces of correspondence, written by the founder of a church back to the now-troubled communities he had established.

In these letters Paul deals with lots of issues, depending, always, on what the problems of the community were. The letters therefore do not provide us with a full expression of everything that Paul thought or taught. They deal only with the situations at hand. But they are invaluable resources for those interested in knowing about what was happening in the burgeoning Christian communities some twenty to thirty years after Jesus' death. And they are our best (and for the most part only) resource for knowing the key elements of Paul's thought.

What Paul thought about Jesus—especially what he thought was important about Jesus—stands miles away from what the author of the Gospel of Judas thought. As you might imagine, Paul has a lot to say about Jesus. Paul was, after all, by his own confession, Christ's own apostle, set apart to obey Christ in spreading his gospel message throughout the lands of the Mediterranean, before the end came with Christ's glorious return in judgment on the world. What is striking, though, is that Paul has almost nothing to say about Jesus' earthly life. For Paul, what mattered about Jesus is that he was crucified and that God raised him from the dead. What happened before then seems to have had relatively little importance.

My undergraduate students sometimes don't believe this, and so I assign a little exercise. I have them read through the letters written by Paul and make a list of everything that he tells us concerning Jesus' life—that is, the things Jesus said, did, and experienced from the time he was born until the time he died. What students are often surprised to learn is that to make a complete list, they don't need even a four-by-six index card.

What does Paul tell us? He tells us that Jesus was born of a woman (Gal. 4:4; a useful datum, I suppose, but one wonders what the alternative would have been); that he was a Jew (Gal. 4:4); that he had brothers (1 Cor. 9:5), one of whom was named James (Gal. 1:19); that he had twelve followers (1 Cor. 15:5); that his mission was to the Jewish people (Rom. 15:8); that he held the Last Supper (1 Cor. 11:22–24); and that he was crucified (Gal. 3:1). In addition to the words Jesus spoke over the bread and cup at the Last Supper, Paul explicitly quotes two other sayings of Jesus, one that indicates that people should not get a divorce (1 Cor. 7:10) and the other that indicates they should pay their preachers (1 Cor. 9:14). And that's about it.

When my students finish this exercise, they are perplexed. Why doesn't Paul say anything more? Why doesn't he quote Jesus' teachings at length? Why doesn't he describe his miracles—his healing of the sick, his casting out of demons, his raising of the dead? Why doesn't he mention his temptations, his transfiguration, his trip to Jerusalem? Why doesn't he talk about Jesus' controversies with the Pharisees? His arrest? His trial before the Jewish Sanhedrin? His trial before Pilate? Or anything else? Is it because he assumes his readers already knew everything else? That's possible—but it's important to remember that Paul was writing before the Gospels were produced, and there's no guarantee that his readers would have known the stories later found in these books. Did Paul know the stories? If so, why didn't he mention them? Surely it can't be because they were unimportant or irrelevant. The few times he does mention events from Jesus' life, it is precisely because it helps him to make his point to his readers—for example, that they should follow what Jesus said or did. Why, then, doesn't he do this more often? When he urges his readers not to fall into temptation, why doesn't he refer to Jesus' temptations?

When he talks about his opponents among non-Christian Jews, why doesn't he speak of Jesus' opposition from the Jewish leaders? When he tells his churches that they should pay their taxes, why doesn't he mention Jesus' saying that one "should render unto Caesar the things that are Caesar's"?

These are difficult questions to answer, and scholars have come up with a range of possible solutions over the years. But on one thing virtually everyone agrees. Even if the rest of Jesus' life was of little interest or relevance to Paul, or even if he may not have known as much about Jesus' life as the later Gospel writers, there was one thing that really did matter to him—possibly mattered to him so much that all else paled in comparison. For Paul, what really mattered was that Jesus was crucified and was raised from the dead.

The reason this is what mattered to Paul—more than, say, Jesus' walking on the water or his Sermon on the Mount—is that Paul had come to see that it was through the death of Jesus that God had reconciled the world to himself. As I have intimated, before his conversion Paul was a religious Jew who considered the Christian claims about Jesus to be blasphemous. Jesus' followers had said that Jesus, who was crucified by the Romans, was the messiah of God. But most Jews, Paul included, found this claim to be ridiculous at best, insidious and insane at worst. This is because—as I indicated in an earlier chapter—Jews who were expecting a messiah were certain that he would be a great and dynamic figure who would execute God's will here on earth, such as by overthrowing God's enemies in a mighty act of power. And was Jesus like this? Quite the opposite—rather than being a powerful warrior who drove the Romans out of the Promised Land, Jesus was an itinerant preacher who had gotten on the wrong side of the law and been unceremoniously tortured and crucified by the enemies of God. He was the furthest thing imaginable from a messiah.

I try to illustrate to my students the kind of gut reaction most first-century Jews had to this claim that Jesus was the messiah. Imagine that someone were to tell you that David Koresh was the almighty Son of God, the Savior of the world. David Koresh? The guy at Waco who was killed by the FBI? Yup: he's the Lord of the universe! Yeah, right.

This claim strikes most of us as so absurd, so far beyond the pale, that we can't even begin to take it seriously. That's how most Jews reacted to the claim that Jesus was the messiah. He was so far from what the messiah would be like that . . . well, that if anyone seriously thought so, they were either deranged or blasphemous. To say that God's messiah had been squashed by his enemies like a mosquito is a slur not only on one's intelligence but on God himself. What kind of God is it that sends a messiah to be nailed to a cross?

Before his conversion Paul tried to stamp out this ridiculous claim and so persecuted those who made it. But then something happened. According to his own account, God revealed the truth to him through a vision of Jesus himself after his death. Paul doesn't go into as much detail as we would like, but it's clear that he believed he had actually seen Jesus with his own eyes (Gal. 1:16; 1 Cor.

15:8). That convinced him that Jesus was still alive—or rather that he had come back to life. And if Jesus had come back to life, that changed everything.

The only way Jesus could come back to life is if God raised him from the dead. But if God raised him from the dead, that must mean that Jesus really was the one specially favored by God. If God showered his special favor on Jesus, why, then, had he been crucified? That doesn't sound like much of a treat from the Almighty. To make sense of it, Paul came to think that the crucifixion of Jesus was necessary before God. God, in fact, had arranged for Jesus to die in this horrific way. But why? Obviously not because of something he had done wrong, since he was the one specially favored by God. It must have been for some other reason, then. Jesus must have been killed not because of his own sins but for the sins of others. Jesus' death was a sacrifice before God, a sacrifice that covered over the sins that others had committed. The proof was in the resurrection. By raising Jesus from the dead, God demonstrated that Jesus' death was all part of his plan to bring salvation to the world (see Rom. 3:21–28).

For Paul, everyone has sinned and so has to pay the penalty of sin: death. But God substituted Jesus' death for others. All those who accept the payment of the penalty that Jesus suffered can have their own sins removed. It is by faith in Jesus' death and resurrection that a person is made right with God.

Once Paul came to see this, it changed everything. Christ was no longer seen as being under God's curse. He really was God's Christ, his messiah. And being right with God could come in only one way—the way God himself had provided in the death of his beloved Son.[2]

This—at least in part—is why Paul hardly mentions other aspects of Jesus' life. They don't really matter to him. What really mattered was Christ's death. That's why when Paul writes to the Corinthians he can say with some pride that "I knew nothing among you except for Christ, and him crucified" (1 Cor. 2:2). And that's why he can later remind his Corinthian congregation the message he had preached as having primary importance:

> For I delivered over to you as the most important matters what I also received, that Christ died on behalf of our sins, in accordance with the Scriptures, and that he was buried; and that he was raised on the third day in accordance with the Scriptures, and that he appeared to Cephas, then to the Twelve, then to more than five hundred others at one time. (1 Cor. 15:3–5)

It was Christ's death and resurrection—not his birth, not his life, not his miracles, not his teachings—that brought salvation. For Paul, these were the only things that ultimately mattered.

Jesus in Our Earliest Gospel

I won't be explaining Christ's significance for every one of our early Christian authors. But it is worth noting that some of these authors shared Paul's understanding of Jesus' death and put it in narrative form. Nowhere can this be seen better than in our earliest Gospel writer, the anonymous author of the Gospel of Mark.

An obvious difference between Mark's view of Jesus and Paul's is that Mark does not think the death and resurrection of Jesus are the only things that ultimately matter. Jesus' life matters as well. And so Mark begins with an account of Jesus' baptism, at the beginning of his ministry, by John the Baptist; the majority of his Gospel describes Jesus' teachings, his healings, his exorcisms, his encounters with his opponents among the Jewish leaders, his final trip to Jerusalem to celebrate Passover, and so on. For Mark, the life of Jesus mattered, in part because it wasn't just *anyone* who was crucified and was raised from the dead. It was this particular person—Jesus, the son of God, whose entire ministry, not just his death, reflected his special standing before God.

At the same time, Mark (and the other Gospels) has sometimes been aptly called a "Passion narrative with a long introduction." What scholars mean by that is that even though the bulk of the account deals with Jesus' life rather than his death, it is his death that drives the plot of the narrative and that is on the author's mind, and imprinted on his page, from the very beginning. Fully six of Mark's sixteen chapters deal with Jesus' final days in Jerusalem. And throughout the first ten chapters Mark is always looking ahead to Jesus' death, as he repeatedly indicates that this is how it will all end. Like Paul, Mark sees this death as what ultimately mattered for salvation. As Jesus himself is reported as saying in Mark: "For the Son of Man [i.e., Jesus himself] came not to be served, but to serve, and to give his life as a ransom for many" (Mark 10:45). In other words, Jesus' life was a life of service for others (hence the miracles and the teachings to his followers); but this life culminated in the greatest act of service of all. Jesus willingly died for the sake of others that their sins might be redeemed.

Mark's Jesus is very human. Some readers have thought he is all too human—as in the Garden of Gethsemane, where he pleads with God three times not to have to go through with his fate. But go through with it he does, even though he seems to be in shock through the entire Passion narrative, saying scarcely anything at his own trial and nothing during his torment and crucifixion—until at the end he cries out to God, asking why he has been forsaken. But even if this is a genuine question of the dying Jesus (see my discussion in chapter 2 above), Mark himself and his reader know the divine answer. In Mark, at the moment that Jesus dies two things happen that show why all this had to take place. Just as Jesus breathes his last, the curtain in the Temple is ripped in half, and the centurion confesses that Jesus really is the Son of God.

No other events better explain Mark's understanding of Jesus. The curtain in the Temple was the thick veil that separated the room called the Holy of Holies from the rest of the sacred precincts. The Holy of Holies was where God himself was believed to dwell (here on earth). No one could go into this room except once a year on the Day of Atonement—Yom Kippur—when the Jewish high priest would enter in order to make two sacrifices, one for his own sins and the other for the sins of the people. According to Mark, at Jesus' death the veil was destroyed, and with it what separates God from his people. Now God is accessible to all; he is not cordoned or closed off. The perfect sacrifice has been made; everyone can be in God's presence.

The centurion overseeing the crucifixion realizes it. Throughout this Gospel, no one could understand who Jesus was—the Son of God who had to die. At his death, though, the centurion makes the confession that no one else could make. Jesus is the Son of God not despite the fact that he had to die but precisely in his death. He is the Son of God whose death is what matters before God.

Confirmation of this view comes in the following scene of the narrative, when three days later several women come to give Jesus' body a proper burial, only to find him missing from the grave. There they learn the supernatural truth of the significance of Jesus' death. God has raised him from the dead. Jesus is the Son of God who died and was raised. This is the view of Paul, put in narrative form.

Jesus in the Gospel of Thomas

This Pauline understanding of Christ became the dominant view in early Christianity. In fact, it literally became the canonical view, in that it is the view that made it into the canon of Scripture, as Paul's letters along with Mark (and Matthew and Luke, based on Mark) make up a large portion of the New Testament. But there were other views about the significance of Jesus that stood at just the opposite end of the theological spectrum, views that came to be excluded from consideration and, as a result, found no representation in the canon as it has come down to us.

One such view is found in the Coptic Gospel of Thomas, which I have referred to on several occasions throughout our discussions. This author claims to be an authority on Christ, just as Paul did. Paul's authority derived from his experience of the resurrected Jesus. Not so with the author of Thomas, who never refers to having seen Jesus alive after his death. Instead, his authority is more directly rooted in who he is, or at least who he claims to be. He calls himself Didymus Judas Thomas. The name *Didymus* is Greek for twin, and *Thomas* also means twin, but in Aramaic, the language of Jesus and his disciples. So this person is Judas the twin. But the twin of whom?

In the New Testament, Jesus is said to have four brothers (see Mark 6:3), one of whom is called Judas, or Jude. Early legends from the church of Syria indicate that this Jude was not simply Jesus' brother but his identical twin. It is not clear how the Syrian Christians who held this view understood it to work: that is, if Jesus' mother conceived him as a virgin, how is it that he could have a twin brother? Possibly these Christians had other myths in mind—for example, the Greek myths about the divine Heracles, son of Zeus, who had a twin brother, born obviously at the same time and from the same mother, a woman named Alcmena. This twin brother, however, was the son of Alcmena's husband, Amphytrion. That is to say, both Zeus and Amphytrion made Alcmena pregnant, and the result was twins. Did the Syrian Christians who told of Jesus' twin brother have something similar in mind, that Mary had become pregnant by the Holy Spirit and also by Joseph, and that the result was twins?

Whether or not that was their thinking, it is clear from such apocryphal texts as the Acts of Thomas that this Judas Thomas was Jesus' twin brother. It appears that the Coptic Gospel of Thomas is claiming to be written by this person. However this twinness was explained, we can understand the appeal of drawing on such authority for a Gospel account. What better authority for knowing the significance of Jesus than his own twin brother?

It is striking that this author seems to have just the opposite view of Jesus from Paul. Not only does the Gospel of Thomas never describe Jesus' death and resurrection, it never even mentions it.[3] Jesus' crucifixion appears to be irrelevant to this author. It certainly is not what makes a person right with God. What matters about Jesus is his secret teachings. And that is all the Gospel provides: there are no narratives here, nothing about what Jesus did during his life or what happened at his Passion and resurrection. The Gospel contains 114 of his teachings. Eternal life comes to the one who understands them.

The key verse for this view is the one that begins his account:

These are the secret sayings of the living Jesus, and Didymus Judas Thomas wrote them down. And he said, "The one who finds the meaning of these words will not taste death."[4]

Salvation comes not by believing in Jesus' death but by finding the truth of his secret sayings.

I argued earlier that the Gospel of Thomas is best understood as a Gnostic Gospel—even though it does not go to great lengths to narrate the Gnostic myths about how the divine world came into existence and how our own, fallen, material world was created, leading to our entrapment here. In my view, rather than explain this myth, the Gospel of Thomas presupposes it, as is evident in a number of its sayings, which are secret. Learning what they mean—having true knowledge (gnosis)—is what brings eternal life.

For this Gospel, the material world we live in is dead and worthless: "Whoever has come to understand this world has found a corpse" (Saying 56). This world came into being not as a pleasant home for spiritual beings but as a place of entrapment for them: "If the flesh came into being because of spirit, it is a wonder [i.e., an amazing insight]. But if spirit came into being because of the body, it is a wonder of wonders [i.e., beyond possibility]. Indeed, I am amazed at how this great wealth [the spirit] has made its home in this poverty [the body]" (Saying 29). Some of us don't belong here in this material world: "If they say to you, 'Where did you come from?' say to them 'We came from the light, the place where the light came into being on its own accord'" (Saying 50). We should not act as if this is our home: "Become passers-by" (Saying 42). For this world is only our temporary dwelling place: "This heaven will pass away, and the one above it will pass away" (Saying 11). To escape it, we must transcend the physical trappings of our bodies: "When you disrobe without being ashamed and take up your garments [i.e., your physical part] and place them under your feet like little children and tread on them, then you will see the son of the living one and you will not be afraid" (Saying 37).

Who is Jesus, then? He is the one who comes from above to teach those who are entrapped in matter the truth that brings eternal life—even though for now they are too far enmeshed in their material selves to see it: "Jesus said, 'I took my place in the midst of the world, and I appeared to them in flesh. I found all of them intoxicated; I found none of them thirsty. And my soul became afflicted for the sons of men, because they are blind in their hearts and do not have sight. . . . For the moment they are intoxicated. When they shake off their wine, then they will repent'" (Saying 28). But those who receive his teachings and understand them will realize their divine nature and understand the truths that bring salvation: "Jesus said: 'He who will drink from my mouth will become like me. I myself shall become he, and the things that are hidden will be revealed to him'" (Saying 108).

Jesus in the Gospel of Judas

And so we have a theological spectrum. On one end is the apostle Paul, who saw Christ's death and resurrection as the be-all and end-all. What mattered was that Christ died for sins and was raised from the dead. Everything else about Jesus was completely subservient to his Passion. On the other end is the Gospel of Thomas, for which the death and resurrection of Jesus had no bearing on salvation. The way to have eternal life was by understanding his secret revelations, the teachings that could liberate a person from the entrapment in this corpse of our existence, the material world and the human body.

It should be clear that if this is the spectrum, the Gospel of Judas falls neatly on the side of Thomas. What matters to this author is explained at the outset:

> The secret account of the revelation that Jesus spoke in conversation with Judas Iscariot during a week three days before he celebrated the Passover.

Just as for Thomas it was the "secret words" that counted, here it is the "secret . . . revelation." Even though these conversations with Judas take place eight days before Jesus' death, what matters to this account is not the death itself but the revelations leading up to it. Despite the fact that this is an expression of the importance of Jesus in narrative form—as was Mark—this account is anything but "a Passion introduction with a long introduction," for here there is no Passion. The account ends with the betrayal of Judas. There is no account of the crucifixion, no mention of the resurrection. For this author, these things are not what matter for salvation. It is Jesus' secret teachings.

The death of Jesus does not matter to this author, in part, because the body of Jesus does not matter. Jesus, in fact, does not have a real human body at all.

He appears to his disciples in various forms ("as a child"). That's why he can leave the disciples at will to return to "another great and holy generation"— that is, to the divine realm, his place of origin and real home. Jesus does not come from this world; he comes from above. He is temporarily here to reveal the truths necessary for salvation.

To the extent he has any kind of body, it is a body that is not destined to die for the sake of others. His body is simply the medium through which he can deliver his secret teachings. That's why the greatest thing that can be done on behalf of Jesus is to give him the opportunity to escape his body, to return to his heavenly home. Judas is the one who makes this possible, and that's why Judas is said to "exceed" all the others: he is the one, says Jesus, "who will sacrifice the man that clothes me" (56:19–21). Jesus' body is simply a temporary dwelling place; once it is sacrificed he will escape the trappings of this material world.

That's why there is no hint of a resurrection in this text. Unlike in Paul and the Gospels of the New Testament, for this Gospel the climax of Jesus' story is not his victorious emergence from the tomb on the third day in a glorified body. There will not *be* a glorified body for Jesus in this Gospel, no resumption of a physical existence, no ascension to heaven, no sitting bodily at the right hand of God. There simply can't be a resurrection for this Gospel. For other early Christian writers such as Paul, the doctrine of the resurrection is an affirmation of the inherent goodness of the physical creation. It is a statement that even though this material world has fallen through sin, the one who created it will redeem and perfect it. But for the Gospel of Judas, the creation is not good and it will not be redeemed. The physical world is flawed at its very core. It is materiality itself that is the problem. Jesus will transcend this material world, this lowly existence created by a bloodthirsty rebel and a fool. When his body dies, his soul will return to the Pleroma and live an eternal existence in the world of the spirit.

For his followers to be saved, they too will need to escape their bodies. They too need to return to "that great generation." Mere mortals can never do that. Only those who have a spark within can do so. Those who come to know who Jesus is—he is from the "realm of Barbelo"—realize that they are like him: they can then "bring out the perfect person" and "stand before" Jesus (35:9–10, 18). The disciples of Jesus "lack the strength" to do that: they know neither him nor themselves. Only Judas does; only he can stand before Jesus; only he will eventually be glorified by escaping his body to return to the realm whence he came.

This Gospel's revelation of how the divine and material realms came into being is, to be sure, full of mystery and enigma. It is hard to follow, let alone understand. But who said the secret knowledge for salvation should be easy? Only true Gnostics can appreciate and grasp this teaching. Those who fail to do so live under the misconception that this world is the creation of the true God. That's the mistake the disciples make, thinking that the creator God is to be worshiped—for example, in the eucharistic celebration. Jesus finds this mistake laughable (34:1–3). This world is not good, and neither are the divine beings who made it. The true God is completely immaterial, the Great Invisible Spirit. Only those who ultimately derive from this God can know who he is, and only they can know who they themselves are, spirits fallen from the realm above, trapped in matter, able to be freed only by learning the meaning of Jesus' secret revelations delivered to his most intimate and faithful follower, Judas Iscariot.

Portrayals of the Disciples

We have repeatedly seen that the twelve disciples, apart from Judas, do not fare well in the Gospel of Judas. To help contextualize this portrayal, I would again like to lay out the spectrum of opinion about the apostles in early Christianity. Most early Christians, of course, understood the apostles as the spokespeople for Christ, the authorized voices of those who knew Jesus and so could be trusted to convey his message. But not everyone thought so.

The Twelve Disciples in the Acts of the Apostles

The earliest narrative to tell about the lives of the apostles—or at least of some of them—is the New Testament book of Acts. As you might expect, here the disciples are portrayed in a most positive light.

As I pointed out earlier, the book of Acts is actually the second volume of the two-volume work produced by Luke, the author of the third Gospel.[5] Whereas the first volume is concerned with the birth, life, death, and resurrection of Jesus, the second narrates events that happened afterward, as the gospel of his salvation is spread throughout the known world, starting in Jerusalem and ending in Rome, the capital city of the Empire. Just as the New Testament Gospels are not disinterested portrayals of the life of Jesus but are written from the theological vantage points of their authors, so too with the book of Acts. This is not a bare-bones account of events as they really happened (if such a kind of history ever could be written). It is told from a particular perspective, with its narrative shaped by the theological views of its author.

In this case, the author's view is that the spread of the church throughout the Roman Empire happened entirely through the power of God's Holy Spirit, who directed the course of the mission and saw to it that nothing could make it grind to a halt. After Jesus' ascension to heaven, the disciples gather together and, at Peter's urging, draw lots to determine who will replace Judas among the Twelve. Judas's death itself, as we have seen, is said to have been a fulfillment of God's plan, as set forth in the Scriptures. So too is the election of his replacement. We're not told why the apostolic band has to be twelve in number; presumably it is because that is the number Jesus had originally chosen. In any event, the remaining eleven decide that someone among the broader group of Jesus' followers, who has accompanied them from the beginning of Jesus' ministry at his baptism by John, needs to be chosen to be, with them, a witness to his resurrection (Acts. 1:21–22). Lots are drawn, and a man named Matthias is elected.

You might think that since this book is entitled the Acts of the Apostles, the rest of the narrative would describe the various activities of the Twelve. But in fact that is not what happens. Most of the Twelve—including the newly elected Matthias—drop out of the picture, never to be mentioned by name again. Only two of them, Peter and John, play significant roles in the early chapters, and the final two-thirds of the book is almost entirely about an apostle not among the Twelve, Paul, who converts to follow Christ in Acts 9 and whose missionary journeys to spread the Gospel are the subject of much of the rest of the book.

At the same time, the apostolic band of twelve is important for the author of Acts, for this is the group that guarantees a continuity between the ministry of Jesus during his life (they witness it) and the spread of the gospel after his death (they authorize it). The apostles are the first to preach the gospel, as the Holy Spirit comes upon them on Pentecost, fifty days after Jesus' death (Acts 2). Miraculous signs accompany their reception of the Spirit, nonbelievers observe what has happened, and thousands convert. The apostle Peter is portrayed as the early leader of the group, and his miracles and sermons lead to impressive results as the small band of Jesus' followers grows by leaps and bounds (Acts 3, 4). The apostles direct the church in Jerusalem, and when the gospel is taken to other cities and lands, they are the ones who sanction the missionary efforts of others and provide stability in the leadership of the church (Acts 7, 10).

Luke's view of the apostles is thus that they are the Spirit-endowed leaders of Jesus' followers after his death, who are able to do miracles and preach to the masses, leading to enormous numbers of conversions. And even though Paul becomes the central figure of the story, one of its key emphases is that Paul did not proclaim a different Gospel than the others did. He is simply the one chosen to take the message further afield—he converts Gentiles in lands as far off as Asia Minor, Macedonia, Achaia, and eventually Rome.

The unity of Paul with the Twelve is one of the most important themes of the book of Acts. This unity matters because the message and mission of Paul in Acts are different from the message and mission of Jesus in Luke. Paul's message is that the death and resurrection of Jesus brings salvation to all people, Jew and Gentile alike. Not everyone agreed on the implications of this message, and Luke wants to show that the disagreements lay only on the margins. There was no discontinuity within the apostolic band itself, even though an outsider is the one who most avidly proclaims the message.

The potential for discontinuity is there even in Acts, however. The problem is that there were people—both as portrayed in Acts and historically—who thought that the salvation of Jesus was meant only for Jews. Some of Jesus' earliest followers stressed that Jesus was the Jewish messiah sent from the

Jewish God to the Jewish people in fulfillment of the Jewish law. The natural implication, for them, was that anyone who wanted to worship this Jewish God through his messiah obviously first had to become Jewish. Not according to Paul, though. Paul maintained—both in his letters and in Acts—that this salvation was for all people, Jew and Gentile. Since all people had incurred a debt of sin before God, all people had to have that debt canceled before God. The way of salvation was the same for both Jew and Gentile. It was Jesus' death and resurrection. As a result, God's salvation goes to all people, whether Jew or Gentile. And so Gentiles do not have to become Jews in order to be Christian.

This was Paul's own message. Luke wants to stress that in this he was not contradicting what the original twelve apostles of Jesus said. Many of the stories Luke tells serve to emphasize the point. In Acts, it is the disciple Peter who first learns that God intends to save the Gentiles without requiring them first to become Jews: God sends him a vision that conveys the message (Acts 10). Peter then is the first to convert a Gentile to the faith (Acts 10). Paul begins his mission to Gentiles only afterward (Acts 13). When questions arise concerning whether these Gentile converts need to begin keeping the Jewish law, a council of the apostles is called in Jerusalem, and there is unanimity and enthusiastic endorsement of the Pauline position: Gentiles are to remain Gentiles. They do not need to convert to Judaism. On this Paul and the Twelve agree (Acts 15).

It is not clear that the real, historical Paul and the real, historical Twelve actually did agree on this matter. At least as Paul himself reports in his letter to the Galatians, he and Peter had a rather nasty falling-out over the issue (Gal. 2:11–14). But for the author of Acts, at least, Paul's mission was completely in line with the mission of the Twelve. All of them were empowered by God for this mission. God is the one who ensured that it would all go according to plan. The miracles performed in the course of the mission demonstrated God's oversight. And there was nothing that anyone outside the apostolic band could do to stop it or even slow it down.

The twelve apostles, then, are the ones who provide the divinely appointed continuity between the ministry of Jesus and the mission of the early church.

The Twelve in the Orthodox Tradition

This view of the disciples in Acts became the normative account. Throughout the writings of church fathers later acknowledged as "orthodox" (i.e., having the "right opinions") this basic view came to be expanded and solidified. The apostles were the heirs of Jesus' teaching and were the guarantors of its truth. This was to become a heated issue in early Christianity, as soon as there were various views of "the truth," all of them claiming to be the *real* truth and all of them claiming to have come from Jesus himself. When there were people such as the Marcionites claiming that there were two gods, not just one, and that this was the view of Jesus, who was to say they were wrong? When various groups of Gnostics emerged, claiming that there were large numbers of divine beings and that the ones who created this world were inferior and ignorant, why *not* believe they were right? Moreover, on the practical level of the nuts-and-bolts management of the church, if there were different church leaders all claiming to represent the truth of the gospel given by Jesus, but they represented different points of view, which ones were to be accepted and followed?

Very quickly the questions of authority and leadership became pressing matters among early Christian communities. In fact, an appeal to the apostles for the support of a particular point of view is already evident in the New Testament itself—witness the book of Acts. Another book, written not long after Acts, deals with the problem head-on. This is a book now known as 1 Clement, an "orthodox" letter, but one that did not come to be included in the New Testament (even though some early Christians did consider it to be Scripture).[6] This letter was written to the Christians of Corinth by Christians living in Rome. The occasion was a kind of ecclesiastical coup in Corinth: the elders in charge of the Corinthian church had been ousted from office, replaced by different leaders. The Roman Christians found this kind of political infighting shameful in its disregard for the unity of the church; even more, it was a violation of the orderliness God had instituted for the community of the faithful. The author of 1 Clement insists that the deposed elders be returned to their positions of power. Part of his argument—it's a very long argument overall, in a very long letter—is that the leaders of the Christian churches had been appointed by those who had themselves been appointed by the apostles. The apostles, in turn, had been appointed by Christ, and Christ had come from God. Thus, those who oppose the leaders of the churches are in fact opposed to God (1 Clem. 42–44).

This is a kind of argument for apostolic succession—the view that the authority for Christian leadership can be traced in a line of descent all the way back to the apostles. The most familiar form of this argument is still seen in the Roman Catholic Church, as the pope is understood to stand in a direct line of succession all the way back to Peter, the first bishop of the church in Rome.

Before there were any popes, there were a number of Christians who appealed to apostolic succession in support of their particular views. A slightly different form of the argument can be found in the writings of heresy hunters such as Irenaeus, whom we have met before, and the third-century writer Tertullian. When Tertullian was opposing groups of Gnostics, he had a very simple argument that ruled their views out of court. According to Tertullian, the teaching of the bishops of the leading Christian churches are the only ones that have been sanctioned by God: Christ appointed the apostles, the apostles appointed their own successors, their successors appointed the current bishops of the leading churches. Whatever these successors taught, therefore, came straight through a line of succession from Christ himself. Anyone who taught anything different—such as those nefarious Gnostics—obviously taught doctrines opposed to Christ (Tertullian, *Prescription of the Heretics*).

As you might imagine, not everyone agreed that Tertullian and Christians like him were the only ones who proclaimed the views of the apostles. There were Gnostics, for example, who claimed that their own views were the ones that stood in the apostolic line. I've earlier mentioned the Gnostic Basilides, who taught that Christ pulled an identity switch at the crucifixion, making himself look like Simon of Cyrene (the man who carried his cross), and making Simon look like himself—so the Romans crucified the wrong man, while Jesus stood aside laughing. This might sound like a terribly strange (and cruel) teaching, but the followers of Basilides claimed that Basilides had been a disciple of Glaukias, who had been a disciple of Peter. So too, the Valentinian Gnostics adhered to the teachings of Valentinus, whom they claimed was the disciple of a man named Theudas, who had been a disciple of the apostle Paul.[7] The doctrine of apostolic succession could be, and was, advanced by different sides, all arguing for a different theological point of view.

The Twelve Disciples in Marcion and the Apocalypse of Peter

There were other Christian teachers, however, who took a different line altogether in trying to authorize their perspectives. These stood on the opposite end of the spectrum from those who thought that the twelve apostles could be appealed to in order to guarantee the truthfulness of a particular view of the gospel. This alternative opinion could point to the early Christian traditions—for example, those that we saw in the Gospel of Mark—where the disciples are regularly shown to misunderstand Jesus and fail to comprehend his message. According to this other point of view, the disciples never did "get it."

We have already seen this view in some of the authors we discussed in earlier chapters. The second-century theologian and teacher Marcion, for example, claimed that the disciples of Jesus, constantly upbraided by their master for failing to understand, continued to think that he came from the Jewish god in fulfillment of the Jewish law. Because they never understood that he was from the other God, the one who had not created this world or called Israel to be his people, Christ had to call another apostle to proclaim his message. That is why he appeared to Paul on the road to Damascus, to reveal to him the truth of the gospel. And that is why Paul regularly contrasted his gospel with the law. The gospel came from the God of Christ, the law from the god of the Jews. These two were irreconcilably at odds. This is why Paul had such heated arguments with Peter over whether Gentiles had to become Jews in order to be Christians (Gal. 2:11–14). According to Marcion, Paul had it right, Peter had it wrong: true faith in Christ renounced the god of the Jews, it did not worship him. The goal of true religion was to escape his clutches, not obey his rules.

A very different theology is found in one of the Nag Hammadi documents, the Coptic Apocalypse of Peter. This is a Gnostic text that presupposes not just two but multiple divine beings. But the attack on the leaders of the Christian churches who claimed to be following the teachings of Jesus are equally harsh.

These leaders, the "bishop and deacons" who claim to have "received their authority from God," are in fact "dry canals" (no living water in them; Apoc. Pet. 79). They are said to "have no perception." Their views are scoffed at and mocked—by Jesus himself, who laughs at their foolishness.

> They . . . hold fast to the name of a dead man, thinking that they will become pure. But they will become defiled. . . . And they will be ruled heretically. For some of them will blaspheme the truth and proclaim evil teaching. And they will say evil things to each other. (Apoc. Pet. 74)

So not everyone agreed that the twelve apostles had a corner on the truth, or that the leaders of the churches after their days could be relied upon to proclaim the real message of Christ.

The Twelve in the Gospel of Judas

We have already seen that the Twelve do not come off well in the Gospel of Judas. If the spectrum of early Christian views goes from the book of Acts and Tertullian, who portray the apostles as guarantors of the truth, to Marcion and the Coptic Apocalypse of Peter, who portray the apostles as misunderstanding Christ until the end, the Gospel of Judas stands firmly on this far side of the spectrum.

It is true that in the Gospel of Judas Jesus picks the Twelve to fulfill a noble purpose. We are told that they were chosen "since some [people] walked in the way of righteousness while others walked in their transgressions" (33:9–14). We might suspect, then, that the Twelve are chosen as representatives of the former group. But there is nothing positive said about them in the rest of the text.

The narrative begins with the disciples' naive celebration of a eucharistic meal, praising "their" god—that is the creator of this world. Jesus laughs and informs them that they are doing this "because it is through this that your god will be praised" (34:6–11) This simply confuses them, since they assume that "you are . . . the son of our god." No, he isn't. And they don't understand. Jesus has no qualms in telling them, "No generation of the people that are among you will know me." Matters devolve from there, as the disciples get "angry and infuriated" and begin "blaspheming him in their hearts" (34:13–22).

When Jesus challenges them to stand before him, they declare with some bravado, "We have the strength." But in fact none of them could "dare to stand before" him except for Judas, the hero of the text. The others cannot stand before Christ because they do not have the spark of divinity within them that can make them his equal (35:6–10).

From that point on, the narrative separates Judas out from the others. Jesus pulls him, and him alone, aside to reveal the "mysteries of the kingdom." Jesus tells him that he will be replaced among the Twelve, so that they "may again come to completion with their god" (36:3–4). That is why later in the text Jesus speaks of Judas as the "thirteenth." He stands outside the Twelve as the only one who truly understands who Jesus is.

Not only do they fail to understand Jesus, they also lead others astray and engage in wild acts of lawlessness that reveal their true character. When the Twelve have a vision of the priests offering sacrifices in the Temple, they see some of them sacrificing their own children and wives, engaging in sexual immorality, and committing "a multitude of sins and deeds of lawlessness" (38:22–23).[8] On one level, of course, this is a castigation of the Jews and their religion, a particularly odious example of early Christian anti-Jewish slander. But the vision functions on more than one level, for when Jesus interprets it, he tells the Twelve that the twelve priests they had seen in fact were themselves. The cattle they sacrifice are the people that the Twelve lead astray. The acts of immorality are the only things not symbolic; as I indicated earlier, these really are the heinous activities of these alleged followers of Jesus.

Moreover, since Jesus seems to indicate that the apostles' followers will behave in a similar way, this text appears to be attacking not just the Twelve but the so-called apostolic successors. In the orthodox writings of the period, apostolic succession was used to guarantee the truth of the claims of the leaders of the Christian churches. Here it is used to show the continued misunderstanding and incomprehensible misbehavior of those who claim the apostolic mantle for themselves. The leaders of the apostolic churches preach error and propagate immorality.

Judas, on the other hand, represents the truth, and so it is no surprise to learn that in his own vision he observes the Twelve stoning him. Error cannot abide truth, and the apostles, the "ministers of error," cannot stand to have Judas in their midst. They kill the apostle of truth and replace him with one of their own. He, then, becomes the thirteenth. On the human level this may have seemed tragic—Jesus tells Judas that it will cause him tremendous grief. On the divine level, however, this is all to the good. Judas rises above his earthly station, he learns the truth of the revelation of Christ—which Jesus gives to him alone—and eventually he returns to the divine realm whence he came. And the others? They are bound to the earth and its creator, and perish as bodies with no souls.

At the end, it is only Judas who remains with Jesus when his enemies come to arrest him. Possibly the others feared for their lives. As material creatures, what else is there to live for, apart from life in the flesh? Give that up, and you give up everything. Not understanding Jesus' teaching that this material world is not the creation of the true God, not having a spark of divinity within them that will transcend their bodies, not having anything to live for but this present life itself, they have all fled. Only Judas stays until the end.

Judas in the Gospel of Judas

The main figure in this Gospel, then, is Judas. As I've noted, this is not the Gospel according to Judas. It is the Gospel about Judas.[9]

For both Jesus and the Twelve, we found it useful to situate the views of the Gospel in the wider spectrum of Christian thought. It would be useful to paint a spectrum of Christian opinion about Judas as well, but in fact there does not seem to be much of a spectrum. Judas is portrayed in a consistently negative light in all of the Christian authors that we have examined.

Our earliest mention of him, in the Gospel of Mark, does not indicate why he betrayed Jesus, but it does indicate that Jesus claimed that "it would have been better for that one not to have been born" (Mark 14:21). The tradition goes straight down from there. In Matthew Judas betrays Jesus because he wants the cash; in Luke he does so because he is inspired by the Devil; in John it turns out that he himself *is* a devil. In the second-century Papias he suffers the horrible torments of bloating, worms, and pus. In the fifth-century Arabic Infancy Gospel he is a nasty Satan-inspired biter of a child from the beginning. In the medieval Golden Legend he is a fratricide and patricide who sleeps with his own mother. In late Christian anti-Semitic rhetoric he becomes the proto-typical Jew: a greedy, money-grubbing, God-denying Christ-killer. The Christian tradition has consistently and increasingly portrayed Judas in a bad light.

The Gospel of Judas provides an alternative vision. It is true that over the years some Christians have wondered if the consistent denigration of Judas was fair. Theologically, some have asked, if Christ had to die for the sins of the world, and Judas is the one that made it possible, wasn't that a good thing? Something that Christ himself wanted? Moreover, some scholars have noted that with the passing of time our ancient traditions portray Judas in *increasingly* villainous ways. Could it be that in the very earliest traditions, which have now been lost, Judas was seen as an intimate of Jesus who simply did his master's will?[10]

If Judas ever was portrayed this way, there is no surviving evidence of it, no text that speaks of Judas in any positive way—until now. The Gospel of Judas stands alone in insisting that Judas was not only close to Jesus but also was the only one among the disciples who understood who Jesus was and did what he wanted.

The Gospel is written to explain the revelation given to Judas, the "secret account," which can bring salvation. Judas alone receives this revelation. The other disciples continue in their misperception, thinking of Jesus as the son of the Creator God. Only Judas knows that he comes from the "realm of Barbelo," that is, the spiritual realm far above that made by the creator. Judas alone can stand in Jesus' presence, for he alone has a spark of divinity within him, comparable to the divine being housed in the body of Jesus. It is true that early in the Gospel Judas cannot look Jesus in the eyes. But at this stage, he has not yet learned the secret knowledge that Jesus is to reveal.

Near the end of the Gospel, all that is changed. After Judas receives Jesus' revelation, he is told that he "exceeds all of them"—that is, all of the other so-called followers of Jesus. Jesus then tells Judas that the "great generation of Adam will be exalted"—exalted, in fact, to that position that it held "from the eternal realms," prior to the creation of "heaven, earth, and the angels" (57:10–14). This is the generation that comes from the divine realm, the people who are fortunate enough to have a spark of divinity within them. And who is the head of this generation? Judas himself.

> Lift up your eyes and look at the cloud and the light within it and the stars surrounding it. The star that leads the way is your star. (57:19–20)

Every eternal soul is connected with a star—a divine being that exists above this world. Judas is told to gaze on the cloud that is the manifestation of the presence of the Great Invisible Spirit. The stars of the saved, of "that generation," surround this cloud. And Judas's star leads them all. As Marvin Meyer has humorously put it, Judas really is the star of this text.[11]

That is especially clear from what happens next. Judas looks and sees the cloud, and then "he enters it." Judas observes his own future transfiguration, his own transcendence from this awful world of matter. He will return to his heavenly home, to dwell with his fellow divine beings forever.

⌘

CHAPTER NINE

Who Was Judas Iscariot?

I n my courses on the New Testament I teach two different approaches to the early Christian Gospels. One involves looking at these books as pieces of literature, seeing how they portray Jesus. Each of our surviving accounts of Jesus' life has a distinctive message, unique to the views of its author. Thus Matthew's view of Jesus is not the same as Mark's, Mark's is not the same as John's, John's is not the same as Thomas's or Peter's or Philip's, and so on. Each author has his own slant, his own theological perspective, his own overall purpose in telling his story.

The other approach tries to establish what Jesus himself was really like, what he actually said, did, and experienced. This approach accepts as a given that each Gospel writer has a point to make in his portrayal of Jesus—or rather, a number of points. But it tries to get behind these books as pieces of literature to establish what actually happened in history. In other words, it is one thing to ask how Mark or John portrays Jesus' words and deeds; it is another thing to ask what Jesus really did say and do. If the first is a literary approach, this second is a historical approach.[1]

The reason we need both approaches is that the Gospels are not simply repositories of data from the life of Jesus. They are not eyewitness testimonies or disinterested reportings of fact. They are not objective descriptions of events. They are literary products that try to make theological points. This is why they are called Gospels instead of histories. The term *Gospel* literally means "good news." These books proclaim the good news of Jesus' life, death, and resurrection. They are more like sermons or proclamations than data sheets.

The clearest evidence that the Gospels do not present objective data from the life of Jesus is that they differ from one another in so many ways, both major and minor. Virtually every story they tell bears the imprint of their authors, who have retold the stories in light of their own points of view and the message (the gospel) they are trying to convey.

Some of my undergraduate students need to be convinced that the Gospels are not simply factual statements about historical events, so I have them do a simple exercise of comparison: I have them take a passage found in more than one Gospel and compare what each author has to say in it. It doesn't matter whether my students choose the accounts of Jesus' birth in Matthew and Luke, of his betrayal and arrest in Mark and John, of his crucifixion in Matthew and Luke, of his resurrection in all four of the Gospels. They will always find differences. Some of these differences are very difficult—impossible, I would say—to reconcile. Why is that? Because each author has his own perspective on the life and death of Jesus.

This means that each author needs to be read for what he has to say—which is my literary approach. It also means that to find out what really happened, we have to apply some critical methods of historical analysis to these texts, recognizing they don't simply present the events as they actually happened—my historical approach. These two approaches are relevant not only for Jesus but also for the other characters depicted in our early traditions, including Judas Iscariot.

In the preceding chapters we have seen how Judas is portrayed in our surviving sources—the Gospels of the New Testament, the Gospels outside the New Testament, the later legends about him, and, of course, the newly discovered Gospel of Judas. These have all been literary studies. We have not, however, asked the underlying historical questions. Who was Judas, really? What did he stand for? What did he do? And why did he do it?

These are the questions that I will now address in this chapter and the one that follows. Our newly discovered Gospel has rekindled an interest in Judas Iscariot, and it portrays him in a way unlike any other ancient Christian source. But what can we say about the man himself as a historical figure?

The Quest for the Historical Judas

It should seem obvious that the only way we can know about figures from the past is if we have sources of information that ultimately go back to their own time. This is true of Abraham Lincoln, Marco Polo, Caesar Augustus, Jesus, and Judas. There are two kinds of stories about figures from the past: stories that contain historically accurate information and those that do not. There is nothing else. Everything you've ever heard about anyone in the past—whether your great-grandparents or Genghis Khan—is either historically accurate or fabricated.[2] The fabrications aren't necessarily malicious; sometimes they just happen—for example, when the people telling the stories simply get the information wrong. Other times storytellers and/or authors exaggerate or use their vivid imaginations. Sometimes they simply make something up in order to make a point.

Given the fact that so much of what is recorded about past figures is not historically accurate, historians have to evaluate what they read and hear in order to get behind the stories to the historical facts. It helps if there are good sources of information. The more there are, the better.

What kinds of sources of information do historians look for when dealing with people from the distant past, such as Jesus or Judas? The best sources, of course, will be from the person's own time, preferably a contemporary who actually knew the person. If you have a lot of eyewitness accounts, you are in relatively good shape. If the accounts are not actually by eyewitnesses but by later authors who knew eyewitnesses, that's not as good, but still not so bad. If they are by later authors who talked with people who once knew someone who claimed to have once heard an eyewitness, well, that's not nearly so good.

What historians want are lots of contemporary reports, if possible. It helps if these reports are independent of one another. If you have two sources of information about a figure from the past but one of these sources got his information from the other one, then in effect you have not two sources but one. If you have two independent sources, that is obviously better than having to rely on one, especially if these sources corroborate what the other has to say. Moreover, it is useful if the sources of information are not overly biased in their reporting. If a source has an obvious agenda, and if the information that it conveys embodies that agenda, then you have to reconstruct the real historical situation, the actual historical data that lie behind the slanted account.

In short, historians want numerous sources close to the events themselves, which are independent of one another, yet agree on the information they provide, while not being biased in their reports.

How do our sources of information about Judas stack up against this wish list? Unfortunately, not very well. We do not have any eyewitness accounts to Judas's activities. Our earliest Christian source, the apostle Paul, never mentions Judas. The Gospels of the New Testament are therefore our earliest accounts. These do not claim to be written by eyewitnesses to the life of Jesus, and historians have long recognized that they were produced by second- or third-generation Christians living in different countries than Jesus (and Judas) did, speaking a different language (Greek instead of Aramaic), experiencing different situations, and addressing different audiences.[3]

The first of our Gospel accounts is Mark, written thirty-five to forty years after Jesus' death. Matthew and Luke both used Mark as a source; they do not appear to have used independent sources of their own for what they tell us about Judas, although, as we have seen, each author modified the reports he received from Mark in light of his own understanding.[4] The Gospel of John probably did not rely on the other three Gospels for its stories, so it is an independent account of Judas, but it dates from near the end of the first century, some sixty to sixty-five years after his death.

Outside the New Testament it is hard to know if the church father Papias is independent of the canonical Gospels. Later traditions—such as those found in the Arabic Infancy Gospel or the Golden Legend—are many centuries removed from the events they narrate, and are obviously highly legendary. The Gospel of Judas itself is much earlier than these, and its author shows little evidence of having used the New Testament Gospels for constructing his account—although he does appear to have known the account of Judas's death from the book of Acts (so he presumably had read Luke as well, and possibly the other Gospels).

In short, we do not have numerous early, independent sources for the life of Judas. What we have are sources from some decades after his life. All of these sources are based on oral traditions that had been in circulation about him. This means two things for historians: (1) if the same tradition about Judas is found in more than one independent source, that increases the likelihood that it is a historical datum (since the sources that attest it could not have made it up, given the fact that it is found independently in different sources), and (2) if there are descriptions of Judas that do not appear to advance the agendas of the sources that narrate them, then these descriptions are more likely to be historically authentic (in that the sources did not make up these traditions to advance their own causes).

This latter consideration calls into question a number of traditions that we have about Judas. For example, Judas is sometimes denounced as a stereotypical Jew in sources that are otherwise anti-Semitic in their tone—where he is portrayed as a money-grubbing, God-denying, demonically inspired Christ-killer. This kind of portrayal does not appear to be disinterested. Moreover, in the one source named after him, the Gospel of Judas, he is portrayed as the ideal Gnostic. But the Gospel of Judas advances a Gnostic understanding of the world and our place in it, and uses the memory of Judas to promote that understanding. And so this Gospel appears to be using Judas to advance its agenda, and is probably not reliable as a historical source, however interesting it is for understanding how later Christians portrayed Judas.

When all is said and done, there is frustratingly little information about Judas from antiquity that we can trust as historically authentic. But that should not lead us to despair of saying *anything* about him. This is because what little firm data we do have about him is illuminating, sometimes in ways that scholars have failed to notice. My argument in this chapter and the one that follows is that we can infer a lot from what little historically reliable information is available to us.

If we are looking for the bedrock of historical fact about Judas, a critical examination of our sources yields at least three pieces of information: his name was Judas Iscariot, he was one of Jesus' twelve disciples, and he "betrayed" Jesus by turning him over to the ruling authorities. I will be dealing with the first two data in this chapter, and the third in the next. Even though the first piece of information gives us almost nothing to go on for further discussion, the other two are in fact worth reflecting on at length.

The Name Judas Iscariot

Sometimes knowing the names of persons from antiquity can give further information about them. People of the lower classes did not have last names, and so to differentiate people with the same first name, descriptive designations were often added. For example, there are several different Marys in the New Testament. Mary was one of the most common names in first-century Palestine. And so each New Testament Mary is given some kind of identifying feature: Mary the mother of Jesus, Mary of Bethany, Mary Magdalene. This last designation indicates that this Mary came from the town of Magdala, which was a fishing village on the Sea of Galilee. Thus, simply by knowing what she was called, we can learn some information about her.

Some people have hoped that the same might be true of Judas Iscariot. What everyone agrees on is that his name was Judas (or Jude, as the name is sometimes translated) and that he is called "Iscariot" to differentiate him from the other Judases of the New Testament. One of Jesus' own brothers was named Judas (or Jude), for example (Mark 6:3), as was another of his disciples ("not Iscariot"; John 14:22), as was the author of one of the shorter letters in the New Testament, the book of Jude (whose author does not claim to be Jesus' brother or any other known Jude).

There is no doubt that the Judas we are interested in was described as Judas Iscariot—this descriptive term for him is found some twelve times in the New Testament, and also in our other sources, including the Gospel of Judas.[5] What is in doubt is what the term might have meant. There have been many, many suggestions made by scholars over the years, but none of them has won general assent.

Some of the suggestions are highly creative. One nineteenth-century scholar suggested that Iscariot came from a Hebrew word meaning "to stop up" (*skr*) and that it referred to the fact that he died by strangling (his throat was "stopped up"). A hundred years later another scholar suggested that the term came from the Semitic words *'isqa' re'ut*—which might mean something like "one who makes money out of friendship." Some scholars have thought that the term showed he came from the region known as Issachar (he was an Issachariot). Others have pointed out that the term *Iscariot* sounds a bit like the Latin word for dagger, *sica,* and is possibly related to the term used of Jewish dagger-assassins known as the Sicarii. This might suggest that Judas was a Jewish zealot who advocated violence against the Roman empire. Others have thought that the name derives from the Hebrew word for "liar," *saqqar,* and that it designates his basic nature. Some have thought that the name goes back to an Aramaic word *'isqar,* which signifies a person with a ruddy complexion; on this basis they have argued that he was a redhead. The possibilities seem endless. But none of these options has persuaded most linguists intimately familiar with the rules of ancient Semitic languages.[6]

Probably the most common explanation is that Iscariot comes from the Hebrew words *ish Kerioth*—which might mean something like "a man who comes from the village of Kerioth." If this view is correct, then the question remains: where was Kerioth?[7] The book of Joshua in the Hebrew Bible mentions a town of this name in the southern part of Israel, the region later known as Judea (Josh. 15:25), so perhaps that's what the name signifies, that Judas was a Judean. If so, that would make him the only southerner among Jesus' followers. On the other hand, there are reasons for doubting that Kerioth still existed in Jesus' day (twelve hundred years after the time of Joshua), and it would seem odd that Jesus, who spent his entire public ministry in Galilee prior to his last week, would have had someone from a completely different part of the country as one of his closest followers. Another city called Kerioth appears to be located outside of Israel in the country of Moab (Jer. 48:24, 41), but it also seems unlikely that one of Jesus' Jewish followers would be from there.

As a result, some of the best scholars have concluded that we simply don't know what Iscariot meant. Indeed, some have argued that even the Gospel writers—some thirty-five to sixty-five years after Judas's death—no longer knew what it meant.[8] In any event, knowing Judas's name does not appear to give us much to go on if we want to learn more about him historically.

Judas as One of the Twelve

Much more fruitful are the inferences that can be drawn from the fact that Judas was a member of Jesus' chosen inner circle, one of the original twelve disciples.

Scholars are virtually unified that Judas must have been one of the Twelve.[9] That is the one thing that all of the traditions have to say about him, whether they are independent from one another, such as Mark, John, and the Gospel of Judas, or dependent, such as Matthew, Luke, and Papias. Moreover, this is not the sort of datum that early Christians would have been likely to make up when telling their stories about Jesus—that one of his own hand-chosen followers was the one who gave him up to the authorities. Would early Christians imagine that Jesus had no more sway over his own followers than that? On these grounds, scholars of almost every stripe and background agree on this basic historical datum.

What many scholars have not seen, however, is that this datum can provide us with some clues concerning who Judas was, and possibly what he did. To make sense of these clues, we have to explore in a bit greater detail what we know about the historical Jesus himself. This will be the key to our investigation. The reason should be obvious: the people who followed Jesus were the ones who were attracted to his message. And those whom he chose to be closest to him, as his inner group of twelve disciples, were the ones who were most closely attuned to this message and committed to it. In order to know anything about any one of these close followers of Jesus, we first have to know what Jesus stood for.

This is a question that has intrigued critical scholars since the end of the eighteenth century.[10] Before then, scholars more or less accepted the literary portrayals of our Gospels as historically accurate, without recognizing the problems that they pose as historical sources. As I've intimated, these Gospels are not ideal for historians interested in knowing what actually happened during the life of Jesus. They were written decades after the events they narrate, by believers in Jesus who were interested in propagating their own views of him, and some of them (for example, Matthew and Luke) are dependent on others (for example, Mark) for many of their stories. Even more problematic, these sources sometimes stand at odds with one another concerning the facts of Jesus' life.

Problems with Our Sources
for the Historical Jesus

We have already seen the problem of discrepancies in the accounts concerning the death of Judas in the New Testament. Several of our Gospel writers, Mark, John, and the author of the Gospel of Judas, provide us with no details at all. The two that do narrate the tale stand at odds on important points: did Judas return the money he received for betraying Jesus to the priests, as in Matthew? Or not, as in Acts? Did the priests buy a field with it? Or did Judas buy a field with it? Did Judas hang himself? Or did he fall prostrate and burst open in the midst? Was the field called the Field of Blood because it was purchased with "blood money"? Or because Judas made a bloody mess on it? On all these points our two sources for Judas's death, Matthew and Acts, disagree.

Similar differences occur throughout the Gospel accounts of Jesus' own life. Just consider the accounts of Jesus' Passion, since this is the part of the story most closely connected with Judas. In terms of the details, did Jesus die the day after the Passover meal was eaten, as Mark indicates, or the day before it was eaten, as stated in John? Was he crucified at nine in the morning or after noon? Did he carry his own cross all the way to the place of crucifixion, as in John, or did Simon of Cyrene carry it for him, as in the other Gospels? Did both robbers crucified with Jesus mock him as in Mark and Matthew, or did only one of them do so, earning the rebuke of the other, as in Luke? Did the curtain in the Temple rip in half after Jesus died, as in Mark, or before he died, as in Luke? Were any of the disciples present at the crucifixion, or had they all fled?

The questions go on and on, and the answers differ, depending on which account you read. The same kind of comparison affects the stories of Jesus' resurrection. On the third day, who actually went to the tomb? Was it Mary Magdalene alone or Mary with a group of women? If other women, which ones and how many were there? When they arrived, was the stone rolled away from the tomb or not? Did they see one man there in the tomb, or two men, or two angels? What did the person(s) in the tomb tell the women (or woman) to do? Did the women do it or not? What were the disciples supposed to do? Were they to go to Galilee or were they not to leave Jerusalem? Did they go or stay? Did Jesus appear to them? When and how many times? Did Jesus then ascend to heaven on the day of his resurrection, or did he do so forty days later?

Scholars since the eighteenth century have seen that these discrepancies must affect how we view the Gospels. These are not dispassionate reports of what really happened: they can't be. They differ too much. And the differences are not merely in the details found in this Gospel or that. They are just as much in the overall portrayal and emphasis of each Gospel. We already saw this in relationship to Mark and Luke. In Mark Jesus is portrayed as if going to his death in shock, silent the entire time, until the very end when he cries out in anguish, asking why God has forsaken him. Not in Luke, however. Here he is not silent, but holds a number of conversations with a number of different people, always exuding confidence that he knows exactly what is happening to him and why—until the very end, when instead of asking why he has been forsaken, he prays to his Father to receive his spirit. These are different accounts, and if you harmonize them into one big account, you obliterate the emphasis of each one of them.

I should emphasize that the enormous differences between the Gospels are not simply in the details of the Passion narratives. Throughout the Gospels we have varying portrayals of Jesus, who he really was, what he really said, what he really did. As a result, scholars cannot simply read these accounts as factual descriptions of what Jesus said and did. These sources need to be used critically if we want to know what kind of person Jesus was and about his historical words and deeds.

The Life of the Historical Jesus

It is precisely because these sources stand at odds with one another that scholars who study them have come up with so many explanations for who Jesus was. Some have argued that Jesus was principally a Jewish rabbi who taught others to love one another. (If so, why did they crucify him—for saying "Love your enemy"?) Others have insisted that he was a political revolutionary out to overthrow the Roman Empire. (If so, why are traditions about his pacifism found in all our sources at every level?) Others have claimed that he urged a social revolution, for example, as a proto-Marxist or proto-feminist. (Aren't these modern concerns more than ancient ones?) Recently some have claimed that Jesus is best seen as a kind of Jewish Cynic philosopher urging his followers to abandon their attachments to material things and to live for things of the Spirit. (If so, where exactly did Jesus, a lower-class peasant in rural Jewish Galilee, run across such sophisticated Greek philosophical traditions?)[11]

The options go on and on. But all of these, in fact, have been minority opinions. For nearly a century now, the majority of critical scholars working in this field have maintained that the best way to understand the historical Jesus is to situate him within the Jewish context of his own time, and to see him as a Jewish apocalyptic prophet. This is the view first popularized by Albert Schweitzer as far back as 1906, and it is the view that has held sway for most of the century since his day.

As I pointed out in a previous chapter, Jewish apocalypticists maintained that there were two forces at work in this world, the forces of good aligned with God and the forces of evil aligned with his personal enemy, Satan. On the side of God were the good angels; on the side of Satan were the fallen demons. God had the power of righteousness and life; the Devil had the power of sin and death. Even though God was ultimately in charge of this world, as its creator, he had for some mysterious reason handed this world over to the powers of evil. That's why misery, pain, and suffering are rife in this age. The Devil and his demons are asserting their control over the world, and matters are getting worse.

They will continue to get worse until God intervenes in a cataclysmic act of judgment, in which he will destroy all the forces of evil and everyone who has sided with them. At the end of this age, God will send a Savior who will make right all that has gone wrong. Some Jewish apocalypticists called this future Savior the Son of Man, a reference to an apocalyptic figure mentioned in the Jewish Scriptures as the future heir of God's great Kingdom (Dan. 7:13–14); others called him the future messiah, who would overthrow kingdoms opposed to God and rule God's people with justice and truth. When this one comes, God will reassert his authority and power over this world, his creation. A utopian Kingdom will arrive, ruled not by kings empowered by the forces of evil but by rulers who side with God.

And when will this apocalyptic end of the ages come? When will the Son of Man/messiah appear? When will the Kingdom of God arrive? According to Jewish apocalypticists, it would be very soon. Indeed, the end was imminent. The people of God had suffered at the hands of their enemies long enough. God was soon to do something about it. As Jesus himself is recorded as saying: "Truly I tell you, some of those standing here will not taste death before they see that the Kingdom of God has come in power." Indeed, "this generation will not pass away before all these things take place" (Mark 9:1; 13:30). If critical scholars are right that Jesus was a Jewish apocalypticist, then he, like other Jews of his time and place, maintained that the end was imminent, the forces of evil were soon to be overthrown, and God would soon set up a good Kingdom on earth, in which his people would be ruled by those who side with God.

Jesus as a Jewish Apocalypticist

Since I have been stressing in this chapter the need to apply rigorous historical criteria to our sources in order to see what they can reveal about the historical facts lying behind their literary portrayals, it would be fair to ask what the evidence is that Jesus is best understood as an apocalypticist. I will not give the full picture here—that would take another book. But I can cite a couple of important points, and expand them a bit in the next chapter.[12]

1. Apocalyptic sayings are abundant on the lips of Jesus in all of our earliest sources. In these sayings Jesus talks about the coming Kingdom of God—an actual kingdom on earth ruled by God's representatives. In his first recorded words he says that "the Kingdom of God is at hand"—that is, it is almost here, because "the time has been fulfilled" (Mark 1:15). This Kingdom will arrive when the Son of Man (the figure mentioned in the apocalyptic vision of Daniel 7:13–14, in the Jewish Bible) appears in judgment. This Son of Man will come suddenly, like lightning (Luke 12:8–9) in judgment on the earth (Mark 8:38; Matt. 13:40–43). Those who have sided with God will be rewarded, and those who have not will be punished: "the first shall be last and the last first" (Luke 13:30). People should repent in preparation for this coming Kingdom (Mark 1:15). For it will come within "this generation," before the death of the apostles (Mark 13:30; 9:1).

2. These sayings are scattered throughout our earliest sources (Mark, the document scholars have called Q, Matthew, Luke). In our later sources (for example, John, the Gospel of Thomas, later Gnostic writings), this apocalyptic message disappears. That is, in sources closest in time to Jesus, this is the view that dominates. When the end didn't come, authors started changing what Jesus said.

3. It would be almost impossible to explain how Jesus began his ministry *and* what happened in the aftermath of it if he were not an apocalypticist. As reported in all of our earliest sources, he began by associating with John the Baptist, who was an apocalyptic preacher of repentance. John's message is found in a saying of one of our early sources: "The axe is already laid at the root of the tree [meaning that the judgment is ready to begin]; every tree that does not bear fruit will be cut down and cast into the fire" (Luke 3:7–9).[13] This is the message that attracted Jesus to be John's follower. Thus Jesus started out in his ministry as an apocalypticist.

Moreover, after Jesus' death, his earliest followers were apocalypticists—for example, our earliest Christian author, Paul, who thought that the end would come in his own lifetime (1 Thess. 4:14–18). Paul established communities of apocalyptically minded Christians in the aftermath of Jesus' life.

Now, if just the beginning of Jesus' ministry was apocalyptic in tone but the aftermath was not, you could argue that Jesus simply changed his mind. Or if the aftermath was apocalyptic and the beginning was not, you could argue that his later disciples were apocalypticists but he was not. The fact that *both* the beginning and the aftermath were thoroughly apocalyptic shows beyond much doubt that what comes between them was as well. Jesus is therefore best understood as an apocalypticist who, like John the Baptist before him and Paul after him, believed he was living at the end of the age.

4. Finally, Jesus' activities make sense if he was an apocalypticist—for example, his "cleansing of the Temple," which he did as a declaration of what God was soon to do to all those people and institutions that stood against him: enter into judgment with them. And so throughout the tradition Jesus predicts that the Temple will be destroyed in God's act of judgment (Mark 13:2–3).

Much more could be—and has been—said about why Jesus is best understood as a first-century Jewish apocalypticist. But what has all this to do with Judas Iscariot? Judas was one of Jesus' closest disciples. On that all our sources agree. Since he was attracted to follow Jesus, he must have been attracted to his message. Since his message was about the imminent end of the age, when God would overthrow the forces of evil to set up his good Kingdom on earth, this must be the message that Judas too subscribed to. The historical Judas Iscariot, like his master, the historical Jesus, was a first-century Jewish apocalypticist.

Jesus, Judas, and the Twelve

One of the most firmly rooted traditions about Jesus is that he had a close-knit band of followers known as the Twelve. This is not only found independently in Mark and John (and in Matthew, Luke, the Gospel of Judas, etc.) but also implied in the writings of the apostle Paul (1 Cor. 15:5). But why did Jesus choose twelve followers? Why not nine, or fourteen?

In fact, it is not hard to make sense of the number twelve within an apocalyptic context. What most scholars have recognized is that the twelve disciples were chosen as a symbolic statement. It has to do with how the people of God had been, and were to be, organized under God's rule. According to the traditions found in the Hebrew Bible, the nation of Israel was organized into twelve tribes, each with its own leader. The nation, of course, experienced numerous setbacks over the centuries; indeed, ten of the twelve tribes had disappeared through wars and catastrophes. But apocalypticists insisted that God would be faithful to his original purposes for his people and would reestablish them as a sovereign state in the coming Kingdom of God. Jesus chose twelve followers to be his special disciples as a symbolic statement that the Kingdom of God was soon to arrive. The Twelve represented all those who would enter into that Kingdom—those who were faithful to God in this age of evil, who would survive the coming onslaught when the Son of Man appeared, and enter anew into God's coming rule. The Twelve were representatives of the faithful remnant of Israel.

But more than that—and this is the key point—these twelve in fact would be the future rulers of the Kingdom. In a saying that is attested in both Matthew and

Luke (which therefore comes from the early source that scholars have called Q),[14] Jesus tells his disciples:

> Truly I say to you, in the renewed world, when the Son of Man is sitting on the throne of his glory, you [disciples] also will be seated on twelve thrones, judging the twelve tribes of Israel. (Matt. 19:28; cf. Luke 22:30)

There can be little doubt that this is something Jesus actually said—that is, it is a historically accurate datum—rather than something that later Christians made up and put on his lips. After Jesus' death, no one thought that the Twelve would be the rulers of the future Kingdom, because the Twelve included Judas Iscariot, and surely *he* wouldn't be a future ruler. He was the betrayer. Since later Christians maligned Judas as the one who was unfaithful to the cause, who had committed an unpardonable sin against Jesus, they would not have invented a saying that would suggest his future rule in glory. That must mean that the saying is found in our traditions because it is something that Jesus actually said. Jesus chose the Twelve and believed that they—Judas included—would be rulers in the coming Kingdom of God.

Judas the Apocalypticist

And so we can draw some important—and widely overlooked—inferences about who Judas was, based on the hard fact that he was one of the Twelve. Like the others, he followed Jesus because he accepted his message. He was so devoted to Jesus and his message that Jesus chose him to be one of the inner circle. Jesus understood this circle—and presumably the twelve members of it understood themselves—to be emblematic of those who would survive the coming judgment to be brought by the Son of Man, who would bring with him the Kingdom of God. These twelve represented the twelve tribes of Israel; in being responsive to Jesus' teaching, they showed themselves faithful to the God of Jesus.

Like the others, Judas anticipated that the end of all things was at hand. Moreover, he must have taken Jesus at his word, that he, along with the others, would be rulers once the Kingdom of God came. This would be soon—within their own generation.

One other point needs to be made. If the Twelve were chosen by Jesus and if he was therefore their master, and if they were the ones who would rule the twelve tribes of Israel (that is, the faithful Jews who made it into the Kingdom), who would rule them? In the present, Jesus was their leader. Would he continue to be their leader? Did Jesus think that he would be the ruler of the Twelve, the ultimate king of this future Kingdom?

If so, what exactly did Judas betray to the authorities that led to Jesus' death? And why did he betray it? Those are the questions we will need to address in the next chapter.

⌘

CHAPTER TEN

What Did Judas Betray and
Why Did He Betray It?

The accomplishments and achievements of a person's entire lifetime can be overshadowed or even obliterated by a single incident. Most of my undergraduate students know about Richard Nixon for one reason: Watergate. And which of us knows anything about the actor John Wilkes Booth apart from the fact that he shot Abraham Lincoln? What do people know about Judas Iscariot? He betrayed Jesus.

But what exactly did he betray? And why did he betray it? To make sense of my thesis—that the commonly held answers to these questions are probably wrong, or at least inadequate—I need to set the stage by reviewing a couple of important background issues.

The Apocalyptic Jesus and
His Apocalyptic Followers

In my opinion, the most important thing to know about the historical Jesus is that he was a first-century Jew who lived in Palestine.[1] The second most important thing to know is that, like so many other Palestinian Jews of his day, he held views of God, the world, and humans' place in it that were deeply and thoroughly apocalyptic.

As I began to explain in the preceding chapter, an apocalyptic form of Judaism was widespread in Jesus' time and place. The community of Jews known as the Essenes, who produced the Dead Sea Scrolls, were apocalyptic, as were many, if not all, Pharisees. So were the followers of the various Jewish prophets who appeared on the scene in Jesus' day, such as John the Baptist, who practiced a rite of baptism to prepare people for the coming end of the age.

Using easily understood apocalyptic imagery, John indicated that "the axe is already laid at the root of the tree"—meaning that judgment (the chopping down of the tree) was about to begin, and that people needed to change their ways and "bear good fruit" if they expected to survive the divinely appointed onslaught (Luke 3:7–9). John was baptizing people who repented of their sins to show that they were cleansed and pure, ready for the Kingdom of God that was soon to arrive.

Jesus of Nazareth began his public ministry by being baptized by John. If nothing else, this shows that he aligned himself with John's message in particular, as opposed to the message of other Jews living at the same time. Jesus, like John before him, preached that the end of time was near and that God was soon to bring his Kingdom. As Jesus says in his first recorded speech in our earliest surviving Gospel: "The time has been fulfilled [i.e., this age is nearly over]; the Kingdom of God is at hand [i.e., God is about to intervene to bring in a new order]; repent and believe in the good news" (Mark 1:15).

This was indeed good news for people who were suffering under the evil forces currently in charge of the world. God was about to overthrow these forces of evil and establish a Kingdom in which love, mercy, and justice would prevail. Not everyone would enter that Kingdom, however— only those who were prepared for it. God in fact was about to send a cosmic judge from heaven, whom Jesus called the Son of Man. The world as we know it would be destroyed, and the elect of God would be brought into a new Kingdom. As Jesus says in our earliest Gospel:

> In those days after that affliction, the sun will grow dark and the moon will not give its light, and the stars will be falling from heaven and the powers in the sky will be shaken; and then they will see the Son of Man coming on the clouds with great power and glory. And then he will send forth his angels and he will gather his elect from the four winds, from the end of earth to the end of heaven. (Mark 13:24–27)

We should not write off such statements as fanciful or metaphorical, as if Jesus did not really mean them. He was an apocalyptic Jew who thought that a day of judgment was soon to come, and the Son of Man from heaven would bring it. In our earliest accounts of his sayings, he appears to be referring not to himself but to someone else when he speaks of this Son of Man, a cosmic judge from heaven.[2]

This is the teaching of Jesus in all of our early sources: Mark, the document scholars have called Q, and the sources that lie behind our Gospels of Matthew and Luke.[3] Consider Jesus' words now found in Matthew:

> Just as the weeds are gathered and burned with fire, so will it be at the culmination of the age. The Son of Man will send forth his angels, and they will gather from his Kingdom every cause of sin and all who do evil, and they will cast them into the furnace of fire. In that place there will be weeping and gnashing

of teeth. Then the righteous will shine forth as the sun, in the Kingdom of their father. (Matt. 13:40–43)

Some of Jesus' parables are designed to emphasize just this apocalyptic point:

The Kingdom of heaven is like a net which was thrown into the sea and gathered fish of every kind. When it was full, they hauled it ashore, and sitting down chose the good fish and put them into containers, but the bad fish they threw away. That's how it will be at the completion of the age. The angels will come and separate the evil from the midst of the righteous, and cast them into the fiery furnace. There people will weep and gnash their teeth. (Matt. 13:47–50)

Who will survive this coming onslaught? Those who have taken Jesus' words to heart and followed his instructions and his demands for repentance.

Whoever is ashamed of me and of my words in this adulterous and sinful generation, of that one will the Son of Man be ashamed when he comes in the glory of his Father with his holy angels. (Mark 8:38)

When will this onslaught occur and the Kingdom come? Right away:

Truly I tell you, some of those standing here will not taste death before they see that the Kingdom of God has come in power. (Mark 9:1)

For Jesus, a judgment day was coming, and people needed to be ready for it. There would be a major reversal when it appeared. The forces of evil would be dethroned, and those who currently suffered would be exalted: "the first shall be last and the last first." That is why Jesus spoke his beatitudes. Why are the poor, the hungry, the hated, and the persecuted "blessed"? Because they are the ones who will inherit the Kingdom when the Son of Man arrives. In preparation, then, people needed to return to God, to do his will, to love God above all other things, and to "love their neighbors as themselves." Those who do so would enter into the Kingdom; those who did not would be sent away to judgment (Matt. 25:31–46).

This Kingdom was coming soon, within his disciples' lifetime: "Truly I tell you, this generation will not pass away before all these things take place" (Mark 13:30). Moreover, the Twelve would be the rulers of this Kingdom: in the "age to come, when the Son of Man is seated upon his glorious throne, you also will sit upon twelve thrones judging the twelve tribes of Israel" (Matt. 19:28; cf. Luke 22:30).

If this was the heart and core of Jesus' proclamation—that someone called the Son of Man, a cosmic judge from heaven, was soon to arrive in judgment to establish God's Kingdom—why don't people today normally think of this as his message? The answer is not hard to find. The expected end did not come.

Jesus died. Then his disciples died. And the end never arrived. As a result, the followers of Jesus started emphasizing other aspects of his message. His proclamation was reshaped away from its original apocalyptic emphasis. The Christian message became the preaching *about* Jesus, about his death and resurrection, rather than the preaching *of* Jesus, about the coming Son of Man. As later storytellers told and retold the stories of Jesus and his preaching, they deemphasized the apocalyptic character of the message. Jesus' teachings, in effect, were deapocalypticized.

We find this happening already in our Gospels. Even though the apocalyptic character of Jesus' message is clear in our very earliest sources, such as Mark, Q, and the sources behind Matthew and Luke, in our later sources there is little of the apocalypse that is retained. The Gospel of John, the latest of the canonical Gospels, does not, as a rule, put apocalyptic sayings on the lips of Jesus. Even later, in the Gospel of Thomas, Jesus preaches *against* an apocalyptic understanding of the world (e.g., in Sayings 3 and 113). Later Gospels have no apocalyptic message at all. When the end didn't come, the followers of Jesus changed his message. Some of them may have felt frustrated. It is possible that for some, the frustration set in even before a long period of time had passed. This may be what lies behind the betrayal of Judas.

The Disciples' Expectations
of the Coming Kingdom

A constant refrain in our earliest Gospel, Mark, is that the disciples never could understand what Jesus meant when he indicated that he would go to Jerusalem and be rejected by the Jewish leaders and crucified. But what is so hard to understand about such a plain teaching? What was the problem?

Could it be that the disciples expected something else of Jesus? It is striking that according to these early records, the disciples—a very poor band of illiterate peasants from the backwaters of rural Galilee—had extremely high expectations for themselves. They constantly argue about which one of them is the "greatest"; they want to know which ones of them will be superior in the coming Kingdom of God; they want to know who will be allowed to sit at Jesus' right and left hands (Mark 9:34; 10:35–37).

Given what Jesus had told them about their future roles in the Kingdom, it is no surprise that they had visions of grandeur: they were to be the twelve rulers in the utopian Kingdom that was soon to arrive. This was a perfect illustration of Jesus' teaching of the Kingdom. When the Son of Man arrived, those who were great, wealthy, and powerful would be humbled, and those who were meek, poor, and powerless would be exalted. Who could be more meek and powerless than his poor followers, a band of nobodies from the hinterland? To illustrate his message about the future reversal, Jesus chose twelve of them and told them they would be the powerful overlords of the coming Kingdom.

The final page of the manuscript; at the bottom comes the title (which normally concluded a book in antiquity): "The Gospel of Judas."

This, then, is what the Twelve—including Judas Iscariot—expected. And so it is no wonder that they could not make heads or tails of Jesus' declaration, near the end of his ministry, that he was about to be rejected and killed. Killed? How could he be killed? The Kingdom was coming, and they would be its rulers. Jesus was their master now. Wouldn't he be their master then? The disciples never did understand that Jesus was about to die. They thought he would be with them in the Kingdom. In fact, he would still be over them. They would be the overlords, ruling the twelve tribes, but he would be the Lord of all, the king of the Kingdom. And what is the Jewish term used to refer to the future king of the future Kingdom, the one who would be anointed to rule over all? It is the word *messiah.*

Jesus as the Messiah

There have been long and hard debates among scholars over the question of whether Jesus understood himself to be the messiah. Most lay people have trouble making sense of these debates, in part because most people don't understand what the term *messiah* meant in ancient Israel. The majority of my students today think that the messiah was somehow supposed to be God come to earth. But no Jew of the ancient world thought the messiah was supposed to be God. The messiah was the "anointed one," the mortal chosen by God to rule over his Kingdom.

The history of the term is reasonably clear. In the Jewish Scriptures God promises King David—the greatest king in Israel's history—that he would always have a descendant on the throne (2 Sam. 7:14–16; Ps. 89:3–4, 26–37). But events in history turned out otherwise. When the Babylonian armies overthrew the kingdom of Judah, they removed the king from power (2 Kings 24–25). What were Jewish thinkers to make of this? God had promised an eternal throne to David, but the kingship had been dissolved. Some of them came to think that God would come to fulfill his promise by restoring the kingship to Israel in the future. There would be a future "anointed one" who would rule God's people.

In Hebrew, the term for "anointed one" is *messiah.* The equivalent term in ancient Greek, the language of the New Testament, is *christos,* or Christ. The messiah (Christ) would be the future ruler of God's people. Many Jews thought that he would be a "son of David"—that is, an earthly descendant who would inherit David's throne when God forgave his people, drove out their oppressors (the Babylonians, the Syrians, the Romans, or whoever happened to be controlling Palestine at the time), and reestablished Israel as a sovereign state in the land.

As I indicated in a previous chapter, there were various expectations among first-century Jews concerning what the messiah would be like.[4] Some, maybe most, thought of him as a literal king who would sit on David's throne. Others thought of him as a cosmic judge of the earth (the Son of Man, for example, whom Jesus referred to). Yet others thought he would be some kind of powerful priest who ruled the people according to the written laws of God. But everyone who thought of the coming messiah thought of him as a great and powerful figure who in some sense would rule God's people in the future Kingdom. He would not be God; he would be God's chosen representative.

Christians, of course, are named after Christ, since they are, and always have been, people who acknowledge that Jesus himself is the messiah. Non-Christians have always rejected this claim, and it is not hard to see why. Jesus never became king, he never returned from heaven as a cosmic judge, he never was a priest who ruled the people. Jesus was none of the things that Jews expected the messiah to be. Calling Jesus the messiah made no sense to most Jews, of Jesus' own day or afterward.

One intriguing question scholars have wrestled with is why the early followers of Jesus began calling him "Christ" in the first place. Is it because after he had died they came to believe that he was raised from the dead and that therefore he must have been the messiah? It may be surprising, but the answer is a resounding no. This is because prior to Christianity there is not a single Jewish tradition that the messiah was supposed to die and be raised from the dead. As New Testament scholar Nils Dahl has convincingly argued, the resurrection would not prove to any Jew that Jesus is the messiah because the messiah was not *supposed* to rise from the dead.[5] Christians later, of course, pointed to passages in the Jewish Scriptures that talked about the death of God's Righteous One and his ultimate vindication by God, arguing that these passages actually referred to Jesus (for example, Isa. 53 and Ps. 22). But prior to Christianity, no one thought that these passages referred to the future messiah who would die and be raised. It is worth noting in this connection that the term "messiah" never appears in these passages. For Jews, what made the messiah the messiah was the fact that he was God's chosen one who would rule God's people. These passages referred to someone else.

Now, if the death and resurrection of Jesus would not lead anyone to say, "Aha! Jesus is the messiah," then why did Christians start calling Jesus the messiah? One of the factors that makes it difficult to answer this question is precisely the fact that our earliest sources—the Gospels of the New Testament, and the writings of Paul even before them—simply assume that Jesus was the messiah. Paul is so convinced that Jesus is the messiah that he uses "Christ" almost as Jesus' last name. The Gospels, written after Paul's day, are written in the full assurance that Jesus is the messiah. Since the Gospel writers were so sure about the point, they naturally speak freely of Jesus' messiahship, so anyone reading these Gospels would simply assume that Jesus and his followers all along knew him to be the messiah.

But for Paul and the Gospel writers Jesus is not the messiah in the *Jewish* sense that he is the one who sat on the throne in Jerusalem, ruling over Israel as a sovereign state in their own land. He rules the world now as its Lord from heaven. To be sure, in the future he will return and rule the earth, so he is also the messiah in a future sense. But for now he is a spiritual messiah, having conquered death by his resurrection and being exalted to sit at God's right hand. In Jesus' own day, however, years before Paul and the Gospel writers came on the scene, there weren't any Jews who understood that *that* is what it meant to call someone the messiah.

In part, that's why our earliest sources—for example, the Gospel of Mark—show that the disciples never understand who Jesus is. Jesus, of course, is portrayed as knowing that he must die and be raised from the dead. But the disciples don't get it. They think he's the messiah—and that means that he will be the future king. The Gospel writers, of course, think that this is the wrong understanding of messiah. For them, Jesus is the messiah in his death and resurrection.

Where did this non-Jewish idea of the messiah come from, that he was the one who would die and be raised? Scholars have come to recognize that the only way to make sense of this idea is to explain it historically. The way it works is this:

- Christians believed Jesus was the messiah.
- Christians knew that Jesus died and believed that he was raised from the dead.
- Christians therefore came to say that the messiah was supposed to die and be raised from the dead.

In sum, the fact of Jesus' death and the belief in his resurrection would not *in themselves* be enough to make anyone think that Jesus was the messiah, because no one thought that this is what the messiah was supposed to do. The only person who would think Jesus was the messiah who died and was raised is one who already thought he was the messiah—before his death.

Expectations of Jesus as the Messiah

There is in fact evidence that this is historically correct, that some of Jesus' followers understood him to be the messiah before his death. When they understood him that way, they must certainly have used their own categories—the Jewish categories available to them—to make sense of this view. They knew he wasn't a priest, so he wouldn't be that kind of messiah. And they knew him as a mortal, here on earth, not as a heavenly angel coming on the clouds of heaven. If they thought of him as the messiah, then, they must have thought that somehow he would be the future king. This would fit in well with Jesus' teaching: if the exalted will be humbled and the humble exalted, it would be no surprise that he, a scarcely known itinerant preacher from unknown parts of remote Galilee, would become the ruler of God's people.

The question persists, however: where did the disciples get the idea that Jesus would be the future messiah? Scholars have long seen why this is a problem: in our earliest Gospel sources, Jesus does not deliver lengthy discourses in which he identifies himself as such—only in later Gospels. And so in John, our latest canonical Gospel, Jesus devotes his discourses to explaining exactly who he is. But what about Mark, our earliest Gospel? Here Jesus does not talk about himself. He talks about God's future Kingdom and what people must do to prepare for it.

The only time in this source, our earliest, that Jesus says that he is the messiah is when he is put on trial after his arrest, when the high priest asks him, "Are you the messiah, the Son of the Blessed One?" Jesus replies pointedly, "I am. And you will see the Son of Man sitting at the right hand of power and coming with the clouds of heaven" (Mark 14:61–62). It is hard to know how a Christian author such as Mark, living forty years later, would know exactly what Jesus said at his trial (remember, none of Jesus' followers was there, and certainly no one was taking notes). But the saying certainly sounds like the sort of thing Jesus would say. It should not be overlooked that he explicitly tells the high priest that the priest himself would be alive when the Son of Man came from heaven. This is not a saying later Christians would make up—at least Christians living after the high priest had died. But for the moment I want to stay with the curious fact that this is the first instance, in our very earliest surviving Gospel, that Jesus publicly declares himself the messiah.

Did the historical Jesus publicly call himself the messiah? If so, it is hard to explain why our earliest sources don't portray him as doing so. On the other hand, his disciples clearly thought he *was* the messiah, even though he didn't do any of the things the messiah was supposed to do. He never raised an army to overthrow the Romans, for example. So where did they get the idea from, and why didn't Jesus say anything about it in public?

I think the best solution to the problem is to conclude that Jesus himself told the disciples that he was the messiah but didn't declare it publicly, to the crowds. The disciples alone knew. This makes sense of just about everything I have been puzzling over in the preceding paragraphs:

- Why Jesus was later called the messiah even though he did nothing the messiah was supposed to do. In fact, he was called the messiah after his death because he had been called the messiah during his life.
- Why Jesus is not portrayed as publicly calling himself the messiah in our earliest sources—because he never did make that proclamation *in public*.
- Why Jesus did not make that proclamation in public—possibly because people would assume they knew what he meant: that he was to be the future king. And this might lead to a violent uprising against the Roman authorities.
- Why Jesus did not mean that he was the messiah in the sense that he would raise an army and overthrow the Romans. He meant it in line with

his apocalyptic teaching. Jesus believed the Son of Man (not himself) was coming in judgment on the earth to bring in God's Kingdom, and he would be the one installed as the king. In this apocalyptic sense, he was the future messiah.

- Why he taught this privately to the twelve he had called to be his disciples. They would rule the twelve tribes of Israel in the coming Kingdom, and he would rule over them.

The idea that Jesus privately told the disciples who he was explains two other critical elements of our early traditions. It explains why he was executed for calling himself King of the Jews when never in his entire ministry did he ever make such a claim about himself, and it explains exactly what it was that Judas betrayed. Judas did not simply lead Jesus' enemies to him privately. He disclosed insider information that the authorities needed to arrest Jesus. Judas betrayed what his master had taught the twelve disciples: that Jesus was to be the future king.

Jesus' Condemnation as King of the Jews

One of the features of the Gospels that has long perplexed scholars is the consistent report that Jesus was executed for calling himself King of the Jews when that is not something that he called himself. There is little question that this was the charge that the Roman governor tried him on. It is the charge independently attested in our surviving sources, where Pilate asks Jesus point blank: "Are you the King of the Jews?" (Mark 15:2; John 18:33). And it is the charge that is inscribed, in different forms in each of the Gospels, on the placard placed above his head on the cross: "This is the King of the Jews" (Matt. 27:37; Mark 15:26; Luke 23:38; John 19:19).

This is a charge of political insurgency. Only the Romans could appoint a king to rule over the Jews, and they obviously never appointed Jesus. If he claimed to be the king, then at best he must have been claiming to subvert the authority of Rome; at worst he was claiming to be about to lead a rebellion against Rome to establish Israel as an independent state. Either way, in Roman eyes, it was a political statement punishable by death. And so the Romans killed him.

But there is almost nothing in our early sources to suggest that Jesus was interested in a political revolt.[6] So how do we explain his death on these political charges?

I should make an important methodological point here. As I stated earlier, there are many, many portrayals of the historical Jesus written by serious scholars. To establish the plausibility of any of these portrayals, a key question to ask is whether the account of Jesus' *life* can make sense of his *death*. Jesus' crucifixion by the Romans is the single most certain aspect of Jesus' life, the one thing that we know for certain about him. Any account of his life must explain it.

If, for example, someone wants to maintain that Jesus was principally a Jewish rabbi who taught his followers that they should love one another, why would Romans kill him for *that*? Did Pontius Pilate say, "Oh no, we can't have you loving one another, and we certainly don't want you to love *us*, your enemies. To the cross with you"? Or if Jesus' overarching concern was with the status of women in first-century Palestine, would Pilate have been angered at the idea and deemed him worthy of death? Or if Jesus principally taught his disciples that they should be like Cynic philosophers and spurn material things in favor of the spiritual, would Pilate have decided Jesus needed to be tortured, mutilated, and crucified? Any account of Jesus' life must explain his death.[7]

If Jesus had been a political revolutionary, that would explain his death. The Romans in that case would have tried him on political charges and executed him. The problem is that Jesus appears to have been a pacifist. He never raised an army and never advocated the violent overthrow of the empire.[8]

Of course, the Romans might have *thought* Jesus was an insurrectionist, even if he wasn't. But there's a better explanation for why they sought to put him to death. He didn't take up the sword against the Romans because in his view he knew that he didn't need to. He knew that the empire was soon to be overthrown—not by the armies he would lead against Rome, but by God himself, in an imminent act of judgment. Jesus was one of those apocalypticists who predicted a future violence, brought not by humans but from heaven. When he went into the Temple the last week of his life and overturned the tables of the money changers and the people selling sacrificial animals, it was a symbolic statement that God's judgment was soon to arrive and destroy that place.[9] The holy place? The sanctuary of God? Yes, God's judgment would hit even there. The rulers of the people had grown powerful and corrupt, they collaborated with the Romans, and they would be destroyed when God's judgment came.

It is no wonder the Jewish leaders did not take kindly to Jesus, fearing he would cause unrest among the people. He was preaching against them, so they decided to have him taken out of the way. That was not particularly unusual. In fact, it was a common fate of apocalyptic prophets of coming judgment. It is what happened to John the Baptist before Jesus. And it is what happened to other apocalyptic prophets in Palestine after his death.[10] The Roman authorities were quick and ruthless when it came to anyone preaching against them, whether they were urging others to take up arms or insisting that God himself was going to intervene. Anyone outspoken and vehement in their opposition to those in power were dealt with in kind.

But, of course, there had to be grounds for prosecution (even if they were wrong or misguided).[11] Which leads me back to my question: if it is beyond reasonable doubt that Jesus was condemned for claiming to be King of the Jews, yet there is no record of him calling himself this publicly in our early sources, how do we explain the charge?

A Reconstruction of
Jesus' Betrayal and Death

The way I understand it is this. Jesus publicly preached an apocalyptic message of judgment. Most of the time he preached this message in his home territory, in Galilee, the northern part of the land. This was a rural area, and Jesus was probably unknown both to the Roman authorities living in the south and to the Jewish leaders in charge of Jerusalem and its Temple.

Near the end of his life he took a pilgrimage with his disciples to Jerusalem in order to celebrate the annual Passover feast. This was a busy and dangerous time in Jerusalem. The Roman authorities viewed it as a potentially incendiary time of year, as Jewish pilgrims from around the world would come to Jerusalem to commemorate the Exodus, which had happened nearly thirteen hundred years earlier, in the days of Moses. That was the time when God had saved his people from their foreign oppression in Egypt. In celebrating this event every year, Jews were not merely remembering the past; many of them were also looking forward to the future, when God would act again, this time saving them from their current oppressors (the Romans). The Roman authorities knew full well that at Passover there could be rebellion in the air, and they took all measures necessary to quell any potential riots.[12]

Jesus came into town and caused a minor ruckus in the Temple, preaching that God would soon intervene in the course of history to overthrow the powers of evil and establish a new Kingdom here on earth. The Son of Man was soon to arrive in judgment. Even the locus of Jewish power and prestige would be overthrown. The Temple itself would be destroyed.

The Jewish leaders in charge of the Temple—the chief priests, whose head was a man named Caiaphas—did not want a riot to start. Riots had happened before at Passover, as the crowds could get worked up over the words of a charismatic preacher. So the Jewish authorities kept an eye on Jesus, a newly arrived charismatic preacher. Over the course of the week before Passover Jesus acquired larger and larger followings, and the chief priests came to think this could lead to trouble. They decided to have Jesus taken out of the way. But there had to be a legal proceeding—they couldn't simply arrest Jesus because they didn't like him. And he wasn't preaching open rebellion. The Jewish authorities needed some charge to pin on him, something that would make the Romans sit up and take notice.[13]

This is where Judas Iscariot came into the picture. For some reason—to be explored in a minute—Judas gave them what they needed: Jesus had privately been calling himself the future king.

Jesus, of course, meant this teaching in a strictly apocalyptic sense. He thought he would be the king when the Son of Man brought in the Kingdom. That kind of nuance didn't matter, however: once the chief priests learned that

Jesus considered himself to be a king, they would have the information they needed. They couldn't get this information from what they heard Jesus preach, of course. It was not his public proclamation but his private instruction to the disciples, his co-rulers in the future Kingdom. But Judas told them what they needed to hear. The Jewish leaders arranged to have Jesus arrested. They used the betrayer to lead them to him. Then they put Jesus on trial, asking him: "Are you the messiah?" He had to answer truthfully, and so he revealed what he considered to be the truth: yes, he was the one who would rule the future Kingdom. The authorities then handed him over to the Roman governor for trial.

That is precisely why Pilate put Jesus on trial for calling himself King of the Jews even though this was not his public message. Jesus thought he would be the messiah of the coming Kingdom, that is, the future king. So when he was asked by Pilate, he either spoke the truth, that he was the king, or at least didn't deny the charge.[14] How could he? This was the heart of his message. The Romans saw this as political insurgency. Pilate ordered his crucifixion. Jesus was flogged and executed on the spot.

And so we have the historical explanation for why Jesus was killed for calling himself King of the Jews when in public he never did so. Judas betrayed the information.

This understanding of what Judas really betrayed makes much better sense than the standard explanation. In the Gospels, the only thing Judas does is show the authorities where they can arrest Jesus privately. But that is scarcely much of a betrayal. If the authorities wanted to know where Jesus was, they could have had him followed; there was no need to hire an insider. The alternative explanation I'm giving here makes sense of all the data:

- Jesus taught his followers, privately, that they would rule in the Kingdom.
- He also taught them that he would be their ruler, as the king in the Kingdom (the messiah).
- He was executed for calling himself King of the Jews, even though he never called himself that publicly.
- He was later revered by Christians as the messiah, even though he did nothing the messiah was supposed to do. The reason they did so: he was known to be the messiah before his death, because that's what he himself taught.

Residual Questions

If the scenario I've just painted of Jesus' betrayal, arrest, and execution is right, there still remain several residual questions. Unfortunately, the answers need to be more speculative than historically certain. As for most events in history, we simply lack reliable sources that can give us the information we want. What follows, then, are some reasonable guesses about what we don't know, based on what little we do.

1. *Did Judas know that his betrayal would lead to Jesus' death?* As we have seen, in the Gospel of Judas that is the point of the betrayal: to allow Jesus to escape his mortal body to return to the realm of the Spirit. But this account was written a century after the fact by a Gnostic who saw liberation from this material world to be the greatest good imaginable, and who told his story about Jesus and Judas in light of his own belief.

   In two of our canonical Gospels, Mark and John, Judas completely disappears from the scene after the betrayal, so there is no evidence of what he felt afterward. But it is striking that in our earliest report, Mark's, Judas instructs those arresting Jesus to take him away "securely" (Mark 14:44; sometimes translated too loosely as "under guard"). This is an odd statement, and some interpreters have thought that it indicates that Judas was afraid Jesus might try to escape. But another option is that he didn't want anything amiss to happen to Jesus, that he wanted him to be kept safe (the term could also be translated "safely" instead of "securely"). If so, then the outcome of the betrayal may have come as a surprise to Judas. Maybe he simply wanted Jesus taken out of the way because he too was afraid riots might start, and he didn't want Jesus—or the disciples—to be hurt in the mayhem. Maybe he didn't expect that handing Jesus over to the authorities would lead to a death sentence, but simply assumed that they would keep Jesus for questioning, find out that he had no political objectives, and let him go as another prophet with high hopes for the future.

   This might make sense of the tradition found in Matthew that Judas felt remorse once he saw that "Jesus was condemned," and that he then tried to return the money he had made off the deal. Why would Jesus' condemnation lead to remorse? Only if that had not been the goal of the betrayal in the first place. Possibly Matthew also understood Judas as being intent not on Jesus' death but only on his being safely removed from the public eye until the festival had ended. When things did not turn out as he had planned, Judas was torn with guilt and grief, and hanged himself.

2. *Why, then, did Judas do it?* The Gospels of course give various answers to this question. In the Gospel of Judas, he betrays Jesus because that's what Jesus wants him to do. In our earlier accounts there are a range of different reasons given: John portrays Judas as inherently evil, "a devil," and so naturally he did what he was inclined to do; Luke suggests that "the Devil made him do it"; Matthew indicates that he did it for the cash.

   But what was the real motivation behind Judas's act? At the end of the day, I'm afraid we can't know for certain. It might be that the scenario I've suggested above is the right one, that Judas simply wanted Jesus removed from public view until after the festival had ended and they could return to Galilee to continue their public preaching.

   But there's another option that might be even more intriguing, possibly hinted at in Mark, our earliest surviving account. Throughout Mark's account Jesus has been preaching about the coming Kingdom of God, speaking about the coming of the Son of Man in judgment, indicating to his disciples that it would happen soon. Then he comes to Judea from Galilee, cleanses the Temple, and is anointed by an unknown woman in the town of Bethany. Apocalyptic fervor among his disciples must have been at its peak. Jesus has just given his lengthiest apocalyptic discourse in Mark 13, describing what will happen soon, at the end of the age. When he is anointed in Bethany, what does it mean? The act, of course, could be interpreted in a number of ways. If Jesus is about to become king, could it not be a symbolic statement that he is about to assume the throne as the Lord's anointed one? Possibly that's what the disciples think. But Jesus does not interpret it this way. Instead he indicates that this unnamed woman has anointed his body "for its burial" (Mark 14:8).

Every time Jesus speaks about his coming death in Mark, the disciples misunderstand him: isn't he to be the future king who will rule, and aren't they to rule with him? So too here. As soon as Jesus speaks of his impending death, Judas goes out to betray him.

Is it possible that we have a historical recollection of the real situation here? For Judas, Jesus' interpretation of his anointing may have been the last straw. Throughout Jesus' ministry, the disciples, including Judas, were looking ahead to the time when they were to rule in the coming kingdom. This would happen soon. How soon? In one of those sayings preserved in Matthew, but which may go back to Jesus himself, Jesus sends his twelve disciples out to preach the imminent arrival of the Kingdom of God, telling them: "Truly I say to you, you will not have gone through all the towns of Israel before the Son of Man arrives" (Matt. 10:23). In its own historical context, what could such a saying have meant? It can't have meant that Jesus himself was going to follow each of the Twelve to all the towns they visited. Is Jesus here referring apocalyptically not to himself but to the cosmic judge of the earth, who will arrive not sometime later in "this generation" but imminently, before the mission of the Twelve is even finished?

If that's what he meant—or at least if that's how he was understood—the disciples must have been bitterly disappointed when the end in fact did not come and things went on just as before.[15] After a while, did all this talk—about the coming Son of Man, the Kingdom of God, the ruling of the twelve tribes of Israel, the entire apocalyptic vision—begin to lose its plausibility? Jesus may well have come to suspect that he would run afoul of the authorities. His predecessor John the Baptist had done so. The prophets of sacred Scripture had done so. Other prophets of his own time had done so. There's nothing implausible about Jesus himself beginning to think that he too would do so. That is, after all, the constant refrain of his preaching in the Gospels.

So why did Judas betray Jesus? It is possible, as I suggested above, that he simply thought matters were getting out of hand and he wanted Jesus securely taken out of the way before any violence broke out.[16] But maybe it was the delay of the end that finally frustrated Judas and made him rethink everything he had heard. He, along with the others, thought they were to be glorious kings. They had made a trip to Jerusalem, raising their hopes that this would be the time, but nothing was happening and nothing evidently was about to happen. Maybe Judas had a crisis of faith, triggered by Jesus' enigmatic references to his own coming demise, and out of bitterness he turned on his master. Maybe his hopes were dashed. Maybe he rebelled. Maybe he turned on the one he had loved out of despair, or anger, or raw frustration.

All of this, as I indicated, must lie in the realm of speculation. As much as we would like to know, we simply will never have reliable information to indicate what it was that motivated Judas, one of Jesus' closest followers, to betray his master. What is clear is that for one reason or another, Judas became a turncoat and handed Jesus over to his enemies—not simply telling them where to find him but giving them the insider information they needed in order to have him brought up on charges before the Roman governor. Jesus had been calling himself the king.

3. *How did Judas die?* We have seen that we have conflicting reports about the death of Judas: those found in Matthew, Acts, and Papias. I think we can discount the legendary account in Papias, that Judas swelled up to an enormous size, that a doctor couldn't even locate his eyes with an optical instrument, that his genitals were grotesquely huge, and that he passed worms and pus every time he needed to urinate. It makes for a good story, but there's not much here for a historian to go on.

Matthew and Acts stand at odds in a number of ways, as we have seen. But they also agree on interesting points. They both indicate that Judas's death was connected with a field in Jerusalem that was sometimes called the Field of Blood. In Matthew it is called the "potter's field." On just about everything else they disagree: Matthew says the priests bought the field with the "blood money" that Judas returned (hence the field's name); Acts says Judas bought it himself. Matthew says Judas hanged himself; Acts says he fell prostrate and burst open, spilling his intestines on the field (hence the field's name).

It is worth noting that these two accounts are independent of one another: that is, neither got any of its information from the other. And so the points they have in common are independently attested. What, then, can a historian conclude?

Here again we have to rely on intelligent guesswork. But one possible solution is this. There was a field in Jerusalem known for its rich clay, which potters used for their earthenware products. Because of the bright red color of its soil, it was known not only as a potter's field but also as the Field of Blood. Judas died on this field, possibly the result of a suicide out of remorse for what he had done. The Christians who came to know about Judas's death considered the name of the field ironic: the field of potter's red clay was where Judas had shed his blood. And so they began to attach a new significance to its name, the Field of Blood: the field connected with the blood of Jesus' own betrayer.

As I say, this is a bit of guesswork, but it makes sense of the known facts. As with most of the information surrounding Judas himself, Jesus' disciple who betrayed him, that is about as much as a historian can hope for.

Conclusion

At the end of the day, reliable information about most figures from the distant past is frustratingly sparse. Most people have lived, loved, suffered, and died without a single trace of their ever having lived on this earth. For some people from the ancient past—Socrates, Julius Caesar, Jesus—we have relatively extensive sources of information, of varying degrees of trustworthiness. In the case of Judas, we have a scant handful of references in books that are far more concerned to tell us about his master and mention him only in reference to Jesus. But these few references may be useful to us because of the inferences we can draw. Jesus was almost certainly an apocalyptic prophet who was crucified on political charges of insurgency. And Judas Iscariot was one of his closest followers, who must therefore have accepted his apocalyptic message. But he was also his betrayer, the one who divulged the information that led to his death. This information probably related to what Judas, as one of the Twelve, was in a unique position to know. Although his motivations may never be fully known—whether he was trying to protect Jesus or was frustrated by the failure of the Kingdom to appear—what can be known is that he alone among the immediate followers turned on his master and handed him over to the authorities. This is the most certain piece of historical information we have about the man. Everything else that he ever said and did disappeared from the public record, eclipsed by the opprobrium attached to the scandal at the end.

⌘

CHAPTER ELEVEN

The Gospel of Judas in Perspective

The newly discovered Gospel of Judas Iscariot has obviously sparked a new interest in understanding the betrayer of Jesus. Throughout this book we have seen how Judas is portrayed in our ancient writings—both those that made it into the New Testament and those of later times. We have also reconsidered who Judas really was, what he stood for, what he believed, what he did in betraying Jesus to the authorities, and why he did it. But the center of our attention, and the ultimate object of our concern, has been the Gospel of Judas itself, one of the earliest surviving Gospels from outside the New Testament. In this final chapter I would like to take a step back and consider the overall significance of this unusual text, which portrays Judas not as a demonically inspired or money-grubbing betrayer of the cause but as the one disciple who both understood Jesus and did his will.

As I stated at the outset, when I first learned of the existence of this Gospel in fall 2004, my immediate reaction was that it could be one of two things— and that its overall significance would hinge on which of these two things it was. On one hand, I thought that it might be a Gnostic Gospel like so many of the other Gnostic Gospels that have turned up in modern times, a document that describes how the divine realm of the aeons came into existence and how this world, and the humans in it, were created as a result of a cosmic disaster. Gnostic Gospels such as this are designed to reveal the knowledge necessary for salvation to the elite few who have a spark of the divine within them. If the Gospel of Judas was that kind of book, it would be highly significant for scholars of early Christianity, possibly as important as such works as the Secret Book of John, the Gospel of the Egyptians, or On the Origin of the World. But it would not be an earth-shattering find. It would be one more Gnostic Gospel to add to the growing list.

On the other hand, I thought that it might be something completely different. It might be a book that discusses the personal relationship of Jesus and Judas in a way that makes it stand out among all our other surviving sources, a book that portrays Judas in a positive rather than negative light. If it was a book like that, I thought, it would be far more significant. It would be the first book of its kind to survive from antiquity, an entirely new view of Jesus in relationship to his disciples and the man who allegedly betrayed him. A book of that kind would matter not only to scholars of Christian antiquity but to all sorts of people, scholars and nonscholars alike. It would be one of the most intriguing Christian texts to be discovered in modern times.

As it turned out, the Gospel of Judas is both things at once. It is a Gnostic Gospel that describes the formation of the divine realm with all its aeons, luminaries, and firmaments, which narrates how this world of matter came into existence not through the creative activities of the one true God but through the work of much lower, inferior, wicked divine beings—a bloodthirsty rebel and a fool. Yet it is also a Gospel that discloses the true nature of the relationship between Jesus and Judas—true, at least, from the perspective of its author. According to this anonymous writer, Judas was the only member of Jesus' apostolic band who understood where Jesus came from and where he was going. Since he alone had insider knowledge, Judas was the only one who could do what Jesus needed: turn him over to the authorities that he might be killed and escape his temporary entrapment in a mortal body.

How do we put a discovery like this in perspective? We should recognize the Gospel of Judas as the spectacular find it is, without sensationalizing it into something that it is not.

What the Gospel Is and Is Not

It will be important for people constantly to bear in mind what this Gospel is not. It is not a Gospel written by Judas, or one that even claims to be. It is a Gospel *about* Judas (and, of course, Jesus). It is not a Gospel written in Judas's own time by someone who actually knew him or who had inside information concerning his inner motivations. It is not a historically accurate report about the man Judas himself. It is not as ancient as the four Gospels that made it into the New Testament. It is not even older than all of our other noncanonical Gospels: the Gospels of Thomas and Peter are probably earlier by at least a couple of decades (although neither of these mentions Judas). The Gospel of Judas was written at least 100 or, more likely, 125 years after Judas's death, by someone who did not have independent access to historical records about the events he was narrating. It is not a book, therefore, that will provide us with additional information about what actually happened in Jesus' lifetime, or even in his last days leading up to his death. And so one might be tempted to ask: if the book doesn't give us any historical information about Judas or Jesus, why in the world should its discovery matter?

The Gospel does matter, a lot. Not because it gives us more reliable information about what happened in the life of Jesus, but because it gives us more reliable information about what was happening in the lives of his followers in the decades after his death. For understanding the early history of Christianity, the Gospel of Judas is tremendously important. It is safe to say that it is the most significant Christian text to appear in the past sixty years.

Gauging the Importance of the Gospel

Scarcely anyone will dispute that the most important institution in the history of Western civilization has been the Christian church—not just for religion but for every facet of life: political, social, economic, and cultural. But the Christian church didn't emerge as a full-grown entity one day in April. It came into being through an enormously complex set of historical circumstances. The religion that converted the Roman Empire and then became the dominant power of the Middle Ages and beyond was not simply the religion that Jesus preached. It was a religion that developed—rapidly in its early years. The religion changed and transformed as it moved from its Jewish matrix into non-Jewish climes. Early on it shifted from being the religion of Jesus himself (that is, the form of Judaism he preached) to being a religion about Jesus (that is, one based ultimately on his death and resurrection).

Given the enormous impact that Christianity has made on our world, it is incumbent upon historians to explain how this religion came into being. Especially important—and especially difficult to document—is what happened in the early years of the faith. The historical foundations of this religion in the first century or two of its existence determined what the superstructure of later times would look like. The more we can understand how Christianity became the religion it did, the better we can explain our own roots as participants in the enormous phenomenon we might think of as Western civilization.

One problem with understanding the early centuries of Christianity is that our sources are so sparse. In part they are sparse because most people living in the Roman Empire—including most Christians—were illiterate, unable to leave us written records of what was happening. They are sparse also because most of the evidence produced by the small minority of Christians who were literate came to be destroyed or lost in succeeding generations.

It is no accident that for centuries, nearly the only written records from the first several centuries of Christianity came to us from the pens of writers who subscribed to essentially the same perspective and conveyed the same message about what Christianity was and how it developed. Alternative versions of the history of the church were suppressed or simply lost. As a result, for most of Christian history we have heard only one side of the story. It is only with the discovery of previously lost Christian writings that we have been able to see more fully just how rich and diverse the early Christian movement was. The Gospel of Judas, as much as any writing from antiquity, shows that there were other points of view passionately and reverently espoused by people who called themselves Christian. These alternative views show us that there were enormous struggles within early Christianity over the proper forms of belief and practice.

Only one side won these struggles. That victorious side then rewrote the history of the engagement. Recent discoveries have allowed us to understand the historical phenomena more as they truly were. In this ongoing act of historical reconstruction, the Gospel of Judas will play an important role.

Heresy and Orthodoxy in the Early Church

There were competing groups within early Christianity; these different groups held different sets of beliefs and practices, and they were all seeking to win converts to their perspectives. These beliefs and practices differed so widely from one group to another that historians have sometimes had difficulty acknowledging all of them as "Christian."

In the early centuries, of course, there were Christians who believed in only one God. But others claimed that there were two gods (the Marcionites); yet others said there were thirty gods, or 365 gods (various groups of Gnostics). There were Christians who maintained that this world was the creation of the one true God; others said that it was the creation of the just but wrathful god of the Jews, who was not the true God; others said it was the creation of much inferior ignorant deities who were malicious and evil. There were Christians who believed that Jesus was both human and divine; others said he was human but not divine; others that he was divine but not human; others that he was two beings, one divine and one human. There were Christians who believed that Jesus' death was what brought about a restored relationship with God; others said that Jesus' death had nothing to do with salvation; yet others said that Jesus never died.[1]

How could all these groups call themselves Christian? In fact, all of them insisted not only that they were Christian but that they were the *true* Christians, and that all the other groups had misunderstood the teachings of both Jesus and his apostles. And each group had books to prove its point, books allegedly written by apostles that supported its various theological views. No one could simply turn to the New Testament to see which group was right: the New Testament didn't exist yet. To be sure, the twenty-seven books that eventually became the New Testament had already been written by the time these disputes erupted in the second century. But the movement to collect these books into an inviolable canon of Scripture came about as a *result* of these various controversies.

Traditionally, one of these groups of Christians—the group that won the battles—has been labeled "orthodoxy," and the alternative groups—each representing an "aberrant" understanding of the faith—have been called "heresies." The term *orthodoxy* comes from two Greek words that mean "correct opinion" or "right belief." The term *heresy* comes from a Greek word that means "choice." Someone who is orthodox, by definition, holds to the right belief; someone who subscribes to heresy has chosen to hold a false belief.

As you might imagine, scholars have come to see these terms as problematic as descriptive categories, because they imply value judgments concerning which group was right and which ones were wrong. It is not the historian's job to say which group had the better theology—that's a theologian's work. The historian can only describe the historical origins and relations of the various groups, and for that, the terms *orthodoxy* and *heresy*—at least in their root meanings—are not all that useful.

Historians have gotten around that problem by redefining what these terms mean. Rather than using the term *orthodoxy* to say that one group was right in what it believed about God, historians today use it to refer to the group that won the disputes over what was right. One group overcame all its opposition and became the dominant form of the religion; it then decided what creeds Christians should recite and what books they ought to consider authoritative. From a historian's perspective, this dominant group is labeled "orthodox" not because it was necessarily right but because it was the one that decided what would be right.

The other groups are labeled "heresies" not because they represented the wrong beliefs, or because the people who held to them were evil or demonically inspired or just plain willful, but because they were marginalized by the group that emerged as victorious. The Gospel of John was preserved throughout the Middle Ages because it was accepted by the orthodox party; the Gospel of Judas was not preserved because it was deemed heretical.

To make better sense of how the Gospel of Judas fits into this modern view of the relationship of orthodoxy and heresy, I should explain further the older, more traditional understanding, whose roots go all the way back to the writings of the first historian of the church, the fourth-century church father Eusebius, sometimes known as the "father of church history."

The Eusebian Model of Orthodoxy and Heresy

In the early fourth century, Eusebius of Caesarea wrote a ten-volume history of the Christian church that began with the life of Jesus and went up to his own day. This history still survives and is a gold mine of information for historians interested in knowing what was happening in the second and third Christian centuries.[2] Eusebius often quotes earlier Christian writings at length, and in many instances we have no access to these writings otherwise. Most of Eusebius's account, however, is his own narrative of the spread and growth of the Christian church, its persecution from local and imperial authorities, and its internal turmoil. It is the internal conflicts that most interest us here, since these were for the most part caused, according to Eusebius, by heretics, who had been inspired by demons to corrupt the true faith passed down from Jesus to his disciples and through them to the church at large.

Eusebius, of course, was not giving a disinterested account of what happened in the early decades and centuries of the church. He had his own perspective, as one whose theological views were those that emerged as victorious from the various conflicts. He was, in other words, staunchly orthodox, and he understood Christians who took other views—such as Marcion and the various groups of Gnostics—to be heretics who attempted to corrupt the faith. Eusebius, in fact, would not consider such groups truly Christian. They did not hold to the true faith.

In Eusebius's understanding of the church, there was and always had been a single orthodox point of view. This had been the majority view of Christians from the very beginning. It began with Jesus, who proclaimed the orthodox doctrines that Eusebius accepted. And it continued in the major churches of Christianity throughout the ages. To be sure, every now and then some strong-willed, disgruntled, demon-inspired teacher would appear who would lead some Christians astray. But the heretical groups that resulted were always, by definition, perverse offshoots of the main church. Orthodoxy had always been the majority and dominant view, from the earliest of times.

Since Eusebius was writing when his views were in fact orthodox—meaning they were the majority views at the beginning of the fourth century—his perspective made eminent sense to most of his readers, who saw heretics as corruptors of an original truth. Later church historians simply took over Eusebius's narrative of the early years of the church, along with his perspective on those years. And so Eusebius's understanding of the relationship of orthodoxy and heresy became the one and only view for many centuries. It was not seriously questioned until the beginning of the twentieth century.

The Alternative View of Walter Bauer

Possibly the most important book on early Christianity to be written in the twentieth century was a densely argued refutation of Eusebius's perspective by one of Germany's great New Testament scholars, Walter Bauer. His 1934 book, later translated into English as *Orthodoxy and Heresy in Earliest Christianity,* took the Eusebian thesis head-on and showed its fatal flaws.[3] Bauer considered the history of earliest Christianity region by region—Syria, Egypt, Asia Minor, Rome, and so on—isolating the earliest surviving records from each region. What Bauer found came as a shock to many of his readers. In almost every instance, our earliest records of Christianity in most of these regions do not embrace the views that later came to be declared orthodox. Instead they appear to have been heretical—that is, they embraced alternative forms of Christianity. And so, according to Bauer, our earliest records of Christianity in Asia Minor indicate that the Marcionite church held sway in the early centuries,

Egypt was dominated by Gnostic Christians, and so on. Moreover, some of these groups had permeable boundaries—there was a lot of cross-fertilization of ideas going on, as one group would take over the ideas of another and incorporate it into its own perspective. As a result, what was seen to be perfectly orthodox at one time later could be declared heretical later, when views had changed again.

Bauer argued that orthodoxy was not the original form of Christianity from which all the other forms derived as secondary. In his view, earliest Christianity was made up of a large number of groups in a number of locations. Each of these various formulations of Christianity had its distinctive set of beliefs and practices; each had its sacred books, allegedly written by apostles, that supported these beliefs and practices; and each had outspoken leaders who advanced the group's perspectives. Each of the groups was attempting to win others to their view of the faith. But only one group emerged as victorious, near the end of the third century or the beginning of the fourth. By the time of Eusebius, the victory had been sealed. When Eusebius described the conflict, he did not describe it as it really was. He wrote about the victory as if it had been a fait accompli from the very beginning. But his own biases had affected his account. In fact, early Christianity consisted of an enormous range of faith and practice, not one solid monolith.

How is it, then, in Bauer's view, that one group emerged as victorious over others, and which group was it? For Bauer, it was no coincidence that the earliest traces of what later came to be called orthodoxy were associated with the city of Rome. Rome, of course, was the capital city of the empire. Early on, it boasted a large church of Christians who used their administrative skills and wealth to propagate their understanding of the faith, imposing it on other Christian communities throughout the empire.[4] Over time, they succeeded in having like-minded persons placed as bishops over the major churches throughout the Mediterranean. Eventually they managed to marginalize the opposing views, denounce them as heresies, and establish their own form of the religion as orthodox. Then it merely took someone of Eusebius's stature to rewrite the history of the conflict. Thus the traditional understanding of Christianity's turbulent early years came to be established as the orthodox perspective, for centuries.

Current Views of Orthodoxy and Heresy

There was a lot to dispute in Bauer's book, and scholars were not slow to take up the task—especially scholars who were personally committed to the Eusebian view that orthodox Christianity (to which most of these scholars themselves subscribed) had always been the majority view of the Christian church from the beginning. Bauer was attacked for making too many arguments from silence: when there was no record of Christianity in a particular region, he would sometimes assume that it was because the region had been controlled by heretics, whose writings were destroyed. And he approached the sources that did survive with a kind of inquisitorial zeal that some reviewers did not appreciate.

At the end of the day, a large number of Bauer's arguments and conclusions came under critical scrutiny, and not everyone was convinced.

Still, even though many of his specific claims have needed to be rewritten, the general perspective offered by Bauer has become a dominant view among scholars of early Christianity today. There was an enormous range of opinion in the early church: lots of different groups represented lots of different perspectives, they all had sacred books supporting their views, they all saw their views as stemming from Jesus and his closest followers, and they all insisted that since they were right, the other groups were wrong. In many instances, there were not hard-and-fast boundaries dividing these groups: what later came to be declared heretical was at one time thought to be perfectly safe within the orthodox camp. In the end, one group did emerge from this wide diversity, and this group did decide on the basic character of the Christian religion for all time.

Evidence that Bauer was right turns up all the time. Numerous archaeological discoveries have been made in modern times of manuscripts of early Christian writings, either by archaeologists looking for them or accidentally by Bedouin who may not know what it is they have found. What is striking is that discovery after discovery simply reinforces our sense that Christianity was remarkably diverse in its early decades and centuries.

It is true that some of these discoveries have been of writings used by orthodox Christians—for example, manuscripts of the New Testament. But one striking feature of these early manuscripts is that many of them incorporate scribal changes that make their texts more useful for refuting the claims of heretical groups. Among other things, this shows that even orthodox Christians were concerned about other views of the faith that were so widespread in their day, and seen as dangerous.[5] What is more, it is important to recall that numerous different groups used the books that became the New Testament—not simply the group that became orthodox. Many groups of Gnostics, for example, loved the Gospel of John. If a manuscript of John turns up in Egypt from, say, the second century, this is not necessarily evidence that orthodox Christianity was dominant there; this may just as well have been a manuscript used by Gnostic Christians. The reverse is not so easily said, however. When a book such as the Gospel of Judas turns up, it is quite clear that this would not have been the kind of book read in a church of the orthodox. This is a Gnostic text, which orthodox leaders would have outlawed as completely heretical.

What is most striking about modern archaeological discoveries is that in most instances they involve manuscripts that are heterodox (representing an alternative teaching to orthodoxy). Why is that? If Eusebius was right, that orthodoxy was the majority opinion in all places and at all times, why is it that the writings that show up are almost always heretical ones, not noncanonical orthodox ones?

There is the Gospel of Peter, discovered in 1886, a book condemned by early church fathers for containing a docetic Christology. Other fragments of the Gospel have turned up in Egypt in the twentieth century. In fact, we have more fragmentary copies of the Gospel of Peter from the early centuries than of the Gospel of Mark. Was Peter the more popular Gospel at the time? There is also the Gospel of Mary, discovered in 1896, which contains a Gnostic revelation given by Jesus to Mary about how the soul can ascend to heaven. Then there are the fifty-two writings of the Nag Hammadi library, including the Secret Book of John, the Gospel of the Egyptians, the Second Treatise of the Great Seth, and the Coptic Apocalypse of Peter—all of them Gnostic writings detailing aspects of the Gnostic worldview—not to mention the Gospels of Thomas and Philip from the same collection. In the 1980s a book called the Gospel of the Savior turned up, which narrates Jesus' last hours and his final words delivered . . . to the cross! And now there is the Gospel of Judas, another Gnostic dialogue that discusses the "secret revelation" Jesus gave to Judas Iscariot.

Is it just a coincidence that none of the noncanonical writings discovered over the course of the past century embody an orthodox perspective? If orthodoxy was so widespread, why is it that only heterodox documents of the second century have been discovered? The answer to this question leads me to consider why, after all, the Gospel of Judas should be seen as so important.

The Ultimate Significance of the Gospel of Judas

It seems to me that this newly discovered account is enormously important for two reasons, one general and one specific.

In general terms, the Gospel provides us yet another ancient Christian writing that does not belong to the orthodox camp. It instead presents a form of Gnostic religion that came to be suppressed by the victorious party in Christianity in the third or fourth century.

Based on its carbon-14 dating, the newly discovered manuscript appears to have been made sometime in the late third or early fourth century. Was it copied much more frequently before that time? This surviving copy is a Coptic translation of a Greek original, and some form of the Greek text was known already to Irenaeus in 180 CE. The book must have been composed, then, in the middle of the second century, copied at least several times, translated into Coptic, and then copied again.

Not only is it a Gnostic text, it also has numerous connections with a range of texts from numerous different Christian groups. Most of its specific similarities are with Sethian Gnostic texts, but it also has striking parallels with non-Sethian Gnostic writings such as the Gospel of Thomas and the Coptic Apocalypse of Peter. It even has interesting ties to non-Gnostic forms of Christianity, such as Marcionism and Jewish-apocalyptic Christianity.

Thus in broad terms this text gives us additional hard evidence that Christianity in the early centuries of the church was remarkably diverse. There were many forms of Christianity, and the boundaries between these Christian groups were not hard and fast. Instead, different groups and the views they represented influenced one another extensively; many of their boundaries were permeable.

Of even greater interest, however, are the specific teachings of the Gospel of Judas. On one hand, it is a Gnostic revelation of the secrets that are necessary for salvation. This Gospel presupposes that some of us are trapped here in our material bodies and that we need to know how we came to be here, who we really are, and how we can escape to return to our heavenly home. Jesus reveals the truth of these things to us; he shows us the nature of reality; he tells us that this world is not all there is. Far from it: this world is a cosmic disaster, the creation of a bloodthirsty rebel and a fool. We need to escape their clutches to return to the divine realm whence we came. Judas himself came to recognize the truth of this revelation, and he is the one who leads the way.

What makes this Gnostic revelation so distinctive is that it is given precisely to Judas Iscariot. Throughout the Christian tradition Judas has been portrayed as the rotten apple in the apostolic barrel. Over the years, some Christians have seen him as eager to betray his master for a paltry sum; others have portrayed him as driven by the Devil; others have claimed that he was inherently evil. Those intent on anti-Semitic propaganda have depicted him as the prototypical Jew in all these ways, a God-denying, money-grubbing thief and Christ-killer.

The Gospel of Judas presents a different view, insisting that Judas was the only one of the disciples who understood his Lord. Jesus came not from the creator god but from the "realm of Barbelo." So too did some of us. Some of us are trapped here in the prisons of our bodies, but once we learn the truth that Jesus delivered to his one faithful disciple, Judas, we will be able to escape to return to our heavenly home. Judas is the one who leads the way. He is the "thirteenth," because he stands outside the number of Jesus' twelve disciples, who never did grasp his teachings and never did realize that their devotion to the creator god is misplaced. Only Judas had a glimpse of the truth. And so to him alone did Jesus reveal all that needs to be known. In return, Judas performed for him the greatest service imaginable. His betrayal was not the act of a traitor to the cause. It was a kind deed performed for the sake of his Lord. He turned Jesus over to the authorities so that Jesus could be killed and escape the confines of his body. In so doing, Judas is the greatest of all the apostles. In the memorable words of Jesus, "you will exceed them all, for you will sacrifice the man that clothes me."

Notes

Chapter 2: Judas in Our Earliest Gospels

1. See my recent book *Peter, Paul, and Mary Magdalene: The Followers of Jesus in History and Legend* (New York: Oxford University Press, 2006).
2. Luke 8:1–3. These verses also indicate that Mary Magdalene was the one who had seven demons cast out of her. It does not state that this was done by Jesus himself, although that might be the implication. In any event, there is nothing in that to suggest that these demons drove her to prostitution—something demons are never said to have done in the New Testament.
3. On this question of whether Paul knew much about the life of Jesus, see my discussion in *The New Testament: A Historical Introduction to the Early Christian Writings,* 3rd ed. (New York: Oxford University Press, 2004), chap. 22. For a fuller treatment, see Victor Paul Furnish, *Jesus According to Paul* (Cambridge: Cambridge University Press, 1993).
4. Scholars today do not think that Paul wrote all of the letters that are attributed to him in the New Testament. For a discussion of the authorship of Ephesians, Colossians, 2 Thessalonians, 1 and 2 Timothy, and Titus, see Ehrman, *The New Testament,* chap. 23.
5. I won't be able to go into great depth in discussion of the portrayals of Judas in each of the Gospels, but will instead emphasize the points that strike me as the most significant. For the reasons for thinking that Mark was the first Gospel written, and that Matthew and Luke used it as a source for their own accounts, and that John was then the last of the Gospels, see my discussion in Ehrman, *The New Testament,* chaps. 5–8, 10.
6. See the preceding note.
7. One of the first to recognize this was William Wrede; see his book *The Messianic Secret,* trans. J. C. G. Greig (Cambridge: J. Clark, 1971; the German original was 1901).
8. See John J. Collins, *The Scepter and the Star: The Messiahs of the Dead Sea Scrolls and Other Ancient Literature* (New York: Doubleday, 1995).
9. This is where the Gospel of Mark originally ended—abruptly, with the women's silence. Later scribes thought this was all too abrupt, and they added an additional twelve verses that serve to put the disciples in a better light. On this ending, see my book *Misquoting Jesus: The Story Behind Who Changed the Bible and Why* (San Francisco: HarperSanFrancisco, 2005), 66–67.
10. Here and throughout my translations, the Greek for "betray" is *paradidomi,* and so could be translated "hand over." But given the dire things Jesus has to say about the one who will

hand him over—"it would have been better for that one not to have been born"—it is clear that he is referring to an evil act of betrayal, not a neutral action.

11. Some readers have wondered if this narrative sequence makes sense. The leaders don't want to arrest him during the festival, but they do so anyway. And they are afraid that the crowds will riot in Jesus' support, but at his trial they have no trouble stirring up the crowds against him. But why would the crowds riot at his arrest but not at his trial? Is Mark giving us a historical account?

12. This approach to Matthew—which can be used for Luke as well, since it too used Mark as a source—is called redaction criticism. A redactor is an editor, and so this method sees how these later authors edited the one source we're reasonably sure they had at their disposal (Mark). See Ehrman, *The New Testament,* chap. 7.

13. Although, as we will see, he misattributes the quotation, for some reason, to Jeremiah.

14. The best complete discussion can be found in Dale Allison and W. D. Davies, *The Gospel According to Saint Matthew* (Edinburgh: T & T Clark, 1997), 3:557–73.

15. See, for example, Mark 1:2 (Mal. 3:1 and Isa. 40:3) and Romans 9:27 (Hos. 2:1 and Isa. 10:22).

16. For a fuller discussion, see Ehrman, *The New Testament,* chap. 8.

17. One key difference between Luke and Mark occurs when Jesus calls the Twelve to be his disciples, for in Luke we are explicitly told that Judas would be the one who "betrayed" Jesus. This is the Greek word *prodidomi,* not the word we looked at earlier, *paradidomi,* which more usually means simply "handed over." For Luke, Judas is explicitly called a "betrayer."

18. They come, therefore, from the source that scholars have called Q. This is a no-longer-extant source (i.e., it is hypothetical) that Matthew and Luke used for the stories that they have that are not in Mark—for example, the Beatitudes, the Lord's Prayer, and the account of the three temptations in the wilderness. See Ehrman, *The New Testament,* chap. 6.

Chapter 3: Judas in Later Gospel Traditions

1. See the foundational works of Albert Bates Lord, *The Singer of Tales* (Cambridge, Mass.: Harvard University Press, 1960) and Walter Ong, *Orality and Literacy: The Technologizing of the Word* (New York: Methuen, 1982).

2. It is true, on the other hand, that even before the printing press, authors of *written* texts were concerned that their accounts not be changed by careless or willful scribes. On this, see my book *Misquoting Jesus: The Story Behind Who Changed the Bible and Why* (San Francisco: HarperSanFrancisco, 2006), chap. 2.

3. For fuller discussion of John's relationship to the Synoptics, see Ehrman, *The New Testament,* chap. 10.

4. See in particular Hyam Maccoby, *Judas Iscariot and the Myth of Jewish Evil* (New York: Free Press, 1992), who goes so far as to argue that there never was a historical Judas, but that he was a Christian invention made up by those wanting to oppose Jews by telling stories of this one, Jesus' alleged enemy and betrayer.

5. For a fuller description of Papias and his work, see Bart D. Ehrman, *The Apostolic Fathers* (Cambridge, Mass.: Harvard University Press, 2003), 2:86–89.

6. This and the following quotation are given in the translation found in ibid., vol. 2.

7. Quotations from G. A. Williamson, trans., *Eusebius: The History of the Church from Christ to Constantine,* ed. Andrew Louth (London: Penguin, 1989).

8. On the death of the anti-Jewish Syrian tyrant Antiochus Epiphanes, see 2 Macc. 9:5–12; on the death of the anti-Jewish Babylonian general Holofernes, see Jdt. 16:17—both from the Old Testament Apocrypha.

9. For an account of how the New Testament came to us in this form, and how the manuscripts that survived were changed by Christian copyists over time, see my book *Misquoting Jesus.*

10. The tale is also modeled, in part, on the life of the infant Moses, as described in the book of Exodus, as my colleague Zlatko Plese has pointed out to me.

11. See, again, Maccoby, *Judas Iscariot and the Myth of Jewish Evil.*

12. Jerome, Tractate 59 on Ps. 108:2; I have taken the translation of this quotation from the interesting book by Michael P. Penn, *Kissing Christians: Ritual and Community in the Late Ancient Church* (Philadelphia: University of Pennsylvania Press, 2005), 115.

13. Ambrose, *Epistles* 1.14–18; translation in Penn, *Kissing Christians,* 62.
14. I owe this reference to Kim Paffenroth, *Judas: Images of the Lost Disciple* (Louisville: Westminster/John Knox, 2001), 38. It comes from Chrysostom's Homily on Matthew 85.2, as translated (with minor modification) by G. Prevost in Chrysostom, *Homilies on Matthew* (Edinburgh: T. & T. Clark, 1851).
15. See Paffenroth, *Judas,* 38, quoting Chrysostom's Homily Against the Jews, as translated by P. W. Harkins (Washington, D.C.: Catholic University Press, 1979), 1.7.1.
16. This and the preceding quotation are from Paffenroth, *Judas,* 38–39; it is taken from Chrysostom's *Homilies on the Acts of the Apostles,* trans. J. Walker et al. (Edinburgh: T. & T. Clark, 1889).
17. Taken from Theophylact's commentary on Matthew, 27; the Greek text is found in J. P. Migne, *Patrologia Graece* 123, 460. The translation is from Morton S. Enslin, "Judas in Fact and Fiction," in *Festschrift to Honor F. Wilbur Gingrich,* ed. E. H. Barth and R. E. Cocroft (Leiden: Brill, 1972), 130.

Chapter 4: Before the Discovery: Our Previous Knowledge of a Gospel of Judas

1. Elaine Pagels, *The Gnostic Gospels* (New York: Random House, 1979).
2. For a full discussion of these and all the related points, see my book *Truth and Fiction in the Da Vinci Code* (New York: Oxford University Press, 2004).
3. See my discussion of these texts in the third section of my book *Peter, Paul, and Mary Magdalene* (New York: Oxford University Press, 2006).
4. For a fuller description of this discovery, and a discussion of its significance, see Bart Ehrman, *Lost Christianities: The Battles for Scripture and the Faiths We Never Knew* (New York: Oxford University Press, 2003), 51–55.
5. We have two surviving Gospels called the Gospel of Thomas, for example.
6. For the full text of the letter, see Eusebius, *Church History,* 5.1.
7. For a standard treatment, see Kurt Rudolph, *Gnosis: The Nature and History of Gnosticism* (New York: Harper and Row, 1984); for a selection of Gnostic writings and of Irenaeus's descriptions of Gnostics, see Bentley Layton, *The Gnostic Scriptures* (New York: Doubleday, 1987).
8. For this view, advanced from two very different perspectives, see Michael Williams, *Rethinking Gnosticism: An Argument for Dismantling a Dubious Category* (Princeton: Princeton University Press, 1996) and Karen L. King, *What Is Gnosticism* (Cambridge, Mass.: Harvard University Press, 2003).
9. See, for example, Frederik Wisse, "The Nag Hammadi Library and the Heresiologists," *Vigiliae Christianae* 25 (1971): 205–23.
10. Irenaeus himself doesn't actually give them this name. He speaks of them as a group of Gnostics who particularly revered Cain; later heresy hunters who relied on his account (such as Pseudo-Tertullian in the third century) gave them the name.
11. Translation of Dominic J. Unger, ed. John J. Dillon, *St. Irenaeus of Lyons Against the Heresies* (New York: Paulist Press, 1992), 102.
12. See the essay by Gregor Wurst, "Irenaeus and the Gospel of Judas," in *The Gospel of Judas,* ed. Rodolphe Kasser, Marvin Meyer, and Gregor Wurst (Washington, D.C.: National Geographic, 2006), 121–36. The translation comes from the same volume.
13. See ibid.
14. See Birger Pearson, "Cain and the Cainites," in *Gnosticism, Judaism, and Egyptian Christianity* (Minneapolis: Fortress, 1990), 95–107.

Chapter 5: The Discovery of the Gospel of Judas

1. Andrew Jacobs has pointed out to me that modern fiction writers of "Gospel thrillers" have occasionally developed the idea of the "discovery" of an iconoclastic Gospel written from Judas's perspective, for example in the 1972 novel *The Judas Gospel* by Peter van Greenaway and the more recent 2001 *The Gospel of Judas* by Simon Mawer. See further, on Gospel thrillers generally, Andrew S. Jacobs, "Gospel Thrillers," *Postscripts* 1, 1 (2005): 125–42.

2. On the entire issue of the antiquities market and the illegal smuggling (and profiteering) involved with it, see the UNESCO statement found at www.unesco.org/culture/laws/1970/html_eng/page2.shtml. I owe this reference to Andrew Jacobs, who informs me that he got it from a fellow scholar of Christian antiquity, Carolyn Schroeder.
3. Like others in this narrative, Samiah was a Coptic Christian. I have used the term *Coptic* repeatedly throughout this account already. Here I might point out that the term itself actually comes from the word *Egyptian* (where *gypt* means "Copt"). Christianity may have come to Egypt already in the first century—Copts claim that the church there was founded by none other than the apostle John Mark, the alleged author of the second Gospel. Today most of Egypt is Muslim, but Coptic Christians make up something like a seventh of the population.
4. See note 2 in this chapter.
5. In a private communication, Herb Krosney has told me that Hanna's business partner informed Krosney that the source of Hanna's original evaluation was a distinguished Italian papyrologist, Manfredo Manfredi, professor at the University of Florence.
6. Quotation taken from Herb Krosney, *The Last Gospel: The Quest for the Gospel of Judas* (Washington, D.C.: National Geographic, 2006), 110.
7. Krosney, *Discovery,* 115.
8. See note 2 in this chapter on the UNESCO statement concerning antiquities.
9. *The Gospel of Judas,* ed. Rodolphe Kasser, Marvin Meyer, and Gregor Wurst (Washington, D.C.: National Geographic, 2006), 60–61.
10. Ibid., 47–48.
11. Ibid., 65.
12. Ibid., 66–67.

Chapter 6: The Gospel of Judas: An Overview

1. For a discussion of this question, see Bart Ehrman, *Lost Christianities: The Battles for Scripture and the Faiths We Never Knew* (New York: Oxford University Press, 2003), chap. 1.
2. Throughout my discussion, I will be using the translation of Marvin Meyer, from *The Gospel of Judas,* ed. Rodolphe Kasser, Marvin Meyer, and Gregor Wurst (Washington, D.C.: National Geographic, 2006). Whenever brackets occur in the translation, these indicate places where there are gaps in the manuscript, where the words have to be supplied by the editor. In places I will suggest alternative translations of the Coptic; these are also indicated in brackets but are followed with a dash and my initials, BE. The reference numbers indicate the page and lines of the manuscript (the Gospel of Judas begins on page 33 of the codex), so that 33:1–6 means page 33, lines 1–6.
3. The word *child* here is very rare and will probably be disputed by scholars who work further on the text. An alternative translation would be that Jesus appeared among his disciples as a "phantom," which would be an even clearer statement of the docetic Christology (see below) that the author appears to embrace. But the editors of the text—Kasser, Wurst, and Meyer—are confident that "child" is the correct reading.
4. Brackets in the translation indicated places where there are holes in the manuscript and the missing words have been hypothetically restored by the editors.
5. Most of the references to stars in the Gospel are negative; the stars appear to *mislead* people. The exception comes at the end, when Judas's own star is said to "lead the way."
6. This can especially be found in Plato's dialogue, the *Timaeus.* See the full and illuminating discussion of Marvin Meyer in *The Gospel of Judas,* 163–65.
7. I am indebted to Andrew Jacobs and Zlatko Plese for this information; Marvin Meyer gives an alternative explanation in his notes to the English translation in *The Gospel of Judas* (n. 106).
8. The Coptic is actually ambiguous: it could be Judas's Gospel or the Gospel About Judas. But it is just this ambiguity that is interesting: unlike other Gospel texts that we have, this Gospel is not unambiguously entitled the Gospel According to Judas. This opens up the possibility that the author wants his readers to see that it is the Gospel that describes Judas.

Chapter 7: The Gospel of Judas and
Early Christian Gnosticism

1. For some of the recent discussions, see the following, along with their bibliographies: Karen King, *What Is Gnosticism?* (Cambridge, Mass.: Harvard University Press, 2003); Riemer

Roukema, *Gnosis and Faith in Early Christianity* (Harrisburg, Penn.: Trinity Press International, 1999); Michael A. Williams, *Rethinking "Gnosticism": An Argument for Dismantling a Dubious Category* (Princeton: Princeton University Press, 1996).

2. This is the proposal advanced in a very fine study by one of the top experts of Gnosticism in North America, Michael Williams, in *Rethinking "Gnosticism."*

3. Karen King's argument is particularly nuanced, as she shows that one problem with the term *Gnosticism* is that it comes to be used by modern scholars in ways that reflect their own views and concerns, rather than as a purely descriptive term. See her book *What Is Gnosticism?*

4. It is of course possible to interpret a text such as the Gospel of Thomas in a non-Gnostic way, as has been done by a number of scholars, such as Richard Valantasis in *The Gospel of Thomas* (New York: Routledge, 1997). I think it is a real mistake, however, to claim that these interpretations are superior because they let the text "speak for itself," rather than importing an alien view into the text. On one hand, texts never do speak for themselves; they are always interpreted by scholars who bring other information to the texts to make sense of them. Anyone who doubts this should simply read an account that allegedly lets a text speak for itself, and see how much interpretive baggage is brought to the task. On the other hand, there are clear indications in the Gospel of Thomas that the Gnostic myth is being presupposed by the author. See my fuller discussion in my book *Lost Christianities: The Battles for Scripture and the Faiths We Never Knew* (New York: Oxford University Press, 2003), 59–65.

5. See *The Gospel of Judas,* ed. Rodolphe Kasser, Marvin Meyer, and Gregor Wurst (Washington, D.C.: National Geographic, 2006), 137–69.

6. A full scholarly treatment is by John D. Turner, *Sethian Gnosticism and the Platonic Tradition* (Sainte-Foy, Québec: Presses de l'Université Laval, 2001). For an account written more for lay readers than scholars, see the accessible discussion in Bentley Layton, *The Gnostic Scriptures,* Section I: "Classical Gnostic Scripture."

7. See the discussion of Gnostic scholar John Turner in Meyer, *Gospel of Judas,* 141–42.

8. All the translations of the Secret Book of John are by Frederik Wisse, "The Apocryphon of John," in *The Nag Hammadi Library in English,* 4th ed., ed. James. M. Robinson (San Francisco: HarperSanFrancisco), 1996.

9. Translated by Alexander Böhlig and Frederik Wisse, in Robinson, ed., *Nag Hammadi Library in English.*

10. Some Gnostic scholars, such as Catherine Barry, have detected some Christian imprint on Eugnostos the Blessed. See her essay in *Les textes de Nag Hammadi et le problème de leur classification,* ed. Louis Painchaud and Anne Pasquier (Sainte-Foy, Québec: Presses de l'Université Laval; Louvain: Peeters, 1995). I owe this reference to Zlatko Plese.

11. Translation by Douglas M. Parrott, in Robinson, ed., *Nag Hammadi Library in English.*

12. From the burgeoning literature, see especially Karen King, *The Gospel of Mary of Magdala: Jesus and the First Woman Apostle* (Santa Rosa, Calif.: Polebridge Press, 2003).

13. If the word *phantom* is intended, the word would need to be spelled slightly differently.

14. Translations from the Acts of John are taken from J. K. Elliott, *The Apocryphal New Testament* (Oxford: Clarendon Press, 1993).

15. Translations of the Second Treatise of the Great Seth are by Roger A. Bullard and Joseph A. Gibbons, in Robinson, ed., *Nag Hammadi Library in English.*

16. There also survives another Apocalypse of Peter in Greek (and in a fuller Ethiopic translation). This is the first surviving account of a guided tour of heaven and hell, given to Peter by Jesus himself—an obvious forerunner of Dante's *Divine Comedy.*

17. Translations of the Coptic Apocalypse of Peter are by James Brashler and Roger A. Bullard, in Robinson, ed., *Nag Hammadi Library in English.*

18. Translations of the Gospel of Thomas are by David R. Cartlidge and David L. Dungan, *Documents for the Study of the Gospels* (Minneapolis: Augsburg/Fortress Press, 1980).

19. For a general study of the phenomenon, see John J. Collins, *The Apocalyptic Imagination: An Introduction to Jewish Apocalyptic Literature,* 2nd ed. (Grand Rapids: Eerdmans, 1998).

20. See John D. Turner, *Sethian Gnosticism and the Platonic Tradition* (Sainte-Foy, Québec: Presses de l'Université Laval, 2001).

21. For some of these Gnostic connections to Jewish thought, see Pheme Perkins, *Gnosticism and the New Testament* (Minneapolis: Fortress Press, 1993).

22. For a similar thesis, see the older work of Robert M. Grant, *Gnosticism and Early Christianity,* rev. ed. (New York: Harper & Row, 1966). More recently see Perkins, *Gnosticism,* and Birger Pearson, *Gnosticism, Judaism, and Egyptian Christianity* (Minneapolis: Fortress Press, 1990). For strong counterarguments, seeing Gnosticism as rooted ultimately in Platonic thinking, see Roukema, *Gnosis and Faith,* and especially the intriguing article by Gerard Luttikhuizen, "The Thought Pattern of Gnostic Mythologizers and Their Use of Biblical Traditions," in John Turner and Annie McGuire, *The Nag Hammadi Library After Fifty Years* (Leiden: E. J. Brill, 1997).

Chapter 8: Jesus, Judas, and the Twelve in the Gospel of Judas

1. I summarize some of these views in my book *Jesus: Apocalyptic Prophet of the New Millennium* (New York: Oxford University Press, 1999); for a brilliant assessment of earlier attempts to write lives of Jesus, see the classic by Albert Schweitzer, *Quest of the Historical Jesus* (New York: Macmillan, 1968; German original, 1906).
2. It was additionally important to Paul that Christ died the way he did—by being crucified. For the Scriptures indicate that anyone who is hanged on a tree is "cursed" by God. According to Paul, because Jesus was crucified—hanged on a tree—he stood under God's curse. But since he himself did nothing to deserve this fate, he in effect took the curse of God on himself for the sake of others. It was the crucifixion, therefore, that brought about salvation for the world of sinners (see Gal. 3:10–14).
3. A possible exception, as Zlatko Plese has pointed out to me, is Saying 65, in which Jesus tells the parable of the vineyard, in which the farmers leasing the land kill the son of the owner. But nothing is made of the salvific significance of the death in the account.
4. Quotations from the Gospel of Thomas are from David R. Cartlidge and David L. Dungan, *Documents for the Study of the Gospels* (Minneapolis: Augsburg/Fortress Press, 1980).
5. As is the case of the other Gospels, we do not know who the actual author of Luke was. Early Christian tradition indicates that Luke and Acts were written by a traveling companion of the apostle Paul, the Gentile physician Luke. We do not have evidence of this tradition, however, until nearly a century after the books themselves were written. For further discussion of the authorship of this and the other Gospels, see Ehrman, *The New Testament: A Historical Introduction to the Early Christian Writings,* 3rd ed. (New York: Oxford University Press, 2004), 58–59.
6. It is included, for example, as part of the New Testament in the fifth-century manuscript called Codex Alexandrinus.
7. This can be found in the writings of the church father Clement of Alexandria, *The Miscellanies* (7, 17, 106).
8. On the attack on "others" for their wild and profligate behavior—a standard stereotype in ancient rhetorical attacks—see my discussion in *Lost Christianities: The Battles for Scripture and the Faiths We Never Knew* (New York: Oxford University Press, 2003), 197–202, and the bibliography I cite there.
9. See note 8 for chapter 6.
10. This is the view, for example, of William Klassen, *Judas: Betrayer or Friend of Jesus?* (Minneapolis: Fortress, 1996).
11. *The Gospel of Judas,* ed. Rodolphe Kasser, Marvin Meyer, and Gregor Wurst (Washington, D.C.: National Geographic, 2006), 44, n. 142.

Chapter 9: Who Was Judas Iscariot?

1. Actually, both approaches are historical, in that the literary approach tries to establish what this literature means in its own historical context. But the other approach tries to see what actually happened in history, and in *that* sense is "historical."
2. Even historically accurate stories are "fabricated," of course, in that they are stories that are told, and stories by their very nature—even historically accurate ones—are constructed. But my point is that the information we receive about the past is either accurate (to some extent) or not.

3. For further information on the Gospels, see Bart D. Ehrman, *The New Testament: A Histori-cal Introduction to the Early Christian Writings,* chaps. 4–8, 10.

4. Matthew and Luke did have written sources at their disposal other than Mark, but it does not appear that their accounts of Judas were drawn from these sources. As I have already noted, both used the document that scholars have called Q (short for *Quelle,* German for "source")—a written account of Jesus' sayings (for example, the Beatitudes and the Lord's Prayer) which no longer survives. Matthew had access to other sources (sometimes just called M), for example for his stories of the wise men visiting the infant Jesus, found only in Matthew. So too Luke had other sources (called L) for passages that he alone has, such as the parables of the Good Samaritan and the Prodigal Son. For a discussion of the sources in the Synoptic Gospels, see Ehrman, *New Testament,* chap. 6.

5. Nine times it is spelled, in Greek, *iskariothes,* and three times *iskarioth.*

6. See especially Raymond Brown, *The Death of the Messiah: From Gethsemane to the Grave* (New York: Doubleday, 1994), 2:1413–6.

7. Some very fine scholars doubt that it is. See ibid., 2:1414.

8. See ibid., 2:1416.

9. There are occasional exceptions. See, for example, Hyam Maccoby, *Judas Iscariot and the Myth of Jewish Evil* (New York: Free Press, 1992).

10. For the classic discussion of earlier scholarship on this question, from the time of its incep-tion at the end of the eighteenth century until his own day, at the beginning of the twentieth, see Albert Schweitzer, *Quest of the Historical Jesus* (New York: Macmillan, 1968; German original, 1906).

11. On these and other options, see my book *Jesus: Apocalyptic Prophet of the New Millennium* (New York: Oxford University Press, 1999).

12. See the much longer elucidation of these points in ibid.

13. This saying comes from the source that scholars have called Q—a source used by Matthew and Luke for the sayings that they share that are not found in the Gospel of Mark. See further note 14 in this chapter.

14. Again, Q is a hypothetical document (i.e., it no longer exists) that was used by both Matthew and Luke as a source for many of the sayings of Jesus. A saying probably came from Q if it is found in both Matthew and Luke but not in Mark (if it is in Mark, that is where Matthew and Luke got it). For further discussion, including the evidence that Q once existed, see my *New Testament: A Historical Introduction,* chap. 6.

Chapter 10: What Did Judas Betray
and Why Did He Betray It?

1. Palestine is the name given to the region later by the Romans; it is commonly used today to refer to the ancient regions of Galilee, Samaria, and Judea.

2. Jesus' teachings about the Son of Man are extremely complicated and have divided scholars for a very long time. My own view is that the earliest sayings, such as Mark 8:38, appear to differentiate between Jesus and the Son of Man. Since later Christians believed that Jesus himself *was* the Son of Man, they would not have made up these sayings. That means these particular sayings must go back to Jesus. And he appears there to be speaking of someone other than himself. See further my book *Jesus: Apocalyptic Prophet of the New Millennium* (New York: Oxford University Press, 1999), 144–48.

3. Recall that Q is an abbreviation for the German word *Quelle,* which means "source." It is a term used by scholars for the hypothetical source (i.e., no longer surviving) used by Matthew and Luke for many of their sayings of Jesus—such as the Lord's Prayer and the Beatitudes—that are not found in Mark.

4. See further John J. Collins, *The Scepter and the Star: The Messiahs of the Dead Sea Scrolls and Other Ancient Literature* (New York: Doubleday, 1995).

5. See his brilliant article, "The Crucified Messiah," in his collection of essays, *The Crucified Messiah and Other Essays* (Minneapolis: Augsburg Press, 1974).

6. See note 8 in this chapter.

7. This is true even if Jesus' execution was a simple miscarriage of justice or a case of mistaken identity. Romans executed criminals for *reasons,* even if some criminals were wrongly ac-cused or unfairly convicted.

8. Some scholars as far back as H. Reimarus at the end of the eighteenth century have insisted that Jesus is best understood as a political insurgent, and was recognized as such by the Romans. A modern proponent of the view is Samuel G. F. Brandon, *Jesus and the Zealots: A Study of the Political Factor in Primitive Christianity* (New York: Scribner, 1967). One intriguing piece of evidence that needs to be considered is the fact that at least some of Jesus' followers were armed when the authorities came to arrest him—one of them evidently drawing his sword to put up a fight. In a politically incendiary time in the capital city, Jerusalem, how would this *not* look like an armed group? Still, however one explains the sword carried by one (or more) of Jesus' followers, the emphasis on peacemaking and on the future intervention of God (not humans) in Jesus' teaching has suggested to most historians that Jesus himself was not a proponent of a violent overthrow of the empire. And it should be noted that Jesus himself is never said to have been armed; that is odd if he was the leader of a group of insurrectionists.

9. The most compelling demonstration of this point is in E. P. Sanders, *Jesus and Judaism* (Philadelphia: Fortress, 1985).

10. See the discussion in Richard Horsley, *Jesus and the Spiral of Violence: Popular Jewish Resistance in Roman Palestine* (San Francisco: Harper & Row, 1987).

11. See note 10 in this chapter.

12. See Ehrman, *Jesus: Apocalyptic Prophet,* chapter 12.

13. Some scholars have suggested that it was Jesus' triumphal entry into Jerusalem as a deliverer, when the crowds acknowledged him as the coming Savior, that led eventually to his arrest and execution as a messianic figure. I do not think, however, that the stories of Jesus' entry into Jerusalem can be taken as historically accurate as recounted. If Jesus really did arrive in Jerusalem on the back of a donkey, in fulfillment of the Scriptures, to the cheers of the crowds who proclaimed him the messiah to come, he would almost certainly have been arrested immediately and taken care of by the authorities on the spot. Yet all our traditions indicate that he spent some days in Jerusalem before the authorities took serious enough notice of him to have him arrested. The account of the triumphal entry, therefore, appears to me to be a story imagined later, by Christian followers of Jesus who wanted to show that he fulfilled prophecy in coming to the capital city and to show that the crowds originally welcomed him for who he was—the messiah—even though they were to turn on him days later.

14. Again, I owe this observation to Nils Dahl. See note 5 in this chapter.

15. This view is set forth in the brilliant—if otherwise completely dated—analysis of Albert Schweitzer in his classic *Quest of the Historical Jesus* (New York: Macmillan, 1968; German original, 1906).

16. This is a view popularized in the English-speaking world by the rock opera *Jesus Christ Superstar* by Andrew Lloyd Webber and Tim Rice.

Chapter 11: The Gospel of Judas in Perspective

1. For a study of these wide-ranging views, see my book *Lost Christianities: The Battles for Scripture and the Faiths We Never Knew* (New York: Oxford University Press, 2003).

2. For an accessible English translation, see G. A. Williamson, *Eusebius: The History of the Church from Christ to Constantine,* revised and edited by Andrew Louth (London: Penguin Books, 1989).

3. The English translation is in Robert Kraft et al., *Orthodoxy and Heresy in Earliest Christianity* (Philadelphia: Fortress Press, 1971).

4. Bauer found evidence for this view in one of our earliest texts to survive from the church of Rome from after the New Testament period, the book of 1 Clement, in which the Roman church tries to intervene in the internal affairs of the church of Corinth, insisting that a certain group of church leaders be reinstated in office after having been removed.

5. See my book *Misquoting Jesus: The Story Behind Who Changed the Bible and Why* (San Francisco: HarperSanFrancisco, 2005), chap. 6; for a more thorough and scholarly discussion, see my book *The Orthodox Corruption of Scripture: The Effect of Early Christological Controversies on the Text of the New Testament* (New York: Oxford University Press, 1993).

Index

Note: Page numbers in italics indicate illustrations.

divinity of, 90, 136, 138–39
enigmatic nature of, 11
as fictional creation, 182n. 4
and 1 Corinthians, 15–16
and the Gospel of Judas, 137–39
and the Gospel of Mark, 17–20, 20–23,
    166
and the Gospel of Matthew, 23–29, 45,
    168
historical information on, 13–14, 142–44
illiteracy, 1
inconsistencies on, 36, 168–69
and the Kingdom of God, 44
name, 8, 144, 145–46
parallels with Peter, 23
and Paul's writings, 14–15
scarcity of sources on, 5
Judas Thomas
    confused with Judas Iscariot, 5, 74
    and the Gospel of Thomas, 86, 113
    and the Nag Hammadi Library, 55
    as twin, 127–28
Jude, 145
judgment day, 149–52, 154–56, 163, 167–68
Jull, A. J. Timothy, 2, 6–7, 8

Kasser, Rodolph
    announcement of the Gospel of Judas, 82
    authentication efforts, 3–8, 69–70
    on the condition of the Gospel of Judas,
        77, 79–80, 86
    and the National Geographic Society, 80
    translation efforts, 103
Kerioth, 145–46
King, Karen, 185n. 3
King of the Jews, 162–63, 165
Kingdom of God. See also apocalypticism;
        end times
    and the disciples, 156–58, 167
    Irenaeus on, 44–45
    and Jesus' death, 164–65
    Jesus on, 150
kiss symbolism, 27, 32, 43, 50
Koenen, Ludwig, 72–74
Korah, 62
Koresh, David, 124
Koutoulakis, Nicholas, 72–73
Kraus, Hans P., 75
Krosney, Herb
    on the antiquities market, 184n. 5
    and authentication efforts, 2, 8, 10, 68–70
    publicizing the Gospel of Judas, 83

"L" document, 187n. 4
Last Supper
    and Corinthian communion meals, 15
    in 1 Corinthians, 123
    in the Gospel of John, 43
    and Judas' betrayal, 20, 22, 41
Latin language, 145
Latin Vulgate, 50

laughter of Jesus, 89, 90–92, 96, 110–11,
    136
Law of Moses, 27
Layton, Bentley, 76
Lazarus, 42
legal issues of the Gospel of Judas, 76
Letter of Peter to Philip
    condition, 9
    discovery of, 69, 71, 74, 82
    found with the Gospel of Judas, 3
Levi, 85, 107
life of Jesus, 126, 162
literacy, 1, 35, 173
literary approach, 141–42, 186n. 1
The Lord's Prayer, 24
The Lost Gospel: The Quest for the Gospel of
    Judas Iscariot (Krosney), 70
lost Gospels, 2. See also noncanonical
    Gospels; specific texts
luminaries, 94, 104, 105–6

"M" document, 187n. 4
Maecenas Foundation for Ancient Art, 3, 10,
    68–69, 78–79, 82–83
Maghagha, Egypt, 70
Manfredi, Manfredo, 184n. 5
Marcionism, 114–15, 133–36, 174, 176–77,
    179
Marcus Aurelius, 56
Martha, 42
Martin Bodmer Foundation, 2
Mary, Mother of Jesus, 47
Mary Magdalene
    and the Da Vinci Code, 53
    and exorcism stories, 181n. 2
    and the Gospel of Mark, 20
    Gospel of Mary, 54–55, 62, 101, 106,
        179
    inconsistencies on, 147
    legends about, 13
    and Paul's writings, 14
Mary of Bethany, 42
mathematical treatises, 71
Matthew, the Apostle, 113
Matthias, 38, 90, 131–32
Mawer, Simon, 183n. 1
messiah and messianic beliefs
    and Acts, 132–33
    and the betrayal of Jesus, 158–60, 160–
        62
    and the end times, 149
    expectations of Jesus, 160–62
    and the Gospel of John, 161
    and the Gospel of Mark, 18–19, 21, 160–
        61
    and Jesus' death, 162, 164–65, 188n. 13
    and Paul's writings, 124, 125, 159
Meyer, Marvin, 80, 87, 103–5, 139, 184n. 2
Micah, 24
Michael (Angel), 95
Middle Ages, 42–43